BLACK COPS

James N. Reaves

Quantum Leap Publisher, Inc.   Philadelphia, Pennsylvania

Published by Quantum Leap Publisher, Inc.
2701 North Broad Street
Philadelphia, Pennsylvania 19132

Manufactured in the United States of America

Library of Congress Cataloging-in-Publication Data

Reaves, James N. (Nauwood), 1915
    Black Cops/James N. Reaves.
        p.   cm.

    African-American police—Pennsylvania—
    Philadelphia—Autobiography.

HV7911.R43A3 1991
363.2'089'96073074811—dc20   91-25218
                                                    CIP

ISBN   0-9627161-4-6

Acknowledgements

Gathering information and pictures for this book was not an easy task, but the desire to do it was an ever driving force. There is so little written about the history of black policemen, therefore, I feel it will contribute to the understanding of their valor, loyalty, and dedication to professional law enforcement for the community.

I am deeply indebted to many people who have been so helpful and encouraging. My wife, Vivienne, who in the early years of my effort to produce a manuscript did my typing. Throughout my struggling to write this book, she was ever present. She helped me to have patience and she encouraged me onward until the final page was completed.

Mary Gagnier, a contributing editor of *Delaware Valley* magazine, devoted many hours in assisting me in the rewriting and word processing of the original manuscript. Orville (Pat) Jones, the former Personnel Director, City of Philadelphia, was never too busy to answer my telephone calls about my research for this book.

The Honorable, A. Leon Higgenbothem, judge, gave to me his full confidence in my research for this book. Through his consultation, I gained many insights to help me reach my goal, its completion. Further, Peter Landry, reporter for *The Philadelphia Inquirer*, did a brilliant story on black policemen from my manuscript. Lieutenant Leonard T. Jones, Philadelphia Police Department, found a way to be available to me, to clarify many incidents that involved police.

The Guardian Civic League and its Board helped me to get this book distributed. Finally my brothers, Lawrence W. Reaves and Walter R. Reaves, were always available to me with resources to help move the manuscript forward into a published book. All in all, I will always feel indebted to the above individuals.

CHAPTER ONE

I felt like I was somebody important that August day in 1940. After six weeks of training at the police academy, I was headed for Philadelphia's City Hall to meet the mayor. I was all dressed up in my new blue uniform with brass buttons, a chrome badge, a sidearm, and a nightstick, and I was about to become an official member of the Philadelphia police. Fifty-one other new recruits to the force would also be attending the ceremony, but I suspected I would be singled out for special attention. I would be the only black rookie policeman in the room. In fact, I was the first black policeman to have been appointed to the force in over eight years.

I had given up a college education at Lincoln University, which I was attending with the assistance of a senatorial scholarship, to take this job. I knew that a college education held the promise of obtaining a comfortable life with a good income and enviable status, but it also meant years of hard work and deprivation. When the opportunity to join the police force and earn $5 a day—paid in cash twice a month—presented itself, and when I thought about the respect that was accorded to policemen in those days, I just couldn't resist the opportunity. My mother was concerned about the danger involved in police work, but I had had a modicum of success as an amateur boxer, both as a teenager and as a young adult; and when I assured her I could take care of myself, she was supportive of my decision.

My family had always lived from paycheck to paycheck because of low wages and bouts of unemployment, but we were never on public welfare. My father was a carpenter and often had to leave town to find work, while my mother did day work in the homes of white families. My two older brothers augmented the family income with part-time jobs after school, but there was never enough money. I knew that when I got my first pay envelope full of $5 bills it would seem like more money than I had seen in my life and that it would provide my family with a better living.

Mayor R. E. Lamberton received my class in his large office, where he inspected and congratulated us, urging us to wear our uniforms proudly and to perform our duties faithfully. Flash bulbs on the cameras of the press photog-

1

raphers in the office went off throughout the ceremony, and when it concluded I was surrounded by photographers and reporters from the four black weekly papers, as well as men from the daily papers, who wanted to get the story of the new black recruit on the force. The mayor dismissed us shortly thereafter, instructing us to report to our respective assignments.

I was so anxious to get started that I went directly to my assigned station, the 33rd Police District at 7th and Carpenter Streets. I lived only a short distance from the station, but I had never been inside it before. It was a typical old nineteenth-century stone building that had become quite tired-looking because it wasn't very well kept up. Upon entering the front door, I was immediately struck by the overpowering odor of alcohol. The roll room was almost half filled with illegal whisky stills and related paraphernalia that had been seized during raids, most of them conducted on private homes.

Sergeant James McCoy, an elderly fatherly-looking man, was the operations room commander. He ushered me into the front room where he introduced me to Captain Joseph Cintenni, another elderly man who was all business. Captain Cintenni told me to do the best job I could and to stay out of trouble. "And," he added, "don't fall for all the bullshit the men will tell you." It was a message I never let myself forget.

At home after dinner, I was so on edge I couldn't sit still for thinking about my first shift. I put my uniform back on and walked to the subway station on Broad Street. I was greatly surprised when the cashier at the station buzzed the gate open for me to walk through without paying the fare, which was only eight cents at the time. I rode the train to City Hall, then changed lines and rode out to 69th Street, beyond West Philadelphia. I didn't do much, just walked around showing off my uniform, but everyone was so kind to me, smiling and tipping their hats.

I was quite full of myself and my new uniform by the time midnight rolled around. Almost since I had entered the police academy, everyone associated with the police force had treated me very well. One day, when we were on the firing range at the academy, a report came in that a fire was raging out of control in a wax factory in Camden, New Jersey, across the Ben Franklin Bridge from Philadelphia. The recruits were ordered to pile into patrol wagons quickly to go assist in the fire fighting effort. We hadn't been issued holsters yet, so we stuck our pistols under our belts and hurried off. After the fire was extinguished, we were ushered into a local restaurant for dinner, where our white sergeant insisted that I sit next to him. All of the other officers were kind to me, and I felt like I fit right in with them.

Perhaps I had too quickly overlooked the warning signs that surfaced when I originally took the civil service exam to become a policeman. The first time I took the test, on October 13, 1939, I came away quite confident that I had scored well. I knew the material in the test and, as a student, I was quite used to being tested. I was dumbfounded when the test results were published and I saw that I was ranked 2,960th. It had long been rumored that civil service tests were manipulated by the notoriously corrupt Republican administration that had a stranglehold on Philadelphia at that time, and after I saw my test results I was convinced of it.

Newspapers soon began publishing reports that members of the Civil Service Commission were feuding among themselves, and that two members of the commission had approved the test results in the absence of the chairman, who was out of town. One newspaper, *The Philadelphia Record*, noted that "Traditionally, a certain number of police jobs are allocated to each [political] ward," but in this test not a single applicant from the commissioner's ward made the list of successful applicants.

The commissioner refused to certify the test results when he returned to town, and he also managed to oust the two commissioners who had manipulated the test in his absence. A new test was given in March of 1940, and when I took that test I suddenly moved up the list to place in the 137th position.

Despite that experience, I reported to my first shift of duty in a positive and optimistic frame of mind, but that didn't last long. When I arrived at my station house, one of the officers on duty introduced me to the street sergeant in charge that night. He glanced at me coldly, gave me a quick scan up and down, and then said something for which I never forgave him. "My God," he hissed, "it gets worse."

I was crushed, and at roll call I stood next to the only other black officer in the squad, Tom Brown. He understood the situation I had walked into, and he immediately took an interest in me. When roll call was over, Tom and I left for our beats. But, while the white foot beat officers in the squad were driven to their assignments in police cars, Tom and I had to walk to ours.

Just four years earlier, an atypical white police sergeant had attempted to mix white and black police officers in a squad car, and it almost ruined his career. Sergeant Edward Reynolds was working in the First Police District—located in the heart of a black community—on the evening of February 18, 1936, when he assigned a black policeman to ride in a patrol car with a white officer. The white officers in the squad bitterly protested Reynolds' action to the district captain, who immediately ordered Sergeant Reynolds to refrain from assigning any black officers to patrol cars. In spite of the harsh words that his white officers directed at him, and ignoring the possible repercussions, Sergeant Reynolds protested the captain's order. But the captain was adamant and insisted that Reynolds obey his order.

When news broke in the neighborhood of this blatant slap in the face, the black community protested loudly. The city's largest black newspaper, *The Philadelphia Tribune*, demanded that the director of public safety launch an immediate investigation. As with many other related requests at this time, however, nothing ever came of the investigation. Nothing, that is, except that Sergeant Reynolds was removed from the district and exiled to a new assignment in the boondocks.

As Tom Brown and I patrolled up and down South Street on my first night, he patiently instructed me on the business of police work. There were a number of bars on South Street, an area of small businesses and retail establishments, and on the midnight shift things quieted down quickly when the bars closed for the night. When the street was deserted, at about 3:00 A.M., Tom told me he had to run an errand and suggested that I take it easy until he returned.

I was walking slowly down the sidewalk when a young white girl came running up to me and said that her parents wanted me to hurry to their store, which was two blocks away. When I arrived, I found that it was a jewelry store, and all the lights were blazing. The owner told me that he thought there was a burglar on the third floor. Without further thought, I hurried up the stairwell and discovered that the door at the third level was closed.

I drew my revolver with my right hand, turned on the flashlight in my left hand, kicked in the door, and rushed into the darkened room. I froze in my tracks as I saw a pile of clothes on the floor in front of me suddenly burst into flames. The family passed me buckets of water and I quickly extinguished the fire. We then figured out that the fire had been caused by an electric iron, which had been left turned on by the maid. The iron had burned through the ironing board and it and the ironing board had fallen to the floor, causing the noise the owner heard.

The store owner heaped praise on me for helping him avert disaster, and I began to forget about the harsh reception I had received earlier that evening from my sergeant. The sergeant had the final word, though. Rather than commending me for my action at the jewelry store when he learned of it, he told me that I was stupid for having gone into the building by myself.

After a short time working with Tom Brown on his beat, I was assigned to a beat adjacent to his. Tom was my mentor, and he constantly advised me on the correct procedures to follow. Our beats were located near my home, which was unfortunate because my neighbors and associates hadn't been very supportive of my decision to join the force. They warned me that I would have to arrest people close to me, but I always countered that my friends were not the criminal type.

As an experienced policeman, Tom Brown was well aware of what the criminal types were like, and he hastened to educate me in identifying which criminals it was OK to arrest, and which ones had bought themselves immunity from prosecution through regular payments to certain top police officials and politicians.

It was general knowledge on the police force, and in the city, that some lawbreakers were not to be tampered with. Generally, these were numbers writers and gamblers, as well as people who ran houses of prostitution and speakeasies, which remained popular after Prohibition because legitimate liquor licenses were expensive and difficult to come by.

The regularly scheduled payoffs were generally made to policemen who were assigned to squad cars, because squad-car men were assigned to fixed sectors. Foot patrolmen were often transferred on a daily basis, and they never knew where they were going to be sent when they reported to work.

Squad-car men also periodically raided the illegal establishments that were paying off to give the appearance of legitimate law enforcement, but the establishment in question would be given ample warning of the raids, and they were happy to cooperate. One speakeasy operator was known to request that raiding officers not break any of his pint bottles because they were too difficult to replace. The corrupt police officers obliged him and even went so far as to help protect the man's territory by arresting anyone who tried to set up a competing enterprise in his area.

In between the staged raids on protected operations, foot patrolmen like Tom Brown and myself were expected to make frequent visits to the protected businesses to ensure that the clientele that patronized them didn't cause any trouble for the owners. Although I didn't like the idea of this selective law enforcement, it was so entrenched that there was absolutely nothing a foot patrolman, and especially a black foot patrolman, could do about it. Members of the community considered the illegal activities to be victimless crimes, and they never complained to their politicians as long as the things they did care about—from parking tickets to government jobs to traffic signals—were taken care of.

The most nerve-wracking aspect of the situation for a policeman was that the identity of who was protected was never officially acknowledged, of course. A policeman could only identify a protected party through word-of-mouth advice from other officers. The most certain—and unpleasant—way of discovering who was paying off was to arrest a protected person, as I discovered when I stumbled upon a large craps game during my early days on the police force.

I was patrolling Delaware Avenue, which adjoins the river of the same name that houses Philadelphia's port complex. It was just after daylight when I observed a large group of men collected on the sidewalk. As I approached them, I thought they were longshoremen awaiting assignment to one of the cargo ships in the port. I became suspicious when some of the men on the outer edges of the group walked away as they saw me approaching. As the group thinned out, I could see that there was a large craps game in progress.

I knew that there were organized crap games that were run as on-going businesses by protected people, almost all of them white, but I didn't know if this crowd was part of that gang. In addition, there were so many men present that I couldn't have arrested them by myself even if I had known their protection status. I decided that the best action to take was to ask for assistance from my sergeant. I found a police call box and started describing what I had seen to the sergeant. I wasn't halfway through my report when the sergeant interrupted to tell me to stay put and he would be right there. Moments later, the sergeant ordered me into his car without a word of explanation, then drove me to a beat on the extreme opposite end of the district. When we arrived there, he told me to get out of the car and start walking, saying that I had just been reassigned.

Like the majority of black police officers, I was usually assigned to predominantly black neighborhoods. As a result, most of the people I arrested were black. There were times, however, when I had to arrest whites and, depending on who was on command that day, this could also be a source of trouble. To some white sergeants, white law breakers were immune from arrest by black policeman, even if the white person in question wasn't paying anyone off.

I was patrolling on the east side of Broad Street one day when I observed an automobile strike a milk wagon and knock it over on the west side of the street, which was out of my district. Willard Johnston, another black officer who was assigned to the district with jurisdiction, also saw the accident from his position on the opposite side of the street. I crossed Broad Street to assist Johnston, something we were not supposed to do unless ordered to by a superior, and I later assisted in arresting the driver of the car that had caused the accident. My sergeant didn't seem to mind when I first told him of the incident, but he later became enraged when he read my report and learned that I had arrested a white man.

Perhaps the most blatant incident occurred when I issued a parking ticket to a man for parking too close to a firehouse. The driver informed me that I had better not give him a ticket, and that I would hear more about it later if I did. I ignored his threat because white people often said that when I arrested them for something. When I returned to the station house to report off duty that day, however, the sergeant immediately confronted me and demanded an explanation for my having issued that ticket. When I told him I was just doing my job, he shook his head and said "You'll never learn, will you?" For the next three weeks, in the dead of winter, I was assigned to stand guard outside the front of a hospital for eight hours a day without any relief.

My mentor, Tom Brown, and the four other black policemen in my district— out of a total of 150 policemen assigned there—counseled me and offered their advice when I got into these situations. Tom Brown, who only had a fifth-grade education, had a lot of "mother's wit," and he warned me not to make enemies with my white superiors, but not to become too friendly with them either. I didn't like having to deal with this tension all the time, but fortunately it was offset by the kindness of many of the residents and businessmen—both white and black—who lived or worked in the areas I patrolled.

One day I arrested a man on South Street who had a gun tucked in the waistband of his pants. I disarmed him at gun point and walked him to a call box to call for a police wagon to come pick him up. I had to release my grip on him while I opened the call box and, while I still had my gun drawn on him, I was worried that he might make a grab for my gun while I was distracted. It seemed like forever until the police wagon came, and my nervousness must have shown, for the next day a man who lived near the call box told me I hadn't had a thing to worry about. The man had seen me make the arrest, he said, and he had gotten a rifle inside his house and kept it trained on the criminal the whole time I was on the phone.

Another piece of advice that Tom Brown gave me was to join a social club made up of blacks who worked for the police and fire departments and the electric bureau. City officials strongly opposed the idea of such a group, knowing the potential trouble that could develop out of group action, and they were correct in their concern. Shortly after I joined the group, the policemen in the association became increasingly vocal about the prohibition against black officers using patrol cars. At one meeting, the men decided to enlist the aid of a black political leader, Dr. John K. Rice of the North Philadelphia Civic League, in their cause.

Dr. Rice and a committee from his organization arranged a meeting with the city's director of public safety, James J. Malone, and his assistant, Herbert E. Millen, who was one of the few blacks with a prominent political job in the city. Director Malone acknowledged that there were no blacks in patrol cars, nor any black sergeants, captains, or inspectors in uniform, nor even any black elevator operators in the electric bureau. But he blamed the lack of promotions on the Civil Service Commission and promised to do everything in his power to end all apparent discrimination on account of race or color in the police and fire departments. Malone never even came close to keeping his word.

The North Philadelphia Civic League then held a public meeting at the McDowell Memorial Church at 21st Street and Columbia Avenue on October 13, 1940. More than 500 people attended the meeting, which—importantly— was held just a few weeks before local elections. Director Malone, who had been warned of the meeting, sent his assistant, Herbert Millen, to the meeting with a hastily prepared announcement. The police department, Millen said, would appoint six black officers to patrol-car duty the very next day. The people in attendance were pleased by the announcement, but they were also skeptical. They warned that the "election patrol-car assignments" might disappear as soon as the last polling place closed.

True to his limited promise, Director Malone had six black officers report to City Hall the next morning where, amid great ceremony and the generation of much publicity, they were assigned to their cars. The men would not be removed from the cars after the election passed, but no additional blacks were assigned to patrol cars for some time.

Just before election day in 1940, my family received a postcard from a distant relative informing us that my father had died on November 1, in Fayetteville, North Carolina. My father had been working as a carpenter on the construction of Fort Bragg, the U.S. military installation that was being built about twelve miles outside of Fayetteville. I traveled to Fayetteville with my mother and my siblings, but when we arrived we were unable to secure lodgings in any of the segregated hotels or motels, and we had to continue on another sixty-five miles to stay with relatives in Dillon, South Carolina.

When we inquired about my father's death, we were embittered but not surprised by what we learned. Although my father had worked side-by-side with white carpenters at Fort Bragg, doing precisely the same work, the white carpenters were provided with lodgings on the site, while my father was prohibited from staying there. He had to rent a room in Fayetteville and commute to work daily in an open-bodied truck. Because of this, he caught a cold, which progressed into pneumonia. He was subsequently taken to Highsmith Hospital, where he died within a few days.

The segregation my father experienced was very obviously a contributory factor in his death, and this event brought about an abrupt change in my racial thinking. Although I had had racial comments cast at me, or made indirectly within my earshot, I still thought my appointment to the Philadelphia Police Department was a sign that racial relations were improving. After this happened to my father, I began to think that things were regressing rather than progressing, and I began to look askance in all of my dealings with white people.

Nonetheless, there were small signs of movement towards equality on the police force during my first years in the department, and I tried to respond to them hopefully whenever they occurred. One incident that gave me some personal satisfaction happened when a white sergeant in my district, Larry Cella, marked his twentieth anniversary on the force. Part of the street wisdom that the older black policemen had imparted to me was that, however cordial some white policemen might be while on duty, there was an unwritten but still quite prominent prohibition against the races socializing when off duty. And, most especially, a black policeman should never expect to be invited to the home of a white colleague.

Thus it came as quite a surprise when Sergeant Cella extended invitations to his twentieth-anniversary party, which was to be held in his home, to all of the policemen in the squad, including the black ones. All of my black colleagues were skeptical and disdainful of the invitation, and all of them declined to attend the event. They also advised me to do the same, saying that white people and black people lived in two different worlds, ones that were separate and unequal. This was one time, though, that I didn't follow their suggestions.

I was uneasy about going to the party, but I told myself that, come hell or high water, I was going to go. I wanted to have the experience of being with my fellow officers in a social setting, and I felt that I couldn't refuse an invitation that, on the surface at least, seemed to have been extended to me in friendship.

I went to the party and had a terrific time, having had a bit more to drink than I should have, as did everyone else. All of the white officers at the party were very solicitous towards me, and made me feel like I was a member of the fraternity of police. Some ice got broken that evening, and the men at the party had the chance to see that I was indeed just like them. It was one of the few times in my early dealings with the overwhelmingly white police department of Philadelphia where race didn't seem to matter.

I didn't have any illusions that, suddenly, everything was going to change as a result of one party but, maybe because I was a student of black history, it gave me faith. I knew that, when change came, it came slowly. It had been that way for the black community for centuries.

Blacks in Philadelphia have long shown an interest in the welfare and safety of the community, beginning as early as 1793 when there were 3,000 blacks in the city. When the yellow fever struck that year, thousands of panic-stricken citizens hastily departed the city for safety in outlying areas. In their haste, they left behind all of their possessions that might have been contaminated. Among those who fled was President George Washington, who took up residence in suburban Germantown, to ride out the course of the dreaded disease in safety.

The hero of this catastrophe was Dr. Benjamin Rush, a highly respected physician who became known as the father of American medicine. Dr. Rush sought out black leaders, including Richard Allen and Absalom Jones, two widely known leaders at that time, and enlisted the men in his efforts to combat the disease. Jones and Allen agreed to assist Dr. Rush, without receiving any compensation. Dr. Rush made them his special assistants, instructing them in administering medicines and caring for the sick. He assured them that blacks were immune to the disease. He was proven wrong, however, since 10 percent of the black population eventually succumbed to the dreaded illness.

During the War of 1812, when the British were threatening the city, Allen, Jones and James Forten put their lives on the line again as they organized more than 2,500 black male volunteers to fight. This represented nearly three-fourths of the entire black male population in the city. The men were mobilized and marched off to Gray's Ferry on Philadelphia's Schuylkill River to put up defensive fortifications. Shortly after that, a battalion for service in the field was formed, but the war ended before they reached the front.

In the early part of the 19th century, new industries sprang up in Philadelphia, attracting new black immigrants, as well as rural white Americans who flocked to the city. They were joined by an influx of both freed and enslaved blacks.

The result was a scramble for jobs, and blacks came out on the short end of the stick. Consequently, crime and poverty increased in black communities. Numerous house break-ins, assaults and petty thefts against blacks were reported. A more stable group of blacks, led by James Forten, spoke out against such crimes. In 1822, blacks held a heavily attended meeting where they denounced crime by black criminals and volunteered information against them.

In 1863, the Union forces in the Civil War put out the call for more manpower. Several hundred prominent black citizens in Philadelphia, led by Frederick Douglass, were given permission by the War Department to form black regiments, with troops being paid $10 a month plus rations. They assembled at Camp William Penn in Chelten Hills on June 26, 1863. By February 1864, five full regiments, known as The United States Regiments of Colored Troops, were ready to march off to battle. They fought well and returned to civilian life after the war, receiving far more respect than they had been afforded before their active service.

With the war over and their emancipation firmly established, blacks believed, and rightfully so, that things would change. The tumultuous years of the first half of the century seemed a thing of the past. They believed they would be accepted by the white community as fellow human beings. They returned from the war with a renewed zeal to hasten their social development in the American society. But, unfortunately, their exhilaration was short-lived. Their new political rights were the very basis for further strife between blacks and whites. Philadelphia blacks registered and prepared to vote en masse for the Republican Party. This sparked murderous election brawls in the 1870s as the Irish Democrats sought to keep blacks from voting in the areas that they controlled. In *The Philadelphia Negro*, published in 1899, W.E.B. DuBois would write, "As the Irishmen had been the tool of the Democrats, the Negro became the tool of the Republicans."

During primary elections in the spring in 1871, there was so much disorder and such poor police protection that the U.S. Marines were called in to preserve order. During general elections in the fall, the city witnessed the cold-blooded assassinations of several blacks, among whom was an estimable young teacher, Octavious V. Catto.

Democratic Mayor Daniel Fox was running for re-election and he used the police department as his own private army. On election day, they were at the polls bright and early, tossing black voters out of the line because they were expected to vote Republican. While waiting to vote, Octavious V. Catto was murdered by a red-haired man with a bandaged head. The red-haired man fired two shots from his pistol, both of which struck Catto. A passerby grabbed the gunman and turned him over to the police. One officer was heard to mutter to the gunman, "Get away quick," and he did.

The October 10, 1871, murder of Catto came at a critical moment. To blacks, it seemed a revival of the type of riots which occurred during the days of slavery, at a time, ironically, when they had their first taste of freedom. To the better classes of Philadelphia, it revealed a serious state of barbarism and lawlessness in the second largest city in the land. To the politicians, it furnished the text for many a speech.

Catto's murder resulted in an outburst of indignation and sorrow, and a determined stand for law and order. Some of the city's most prominent citizens held a meeting to express their outrage, and the funeral for Catto was perhaps the most imposing ever arranged for a black person up to that time in American history.

Modern Philadelphia police history began in 1850 when a Police Marshall was appointed to oversee all policemen in Philadelphia county. In 1854, the police force underwent a complete reorganization and mayors took a special interest in the supervision of the force on the streets. They often walked the beats at night with the officers. One mayor boasted that he knew every one of his 700 men, either by name or by face. Legend has it that one cold night in the 1880s, Mayor Samuel G. King was out walking the beat with some of his policemen when he looked through the window of a private home where blacks lived. The mayor saw that they "were warm and comfortable while white officers shook and shivered on the outside," protecting the blacks. Mayor King reportedly said blacks "should be out here protecting their own." Whether the Mayor King story is fact or fiction is a matter of conjecture at this point. But it is a matter of record that blacks were appointed to the department as turnkeys as early as the middle 1870s.

Apparently, blacks were hired as turnkeys because of the nature of work assigned to this position. Regular police officers certainly had no desire to do the laborious and oftentimes dirty work of a turnkey. Turnkeys were responsible for keeping the station house clean, keeping the furnace stoked in the winter, and putting out the trash and heavy ashes. Eventually, turnkeys were made responsible for prisoner security, but it is not known when.

The appointments of the first four black policemen occurred on August 5, 1881. It was surprising that Mayor King, a Democrat, made the first appointments, since virtually all black voters at that time were Republicans. The appointments were widely reported in the press. On August 6, 1881, the Philadelphia Times reported in a front page article: "Mayor King yesterday appointed four Colored men to his police force and early next week they will assume the club and shield and go forth to battle against crime and disorder. Whether they will figure wholly as peace preservers is a matter on which some affect to be doubtful . . . the members of the force are for the present dissatisfied at the innovation."

The Evening Telegraph reported: "Mayor King said that he would appoint colored men on the force and he has done just what he said he would do." An

Evening Telegraph editorial revealed that some whites believed blacks should not expect nor desire any further advancements. Some whites believe, the editorial stated, "our colored citizens ought to be content with emancipation, the suffrage and other good things which had been bestowed upon them."

The Weekly Item reported: "Soon the colored man will figure on the police, and immediately thereafter Mr. Huidekoper [the Postmaster] will appoint some colored men as letter carriers . . . Progress!"

A news story in *The Press* read: "*The Press* reporter made an effort to see the new appointees in their homes, but found all of them absent celebrating their promotion as suited them best." An editorial writer in the same paper, however, stated, "But neither prejudice nor the willingness of white men to appropriate everything should have delayed so long an act of simple justice . . . The Mayor has done well. The Press honors him for his courage and congratulates him on his sense of justice . . . These men are not appointed because they are black, but because they are believed to be fit for the position, and, if they are fit, the color of their skins should be no more considered than the color of their eyes or hair."

Charles K. Draper had the distinction of being the first black man in police uniform to patrol the streets in Philadelphia, when his patrol duty began August 9, 1881, at 6:00 P.M.. When news of his impending patrol duty spread in the black community, blacks converged on the area surrounding the 19th Police District at 12th and Pine Streets.

The Philadelphia Times reported: "By the time six o'clock struck from headquarters the entire street was blocked. The crowd was inclined to laugh a great deal, colored folk generally are, but there was no mistaking the fact that their heads were, figuratively speaking, bumping against the clouds, as they greeted their hero of the hour on his appearance on the steps of the station house. With him moved the crowd, elbowing and pushing for a good look. Every window along the way was filled with faces to gaze and wonder."

The Times even more poignantly reported, "The fact that the first of their race who ever donned a uniform in defense of the city's peace was in their midst was more than the excitable Africans of the neighborhood could stand quietly. The pride of the men insisted that they be on hand to give their representative an encouraging start. It did not take the crowd long to overflow the sidewalk . . . 'No one'll have a chance for a gal agin his buttons,' said a particularly ugly darkey in an injured tone, but a sable damsel's reply: 'You'd ha' no chance nohow,' proved an effective damper to this critic."

Among the first black members of the Philadelphia Police Department, Alexander G. Davis was one of a kind. Initially, he had the unique distinction of having been a slave, though he seemed a most unlikely candidate for involuntary servitude. Davis was born June 12, 1851, on a plantation near Greenburg, North Carolina. After emancipation, his family moved north and he enrolled at Lincoln

...mes N. Reaves, sworn in as a policeman
...to R: Howard P. Sutton, Supt. of Police, Mayor Robert E. Lamberton shakes Reaves' hand -
...ly 8, 1940

...lks Parade on Broad Street - 1942(?) - led by Sgt Robert Forgy (photo - courtesy of Gaston
...evigne)

Detective Sgt. Richard H. Anderson presents a retirement watch to Clarence Hatcher, plain-clothesman, 1946.

University in 1871. After graduation from Lincoln, he went on to graduate from Howard Law School in Washington, D.C. But he was denied admission to the bar, so he became an educator. He taught first in Gordonsville, Virginia, followed by a stint as a school principal in Wayne County, Georgia. Because of a health problem, Davis moved to Philadelphia and began publishing a small newspaper, *The Spectator*. This brought him to the attention of Mayor Samuel G. King, who included Davis in the first group of black police appointees.

The number of black policemen on the Philadelphia force grew as blacks migrated steadily from their harsh treatment as sharecroppers in the South, to less laborious domestic jobs in the North. The black population in Philadelphia jumped 45 percent from 1860 to 1890. Only 32 percent of the black population in 1890 were native-born Philadelphians. Because of this influx of black residents, it is not surprising that the force of 34 black policemen dating back to Mayor King's administration grew almost twofold, to a total of 62 by 1890. The state legislature had set a standard of one policeman for every 600 citizens in 1854. The number of black policemen in 1890, in comparison to the number of black residents, nearly met that standard.

By 1913, the number of black officers again more than doubled, reaching a total of 124, almost all of the assignments coming by political appointment. Ten years later, the number again more than doubled. The total number of black policeman finally reached 268 by 1923. Unfortunately, progress suddenly came to a halt, and the 1923 figure remained the record high for the next thirty-five years.

CHAPTER TWO

Richard H. Anderson became, by far, the most widely known black policeman in Philadelphia in the early 1920s. He was a tall, dark-brown-skinned man with broad shoulders, who was heavily built but well proportioned. He had high cheek bones with jaws well set and heavily lidded eyes that belied his ever-alert predisposition. He could easily have passed for Paul Robeson's brother, and Anderson did have a good relationship with Robeson himself. A veteran of the Spanish-American War, Anderson was appointed to the department on July 23, 1913. Little is known about his life or career prior to 1921 when he catapulted into instant fame as a result of killing William Drayton, alias "Alabama Joe," in a shootout.

This police action on February 10, 1921 was perhaps the most celebrated ever involving a black policeman in the city of Philadelphia. To this day, there are hundreds of people who vividly recall this highly publicized incident that took place near 17th and Lombard Streets in the central portion of the city. At about 2:00 A.M., the 19th Police District received a call about a shooting in progress. On arrival, the police found a woman, Grace Coleman, who had been shot and who was later taken to Polyclinic Hospital. The woman told police that her attacker was still inside the building she had escaped from, and that he was holding two other women and a child hostage.

When police attempted to enter the house, they were met by several gunshots. They returned the fire, then beat a hasty retreat out of the building to call for reinforcements. After additional police arrived, a second attempt was made to storm the building, but the police were again repulsed by gunfire, which seemed to be coming from both the first and second floors of the building simultaneously. The police commander in charge then sent for a fire department ladder truck, in an attempt to get a clear shot into the building but, even when this additional equipment arrived, the police were unable to enter the building and the standoff continued amid much tension. About 200 policemen had been called to the scene by that time, and three of them were injured by the heavy gunfire.

At about 7:40 A.M., patrolman Dick Anderson, who was en route to work the day tour of duty in that district, entered the area and observed the commotion.

Anderson walked up to the scene and, upon learning that the standoff had lasted for almost six hours, decided to take decisive actions. As a war veteran, Anderson apparently was not fazed by gunfire, and he snuck into the house in the middle of the battle. From that vantage point, Anderson observed that the gunfire wasn't coming from both floors simultaneously, but that the gunman was running from floor to floor, giving the impression that there were additional gunmen inside.

Anderson hid behind a door until the man came back downstairs, then jumped out and opened fire. He hit the gunman four times in the ensuing gun fight, then disarmed him. He took the man's two revolvers and dragged him outside to a waiting patrol wagon, ably assisted by formerly cautious policemen who were now anxious to claim credit for the arrest. As he was lead from the scene, Alabama Joe began singing out "I'm going back to Alabama now." Alabama Joe was taken to a hospital, where he later died at 4:30 P.M.

Because of the wide newspaper coverage of the incident, more than 50,000 people came to view Alabama Joe's body at the funeral home. The visitors were asked to pay twenty-five cents apiece for admission to the funeral parlor, with the money allegedly being used to pay for Alabama Joe's burial expenses.

Later, a reporter for the black newspaper *The Philadelphia Tribune* complained that other policemen received more recognition for the arrest than Dick Anderson did, while Anderson was the one who took the greatest risk. "Anderson did far more in a few minutes than half of the police department could do in almost six hours," the reporter wrote. Other newspapers frequently made reference to the Alabama Joe incident in the following months, with the news media generally using Dick Anderson as a model for what a policeman, white or black, should be like.

Despite his new-found fame, Anderson had very little formal education and usually had problems passing promotion examinations. Nonetheless, politics played a very important role in the Philadelphia police department at that time— as it would for years to come—and that may have had both a positive and negative impact on Anderson's career. The first known record of Anderson's attempt to seek a promotion was when he took the sergeant's exam on August 20, 1921. His results placed him 162nd on the promotion list, and he was not promoted.

Anderson was well liked by his superiors, who often used him as an undercover plainclothesman, and he was eventually promoted to detective in 1930 and to sergeant the next year. Nonetheless, Anderson was demoted back to policeman in 1932 for political reasons, after having served as a sergeant for only a few months.

Blacks received very few promotions in the Philadelphia Police Department, up to and including 1930, as the department practiced the same institutionalized racism that was rampant in all aspects of life at that time. When Anderson was promoted to sergeant in 1931, his advancement was hailed by the black community as being long past due. The white members of the police department, however, were not pleased by it at all. They made no bones about it, they simply told their commanding officers that they would not work for a black supervisor. The white police officers were so vocal about Anderson's promotion that the white police captain in the district Anderson had been assigned to became concerned. He sent word from his office at 20th and Fitzwater Streets to the police superintendent, informing him that he did not want Anderson in his command and that his white officers wouldn't work for him. The superintendent was apparently sympathetic to the captain, because he immediately withdrew Anderson from uniform patrol work and reassigned him to plainclothes work at City Hall.

Anderson continued at this assignment for a short while, then he began having difficulty with a Republican magistrate in City Hall, Edward W. Henry. Henry was a tall, light-skinned black who was an old-line Philadelphia Republican. He had once worked as a headwaiter at the Union League, Philadelphia's most exclusive and reclusive bastion of the monied white community. Henry managed to win his way up the social ladder by becoming the Exalted Ruler of The Quaker City Elks, and the Republican Party in Philadelphia was able to get him elected as a magistrate. At that time, he became only the second black magistrate in the city's history.

Both Anderson and Henry were strong willed, and they ultimately came to conflict over Anderson's arrest of one of Magistrate Henry's friends. Henry attempted to learn the details surrounding the arrest before the man was brought to a hearing, but Anderson refused to explain the arrest outside the courtroom. Shortly afterwards, Anderson lost his rank and was returned to uniformed duty at the 12th and Pine Street Station.

While black policemen were legally entitled to all of the rights and respect that white policemen received, there were unwritten rules and common practices that tended to restrict the full exercise of their official duties and personal privileges. Black policemen were denied promotions, and many civil service lists were frozen when a black policeman's name reached the top of the list. Black officers were denied entry into special police units, they were denied patrol car assignments, and they were seldom assigned to office desk jobs, regardless of how well qualified they were. If black policemen were assigned to work inside the station house, they were given the dirty jobs of stoking fires, putting out ashes, washing windows, and scrubbing floors.

Being a black policeman at that time was considered to be a job that was a level above the nonskilled work most black men were restricted to. It was considered as being of equal status with the black schoolteachers and postal workers of the day—jobs of some significance for a black person. This social recognition made many black policemen feel they were different from other blacks. In another way, it made some black policemen feel satisfied to have come that far; and for whatever reasons, it seemed that the majority of them did not sustain the drive to advance themselves further. It's difficult to say, however, whether this thinking was really a lack of ambition, or a recognition of reality, since it was official policy that black policemen were seldom considered for advancement within the department.

Several of the old time policemen who lived through those days have told me that white policemen never hesitated to remind them of their place in the scheme of things. "This is a white man's job," they'd say. "Negroes don't have any place in the police department."

One of the old-timers smiled and said to me once, "In fact, many of the white policemen back in those days hated being a policeman. Some of them didn't even want to wear the uniform. They regarded themselves as servants in uniforms. Some of them were really a mixed-up bunch. We colored officers figured that one day, since we were on the bottom of the ladder in America, those jobs would become available to more coloreds like us."

Dick Anderson was finally reinstated as a detective, after eight years as a uniformed policeman, in 1940. Black community groups were becoming increasingly vocal about their demands that City Council force the hiring of more black policemen. At that time, the number of black policemen was actually declining from the high of 268 in the late 1920s, while the city, in the prelude to World War II, was actually experiencing an expansion of the job market.

Blacks were entering skilled jobs in industry on the same basis as whites, and people wanted to know why that wasn't happening in the police department. When the four newspapers of the black community joined in with other groups to protest, the pressure on the department to change became enormous. These same groups also wanted to know why black policemen were not being promoted into the higher ranks; and, Dick Anderson, who was still famous for his bravery in the Alabama Joe incident, was the man they always used to illustrate their point.

Black Philadelphians wanted to see their hero progress, and this was highlighted by the letters community newspapers ran calling for change. Those newspapers also ran stories with headlines that read, "We want more black policemen." "We want a black judge." Eventually, after a lot of pressure, Dick Anderson was given back his former rank of detective.

I came to know Anderson a few years after that, when I was assigned to a new squad that he headed. In 1943, I was still patrolling in the district I had first been assigned to, the South Street area of Philadelphia. Crime was increasing in the district at an unprecedented rate, and more and more I dreaded working a beat alone there. I spent a lot of time around Broad and South Streets, since that was an intersection at which three police districts shared corners—the 1st, 19th and 33rd Districts. Usually, I was able to see other officers from this vantage point, and I could share police information with them and get help if I needed it.

It is difficult to understand now how perplexing it was to conduct police work in those days, particularly when officers were assigned to foot patrol alone. Policemen worked without radios, and without a sufficient fleet of motorized equipment. A lone policeman walking a beat or conducting an investigation could often feel very isolated, and he had to use a lot of ingenuity in making arrests. All too often, no telephone was available when you made an arrest, and call boxes always seemed to be an eternity away when you had an unruly prisoner. Sometimes, to attract attention, a policeman would fire his revolver in the air in hopes that some nearby policeman would respond, or that a nearby resident would call police headquarters and report that a policeman needed assistance. As a last resort, a policeman would use physical force to subdue or restrain prisoners.

World War II was at its peak then, and a lot of new characters had floated into the area. There were people who had come looking for jobs, which were plentiful with so many men having left the city to serve in the armed forces, and a good portion of the job seekers were law-abiding people. But, far too many of the new arrivals were con men, burglars and outright thieves looking for an easy buck.

Seldom did a night pass that the plate glass window of a store wasn't broken. Speakeasies proliferated, and street fights among drunk or disorderly men were daily events. Streetwalkers attracted motorists to the neighborhood, who, often as not, were then taken into back rooms and robbed. Pocketbook snatching, petty theft, and wanton shoplifting were a constant. The businessmen in the South Street area, who felt that their very livelihoods were threatened, finally made an urgent appeal for help to the Superintendent of Police, Howard P. Sutton.

The merchants, who were white, were the owners of thriving retail businesses that were being victimized by criminals who, because they lived in the surrounding neighborhoods, were largely black. Almost immediately after the merchants made their plea, a special black plainclothes squad was formed within the police department, and Dick Anderson was chosen by Herbert Millen, the Assistant Director of Public Safety, to head it. Millen was the first black who had been appointed to a position of such power, and he was determined to show his power and effectiveness in helping the merchants ward off the criminals.

There wasn't any doubt in Millen's mind that the way to deal with black crime on South Street was to use tough black cops working in plainclothes. Millen also figured that black community leaders would accept the black squad without feeling that white policemen were trying to control their community, and it provided a perfect opportunity to give Dick Anderson the command the community had been calling for.

In early March of 1943, Detective Anderson was made an acting sergeant. Anderson was then instructed to organize the Special Investigation Squad (SIS), as the new group was to be called. The black press in Philadelphia immediately began running stories on the special squad, all of which made Millen and the police department look good. When the squad first organized, it was composed of thirty officers who were assigned to plainclothes duty. Ultimately, sixty men served in the squad at one time or another.

My friend and fellow officer Willard Johnston heard about the formation of the squad from his father, Hillery, who worked for Herbert Millen. One day in mid-March, Willard and his partner, Theodore (Ted) Jordan, saw me while I was on duty, told me about the squad and asked if I was interested in joining. I readily agreed because I believed the Special Investigation Squad would give me an opportunity to do something really exciting. I could imagine myself in all kinds of dangerous situations, saving society from being taken over by criminals.

Because I knew there would be other black policemen on the squad, I thought that I would be able to trust them to back me up. Like some of my fellow black officers, I wanted to be promoted and I felt this assignment would help me move in that direction. It seemed to me that everything would be going my way if I were able to join the other fellows on the new squad.

I went to see Sergeant Anderson in his office at Twelfth and Pine Streets without asking permission from my superior officers. Anderson's appearance and demeanor were both authoritative and intimidating. I was not impressed with his office setup, however. It seemed to be much too small and ill-furnished for a serious police operation. He interviewed me for about ten minutes, taking all of my personal data, then he said that I would hear from him later.

I was at home that night when I received my acceptance memorandum into Anderson's squad. It was a promotion without money, but I still felt good. I knew I was going places, and I shared my feelings with my family and friends. They were very happy for me. Finally, after three years, I felt I was on the move in the police department. It really was a turning point in my career. Here I was a black policeman who had always worn a uniform, but now I was being trusted to be a policeman in plainclothes.

I reported for duty and met other members of SIS in a small room. It seemed as if everyone was talking at one time with the excitement of the moment. Dick Anderson sat his tall frame on the edge of a desk in the front of the room. "What you boys think this is?" I remember him saying in his deep voice, and we quickly fell quiet.

It seemed as if I couldn't get enough air as I stood packed into that crowded room and listened to Dick Anderson talk about our responsibilities and what he expected from us. I felt even more elated as I learned during his talk that he had personally selected each one of us based upon our personnel file.

Sergeant Anderson had chosen John Roane to assist him with the paperwork.

Roane was seated at an old table that served as his desk. I only knew a few of the older men, for many of them had worked in North and West Philadelphia, a good distance from my beat. I did know most of the younger men, though, for they had all been on the same appointment list as me when I joined the department.

Sergeant Anderson spent well over an hour talking to us and answering questions. He was very stern in giving out orders and warning us of severe disciplinary action for violation of the rules and regulations. He knew that, as the city's first all-black police squad, there was the undeniable sense that all eyes were upon us. Anderson said he wanted his men to be tough, and one reason for this was the prevailing societal temperament towards crime and criminals at that time. There was generally great respect among citizens for police and the law, and criminals were seen as evil people who needed to be rooted out of the community and punished. Policemen were afforded a wide latitude in exerting force in effecting arrests because criminals, regardless of their race, were not seen as having civil rights.

This societal attitude meant that the actions taken by police were seldom questioned by the average citizen, who would have been almost powerless to change police practices even if they had wanted to. The sometimes rough treatment of suspects was an established method of operation within police departments, one that had been passed down through the generations of police work. The civil rights of suspects would not become an issue until the post-World War II era.

Likewise, it was an accepted course of action for police to enter homes without a warrant, even when they knew they wouldn't be able to obtain one legally at a later time to cover their actions. People who were thought to be guilty of things were often arrested solely on the basis of suspicion. They could be held "on ice" for up to four days while an investigation was conducted. And, if the evidence needed for a conviction wasn't forthcoming, confessions were sometimes forced from suspects while they were incarcerated out of the public view.

Sergeant Anderson included two categories of men in his squad. About one-third were old timers with whom he had done uniform work. The rest were aggressive young bucks who were proud of their jobs and anxious to make names for themselves. The older men, most of whom had twenty years experience, served as stabilizing influences for the younger men. The result: very few of the younger men got into any departmental difficulties in later years. The men were paired in twos and given their assignments. I was teamed up with George Arnold, whom I had only met a couple of times. Our first area was on South Street between 18th and 20th Streets. We were of like temperament and worked well together.

A true feeling of brotherhood developed among the members of SIS. We never failed to help one another in dangerous situations, and we shared information about criminals and suspected criminal activities on a daily basis. And, we were always assigned in pairs with small areas to patrol, so we got to know each other well.

There had been plenty of pocketbook snatching, mugging, store theft, and disorderly conduct every night on South Street until SIS arrived, but that changed very quickly. Being in plainclothes gave us the huge advantage of surprise in keeping the streets safe for every individual. We would tend to stay in the shadows, then move in and identify ourselves as police by flashing our badges to make arrests. After a while, we became known, which in itself acted as a deterrent against criminal activity on South Street. Community people came to us with good information about criminals and their activities, which helped us make even more arrests.

Many of the merchants put in burglar alarm systems, which helped to multiply our coverage of the area. The Holmes Protective Agency wired most of the stores, and they answered their own alarms, often while a SIS member stood by waiting for them to arrive and open the establishment to hunt for burglars. Racial relations being what they were, however, we never went inside the stores with the white guards from Holmes, because we worried that we might be accused of stealing if something turned up missing from the store.

We mostly worked split shifts, 7 A.M. to 10 A.M. and 3 P.M. to 8 P.M., between 5th and 22nd Streets on South Street, where most of the crime took place. From time to time as we patrolled our beat, we ran into white, uniformed policemen, who also had been assigned in the area. They acted friendly towards us with short chats. Whenever they arrested a black criminal, they were happy to have a member of Dick Anderson's special squad back them up against any other person who might attack them during the arrest.

In the areas we patrolled, the vast majority of the criminals were black. However, from time to time, we did arrest some white criminals, mostly for shooting craps on the corner of 5th and Bainbridge Streets. They were always surprised to find out that we were plainclothes policemen, but we never had any problem with the white policemen who transported the suspects to the police station.

The black community readily accepted our presence since, just like in any other ethnic group, the vast majority of people were law-abiding citizens. There isn't any doubt in my mind that the black community wanted to see the law upheld against whomever. Many black people identified with the Dick Anderson Squad as their contribution to law and order. This helped us to get many black eyewitnesses to crimes to testify before a judge without fear for their own lives. On other occasions, their testimony supported the action of SIS members when their actions were questioned by the defendants' lawyers. Over a period of time, even the judges believed in our fairness and most of the time the accused were convicted. There were politicians who could get people released later but, nevertheless, they were found guilty first. Our arrest resulted in a conviction rate of 90 percent.

Even today, I still feel on edge about living up to Dick Anderson's expectations for SIS. He knew, and he let us know in a tough tone of voice, that we would be watched closely by others in the police department for the least little thing to bring disgrace to SIS. How we carried ourselves and looked, he felt, would contribute to our success or failure.

Every member was required to wear a well-pressed suit with shirt and tie. In other words, to be well groomed all the time. Anderson himself was always handsomely dressed and spoke in a stentorian manner. We usually looked better than the streetwise dandies we often arrested. Even slick criminals were caught off guard by the way we looked.

Whenever Dick Anderson spoke with us, he talked about doing a good job. He let you know that he was the boss and he expected you to follow his directions. Having to work with a lot of different people in and outside of the police department was difficult for all of us. Anderson always emphasized that we were not to take back talk from anyone and that we were not to fear anyone. He also made it very clear that you would not remain a member of SIS unless you got results. Getting rid of crime in the area was our mission, and he said that any SIS member who felt that he couldn't do that should request a transfer.

There were many knife and gun carriers in the community, and Anderson said he wanted to stop attacks by those weapon carriers in particular. Arrests were made rapidly, six or seven a week by some SIS members. If you had one or two arrests, or none, over a couple of weeks, Anderson would have you transferred out of SIS.

Our arrest record was reviewed weekly by Anderson. If you were low in arrests, you would get a personal admonition from him. SIS members with high arrest records were praised by him. "The crime is out there. Your job is to make arrests," I remember hearing him say frequently. There was one SIS pair, John King and Theodore Jordan, who were very good at making arrests. We called them Kingy and Jordan. Almost every night, they made arrest. During the day, there was another SIS pair in West Philadelphia, Frank Winfrey and Herbert Locklear, who also made large numbers of arrests on a daily basis. We understood that we had to fashion ourselves after them in terms of production.

I was once assigned to work with two fellows that I had not known in the department, both of whom were older than me. I think I was assigned to them to learn more about police work. As it turned out, they tended to learn from me. Within a month, Dick Anderson put me in charge of four other men in West Philadelphia. He knew from my SIS reports that I was an achiever, and he had watched me work well with other SIS members.

When I was teamed with George Arnold, we made an average of three to four arrests per week. In fact, we were the first to make an arrest on a trolley for smoking. The ordinance had been passed in 1943 to stop cigarette smoking by defense workers on the trolleys. Passengers had complained about the heavy cigarette smoking affecting their children and older people. For some unknown reason, the SIS was given certain routes on which to make those arrests. We did our job readily, and the transportation company gave each policemen $2 for expenses. The smoking stopped quickly on those routes after the word got around that plainclothes policemen were on the trolleys.

SIS did good police work. We never were unprofessional as I had heard about other special squads. We never told lies on anyone. It was our values and our being from a minority group, I believe, that guided us towards always giving an individual a fair shake, even a criminal. The members of SIS were real macho guys, but they didn't have a need to beat on anyone unless that person resisted arrest.

The reputation of the squad quickly became such that the mere mention that members of the squad were in a given area sent the criminal elements scurrying into hiding. Even to this day there are legions of old-timers who lament the fact that the squad is no longer operating, and they can tell stories of their escapades. Granted, squad members violated many a suspect's rights, but at that time it was normal, accepted police behavior. And, their methods proved most effective in stemming the tide of crime, resulting in departmental commendations being issued to a squad member almost daily.

The effectiveness of this hard-nosed approach to law enforcement was noted more than a decade later in the book *Racial Factors and Urban Law Enforcement* by William M. Kephart (published by the University of Pennsylvania in 1957). In this book a white policeman was quoted as saying, "When we had the Special Investigation Squad, the Colored hoodlums were afraid to cut loose. The squad kept things under control because they knew how to operate. They weren't brutal by any means, but they didn't stand for any monkey business. After the squad was broken up, they [black criminals] all started carrying switchblades."

Working on the Special Squad was also satisfying for me in another way. For the first time since I joined the department, I never had to worry or be concerned as to whether or not my supervisor was prejudiced as to color. I always had a partner to work with whose interests were similar to mine, which made for easy conversation. Although I had more time in the department than one of my partners, Arnold, he was somewhat older than I was, and I usually respected his judgment, which often proved beneficial. Often when I was on patrol, I would go right into a group of toughs standing on the street corner and frisk them. George would suggest caution. "Now wait. Let's see if we can't get some help," he would say. Most of the time he was right.

SIS was so successful that within a very short time its territory was expanded to include some other sections of the city that were experiencing similar problems. This included areas such as 40th and Market Streets, 40th Street and Haverford Avenue, 52nd and Market Streets, and Columbia, Ridge and Point Breeze Avenues. In West Philadelphia during World War II, barriers of segregation were coming down, and more blacks were going into restaurants and bars and demanding service. There were a lot of disturbances caused by this.

One of the most interesting stories told of the exploits of the SIS was the one about Officers Frank Winfrey and Herbert Locklear. They suddenly came upon a group of men shooting craps in the street at 42nd Street and Fairmount Avenue one day. Winfrey and Locklear ordered the men up against the wall, searched them and wrote down their names. They then asked a bystander to call for a police wagon to take the men to the police district.

When the patrol wagon did not arrive in a reasonable amount of time, the policemen began to get uneasy. Fearing that their prisoners would provoke a disturbance in the neighborhood or try to escape, Winfrey and Locklear told the prisoners that they had all their names written down, and that they were going to walk to the police station, which was about four blocks away. If any one of them tried to make a break for it, the policemen warned, they would be sorry when caught later. The threat worked, and every one of the men remained orderly during their walk to the police station. (Some overzealous buffs of SIS activities now swear that the men walked to the station in a lockstep fashion.)

By far, the most serious police action that I was involved in while a member of the SIS squad took place on April 9, 1943, on Broad Street near Bainbridge. At about 7:00 P.M., Arnold, my partner, left me to go to lunch. As active as I was, I just had to go on patrolling alone. A short time later, I saw a group of men gathered on the sidewalk, and I noticed that a man at the center of the group had a gun. I moved toward the men while pulling my own gun. When the man in the group who had the gun looked up and saw me, he raised his pistol and fired at me. I fired back almost simultaneously, but his shot missed me, and it seemed that I had missed the men as well. The group ran down the street, then split up and headed in different directions as I fired another shot, trying to wound rather than seriously injure the fleeing men.

I pursued the man with the gun, firing my revolver at him as I ran. I chased him to 15th and Bainbridge Streets then south on 15th.. When I was about halfway down the block, I fired what was my fourth shot and the man, later identified as Vincent Mason, pitched forward and fell to the ground. I ran up to him and quickly frisked him for the revolver. I was shocked when I did not find one, because I knew I might be accused of shooting an unarmed civilian. Upon noticing blood on his midsection, I knew that he was seriously wounded, and I really became frightened. Just at that moment, a police car came along and the driver called for a patrol wagon to transport us to the emergency room.

While Mason was being worked on, I immediately called Sergeant Anderson to inform him as to what had happened. He quickly arrived at the hospital with two other men from our squad. The other officers told me that they had caught one of the men who had escaped from the initial scene. Their prisoner had been wounded in the right arm, which accounted for the second of the four shots I fired. A few minutes later, a police car crew brought in still a third man, who had been shot in the left arm. It was later established that I had shot all three men, the latter two of whom were not seriously hurt. Sergeant Anderson sent out several of our men to search the area for the missing gun, and officers John King and Elbert Bannister found it.

On another occasion, Arnold and I were given instruction at roll call to concentrate our patrol on the lower end of South Street, between 5th and 10th Streets, and to venture north toward the Pennsylvania Hospital, two blocks away. There had been a rash of auto break-ins and pocketbook snatchings in that area. As we were both young and active, we relished having such a wide area to patrol. At about 8:00 P.M., we were on Bainbridge Street near 8th when we observed two men walking south on a small side street. Each of the men had a small briefcase of a type generally carried by physicians, and neither of them looked as though they were doctors.

When the men saw us they seemed nervous, and they asked us the name of the large street that they were approaching. I hesitatingly said, "Bainbridge." They said nothing, but walked away rather hurriedly. We reasoned that for them to be walking in a small street in that area, they should have known Bainbridge when they came to it, and we decided to stop them.

As we walked swiftly after the men, they increased their pace. We then did the same, whereupon they began to run. We ran after them, calling to them to stop and, because we were in plainclothes, identifying ourselves as policemen. We ran after them for about two blocks and, at a location that was clear enough to risk firing a shot at them, I drew my revolver and aimed it at the legs of one of the suspects, all the time calling for them to halt. I fired one shot and one of them tumbled forward and fell. While I approached the fallen man, Arnold finally overtook the other. My suspect said in a complaining voice, "You shot me." When I saw that he was limping and probably not seriously hurt, I hollered at him, "I'm glad that I did. You should have stopped."

We called for a police patrol wagon to transport them to the emergency ward at Pennsylvania Hospital. The doctor examined the foot of the "injured" man, but found no injury. I picked up his shoe and found that a spent bullet had lodged in its rubber heel. The doctor immediately released him, and we took both men to our station and charged them with burglary of auto after they admitted to having stolen the bags from a doctor's car.

At another time I was standing alone at 13th and South Streets on plainclothes duty when I heard a call for help. As I turned and looked toward Lombard Street, I saw a man running south on 13th Street followed by a short, stout man wearing an apron and yelling, "Hold-up! Hold-up!"As the suspect passed me, I lunged toward him, seizing his arm, but he freed himself with a quick twist. In the process, however, he dropped a cigar box containing the money he had stolen. I resisted the temptation to pick up the money, and ran after the man.

After about three blocks of running, I became winded as he ran into a darkened alley.As I reached the alley, he was about to exit the far end of it. Fearing that I would lose him, I fired at his legs. When he kept going, I thought that I had lost him and I stopped running. But when I walked to the end of the alley, I found him doubled up on the ground. He was cradling his left foot which was bare and appeared to have been injured. I hadn't missed my shot after all. I called for assistance and had him taken to the hospital. At the hospital the doctor treated his foot for a gunshot wound and discharged him. I arrested him and charged him with hold-up, robbery, and related charges.

Our job was plain and simple, enforce law and order. We wanted to instill our values among the underworld element, those tough guys who hung out on the corners and insulted people. They snatched purses from old ladies and they held people up for their week's pay. We just didn't allow them to do those things without them paying the penalty. The word got around about my partner and me, "Man those guys will lock you up. Don't mess with them." After a while, the mere mention of our names stopped some young men from getting into trouble.

We would go into bars on the invitation of the owner to stop potential troublemakers. We would search for knives and guns in the pockets of the patrons. Often, we found weapons in their possession. After a while, we made routine checks in the neighborhood bars for weapons. Many times as we walked in, we could hear weapons hitting the floors. Soon, people respected us for trying to keep their social places and their neighborhoods safe from thugs.

CHAPTER THREE

While in SIS, my social life took on added dimensions. My new status as plainclothesman gave me a feeling of self-assurance and I became more prone to speak out on my views in and out of the police department. I felt more comfortable approaching people. Just prior to joining the S.I.S. squad, I traded in an old automobile for a new Chevrolet with nominal payments. I got a lot of enjoyment taking my lady friend of several years out for rides and meeting people. I noticed that I was sought out for conversation by many more well-known people.

My reputation as a single man made it easy to strike up relationships with the opposite sex. Often my SIS assignment was in the same area as my uniform beats had been, which meant that I was no stranger to many of the residents. South Philadelphia at the time was the center of black social activities. The Standard Theatre at 12th and South Streets, and the Lincoln Theatre at Broad and Lombard Streets featured all black shows with big bands such as Duke Ellington, Lionel Hampton and Don Redmond. While most of the patrons at these shows were black, some whites attended also.

The Strand Ballroom at Broad and Bainbridge Streets was frequented by well-dressed people. There were always attractive single girls in attendance. Many taprooms were located nearby that had well-appointed lounges with high-class entertainment such as Catharines, the Postal Card, and Budweisers on South Street, along with the Showboat Club at Broad and Lombard Streets. All of these were either on my beat or near it. Though I was not a drinking person, I often stopped in those places to see and be seen. As a policeman, there were no cover charges for me, and almost always there was someone who wanted to buy me a drink or even a meal. This also included women who were well paid in the war industries.

The place that I found most interesting was the USO at Broad & Lombard Streets. It was established primarily for black servicemen, who were permitted to visit the white USO but were not made to feel too comfortable. The black USO was located in an old private mansion that had large rooms with antique moldings and woodwork. It gave the appearance of cultural surroundings.

While on duty almost every night, George Arnold and I would stop in to socialize with the ladies who were present to entertain servicemen. Since most of these girls came in groups, I was familiar with many of them. We made some lasting relationships with both the girls and the servicemen. The USO officials were always glad to have us around. They even expected us to come in. Occasionally, white servicemen and white ladies would be there, but not many. There was never any trouble that required police action.

When the theatres were about to close for the night, we would go in for the last part of the last show and stand around outside as the patrons came out to see that there were no disturbances. Since most people then travelled by streetcars or subway train, we waited to see them safely aboard.

There were times that we squad members really had to earn our pay. The Strand Ballroom often rented out to groups that catered to the public. Anyone could come in to dance at an entrance fee as low as twenty-five cents. Although no alcoholic drinks were sold, or allowed, some of the rougher elements would start fights. The management always wanted the SIS to be around in case of trouble. They never wanted uniformed policemen for fear of giving the place a bad reputation. If the place became too rowdy, there was a possibility that the uniformed policemen (usually white) would close it down.

One day in mid-October of 1943, my career in the SIS came to an unexpected end. I reported for duty that day at 4:00 P.M., wondering with whom I'd be paired. Before roll call, John Roane, the acting house sergeant for SIS, gave me my area of assignment. It was all of West Philadelphia, and to my great surprise and excitement I was placed in charge of the other four men who were assigned there, all of whom were older than I.

During the roll call, Sergeant Roane read all of the written orders received from the police superintendent's office and added his own. We were told to look primarily for persons with weapons, hold-up men and muggers. After roll call, the five of us agreed to travel out to West Philadelphia separately, and then to meet up at 40th and Market Streets, where we would divide ourselves up in two of our private cars. We met at the appointed time, loaded into the cars and toured separately, agreeing to meet later at 47th Street and Woodland Avenue. When we met later at 47th Street, there was quite a bit of noise emanating from a neighborhood bar on the southeast corner, and we decided to check it out. Three of us entered the front door, while the other two came in the side door. I was the first man into the building, and I immediately noticed two men standing at the bar and leaning over the top of it. One man was writing in a quite open manner in what I recognized to be a numbers book, and he was obviously accepting a numbers bet and money from the other man.

I quickly grabbed the numbers writer and spun him around, while announcing that I was a policeman. One of our men displayed his badge to assure the man that we were legitimate officers. I seized the numbers book, frisked the suspect and found a revolver stuck in an unusual place. The man had placed it under his belt, in the middle of his back.

I placed the man under arrest, and the patrons in the bar all stopped their fun-making to see what was going on. The other officers took the man out to one of our cars to transport him to our office at 12th and Pine Streets. We questioned the man as we drove, but he had little to say other than asking us to give him a break, saying that he was out of work and had to support his family. His sob story was a routine one that we were used to hearing from prisoners, and we disregarded it. Finally, the man said that he had a friend who would make it worth our while for us to release him, and that all he needed to do was make a phone call to him. We asked who the friend was—looking to make a second arrest, not to accept a bribe—but the man refused to tell us. We showed no further interest in what he had to say.

When we arrived at headquarters, we turned the man over to Sergeant Anderson. After being given a routine questioning, the man was charged with violation of the Uniform Firearms Act and running an illegal lottery, and he was held for a hearing to be held the next day. All of the officers involved in the arrest were then sent home for the rest of their tour of duty that evening.

While waiting in Courtroom 625 for the hearing to begin the next morning, LaBarr Potts, a West Philadelphia politician, walked over and asked me to accompany him to the men's room. Once inside he said that he was interested in helping the prisoner, and he asked me to be cooperative by not mentioning the numbers book I had found to the judge. I told him that I couldn't do that, as the numbers book was an important part of the evidence against the man. Potts was not pleased by my answer, and he asked me to remain in the men's room for a minute, as he had someone else who wanted to talk to me.

A few minutes later, Magistrate John O'Malley, whom I knew from other hearings, came in. He informed me without hesitation that the prisoner had someone important who wanted to help him out in this case. When I said that I had a problem with that, the magistrate told me in a firm tone of voice that I was under orders not to volunteer any information during the hearing. Rather, he said, I was only to answer the questions that were put to me.

When the hearing began, I was not asked about the numbers book, and the few questions that were put to me were limited to my confirming that I had arrested the man for being in possession of a firearm. The magistrate then asked the prisoner why he had a gun in his possession, and the man replied that he was employed as a bouncer at the bar where he was arrested. He said that he needed to carry it for his own protection. The magistrate then instructed Sergeant Anderson to verify the man's claim, saying that he was continuing the hearing until the next morning when he would hear Anderson's report.

If I was disappointed at the direction that the case was taking, I was almost devastated at the final result. When our case was called the next morning, Sergeant Anderson stood with me before the court. Upon being sworn in by Magistrate O'Malley, Anderson was asked only one question. "Sergeant Anderson," the magistrate said, "did you find out if the defendant works at the taproom in question?"

"Yes, your honor," Sergeant Anderson said, "he is employed there." When Anderson failed to elaborate, I whispered to him, "What about the numbers book?"

Anderson turned to me and said in a gruff but lowered voice, "Shut up."

The magistrate banged his gavel and said, "Case dismissed."

I returned home a bit downhearted, wondering how this had happened to me. Later that afternoon, a uniformed policeman came to my home with a teletype message from police headquarters. The message ordered me to report for duty at midnight, in uniform, back to my old assignment in the 33rd District. I was no longer a part of the SIS.

I freely admit that my experience in the SIS had made me feel like I was a cut above uniformed policemen who walked a beat. I had also really enjoyed the freedom of choosing many of my assignments, freedom from hourly call-ins while on the job, and the freedom from working the 12-8 tour of duty, which the SIS didn't work. In spite of Sergeant Anderson's gruffness and overreaction toward prisoners, he treated his men with respect and compassion.

My respect faded for Dick Anderson, however, with his decision to transfer me out of SIS. I had worked hard, and many times I had gone beyond what was expected of SIS members. I remember thinking at the time, I deserved better than being bounced out of the squad. I couldn't get it out of my mind that he hadn't supported me. It was difficult for me to leave SIS, and I imagined all of the SIS members later pointing their fingers at me on the street as an ex-member of the Dick Anderson Squad.

I was wrong about the others' feelings. My partner, George Arnold, told me that he was shocked. We had become close in doing police work. He told me that his heart would not be in working with someone else. Many of the other SIS members expressed the same type of feelings. The irony of my situation was directly linked to Dick Anderson's high standards for the SIS. He always talked about not getting tainted by any illegal activities. And yet, when I rebelled against the discharge of the charges against the numbers man, I was bounced out of SIS. It really made me question the justice and fairness of the system. I felt I got the worse end of trying to do what was right at that time.

Dick Anderson also had difficulty with SIS members like me who showed strong leadership. He wanted to be the top dog, and he didn't want any SIS member to get ahead of him. With my college work at Lincoln University, he probably knew that I had the potential to move ahead of him. Although he assigned me to be in charge of other SIS members, he apparently felt I was doing too good a job. Sometimes I was the one to receive the publicity for an arrest, and he didn't like that. He let this particular case stand as the reason for my transfer, implying that it was the powers above him who had ordered it.

It was extremely difficult for me to return to uniform. I was bitter towards Anderson and the system. When I left the squad room, I drove around in my car while I tried to get my thoughts together about the future. I stopped the car in front of a restaurant and bar in Paoli, Pennsylvania. I knew the bartender there and we had become friends over the years. He listened to me talk about what had happened while I drank several sodas. After talking back and forth for an hour, I felt better. I drove home to my mother, who was wondering what had happened to me.

Returning to uniformed duty in the 33rd District was one of the most difficult things I ever had to do as a policeman. I felt that I would be walking into a situation where all of the other officers would know what had happened to me, and I worried that they would look down on me as someone who could not quite make the grade in my former plainclothes assignment. I was sure that the men in my old squad would degrade and make fun of me. I just wanted to get out on my beat and hide.

As I entered the roll call room only those whom I walked past or encountered had anything to say. As time passed, all of them were friendly and seemed to welcome me back. The men greeted me back with sympathy. They were aware of the politics of the internal police system. Any supervising officer could utilize you in whatever capacity he desired. This meant you were in and out of squads at his whim. There wasn't any appeal process. You had to obey orders just like in the military, with the exception that you could quit if you didn't like the assignments you were given.

Initially, I was disappointed and frustrated at having to return to the district. I suppose for that reason, I felt that I would not take any insults, particularly if they were racial. I still felt I was a police officer in every respect and I wanted to continue to do a good job. Controlling my feelings was difficult, but I didn't want to give anyone an opportunity to get me further into trouble. I worked even harder and I was on guard for racial slurs. Before coming back, I never felt they were talking about me as a black person, but I now understood the meanness of some of the white policemen who had to tell racial jokes and make fun of black prisoners. "Darkies, and "dusty" were their favorite nicknames for black prisoners.

I had to walk a beat in the cold winter while the white police officer rode around in warm police cars. And then there was the boring duty of standing on the corner for hours in the cold weather without relief while military convoys travelled through the community. It was just another way of letting you know that white policemen were in power.

When it came to assignment of patrol cars, I was not given one. It was an unwritten policy of the police department that black policemen would never be assigned patrol car duty. On one occasion, when the district was short of manpower, I was made the number two man on a patrol wagon. The white policeman in charge of the patrol wagon was ashamed to be seen with me. We spent a great deal of the time parked in a dark street. But when I became the tail man, which is the number three man on the wagon, I had to handle all of the unruly prisoners.

After the initial shock of returning to uniformed duty was over, I no longer felt that I was a rookie, but a full-fledged policeman. I now had a new sergeant, a man named Joseph Cappolino. He was extra nice to me for he and my first police partner, Tom Brown, had been long-time friends.

Although I was upset about leaving SIS, there were some things about being on regular foot-patrol duty that I liked. I developed a lot of friendships as I walked along the streets on my daily routine. Many of the contacts that I made resulted in close relationships. I became the best man at two weddings involving black families on my beat. The contacts also served me well in that people often confided information to me on troublemakers and criminals and their sub rosa activities. I enjoyed being helpful to the people on my beat by answering their questions, giving advice, and being extra watchful when requested. It is generally agreed upon by law enforcement officers that 85 percent of the action they take results from information given to them, with the other 15 percent resulting from activities they observe themselves.

The closeness between the policeman and the people on his beat was often exemplified by friendly greetings, frequent conversations and inquiries as to family health. Because of this closeness between citizens and police, there were often times that policemen in the district would catch a youth committing minor crimes—taking fruit from produce stands, turning on fire hydrants, or getting into street fights—and he would give the youth a whack with his hand and send or take him home. Parents were very appreciative of this consideration, and they always promised to thoroughly punish or reprimand their son.

A big problem I had on one beat was the pilfering of coal from railroad cars on Washington Avenue. I would take boys who were caught doing this home to their families, only taking them into the police station when it really seemed necessary. This usually broke the young man out of the habit and the problem subsided. Police officials accepted this as crime prevention. It was the type action that some policemen always preferred to take, and they often boasted of controlling crime in their area without making arrests.

Sad to say, such simple solutions to juvenile delinquency are just one part of a far different world that is no longer with us. Before air conditioning, people often slept in hallways with doors open in the summertime, or even in lounges on the front porch or sidewalk, and they could do so with no fear of molestation. People left their windows open at night with only screens in them, and many times they would leave their homes to go shopping or run errands without locking up the house.

In former years it was considered a disgrace to be arrested, as one would be an outcast who was called a jailbird. Even worse was for a girl to become pregnant out of wedlock. In either case, families often disowned their errant children, and other families would prohibit their children from associating with the fallen ones.

Businessmen also used to make it a point to cultivate the foot patrolman's friendship in the hope that the officer would keep an eye on his property, both day and night. Often, a policeman would be given keys to businesses to come into at night, look around and take a short rest if he needed one. Restaurants often gave free coffee and in some cases free meals to the man on the beat. Almost every taproom offered free drinks and, in many cases, free bottles of liquor if the policeman refused drinks on duty. Area residents would offer coffee or ice tea according to the weather. They even felt disparaged if the policeman refused. I once worked a beat where 7-Up had a bottling works. Just inside the front door was an ice box of 7-Ups. Policemen were free to help themselves at any time to drink it on location.

The little tips and gifts freely given from law abiding citizens were graciously accepted, as was also the case with off-duty employment. Usually, this meant extra pocket money for the men with families who found it difficult to subsist on a policeman's pay of five or six dollars a day. Produce store owners would give men small bags of food to take home. While this was not condoned by the police department, supervisors usually looked the other way because these material things were usually not offered as bribes but as small gifts.

While patrolling in the area of Philadelphia's open-air Italian Market, I became friendly with a policeman named Ralph Rizzo, whose son was later to become Police Commissioner and Mayor of the city. Ralph Rizzo was one of the early members and a district representative of The Fraternal Order of Police (FOP). He signed me up as a member of the FOP while it was still unpopular to be a member, as the organization was frowned upon by the city's administration, which did not want police organizing as a labor union.

A bright spot for me while in the 33rd was when Ralph introduced me to Frank D'Angelo, a private area watchman. We became very friendly with each other as we often worked together on the 12-8 tour of duty. He invited me to his home where his family treated me very respectfully after serving me coffee and rolls. Each year he made a lot of wine in his basement and I could always expect a gallon jug of it even for a number of years after being transferred out of the district.

In early 1944, while working the areas around Palumbo's Restaurant in South

Philadelphia, I became acquainted with the owner, Frank Palumbo. Palumbo's was a famous Philadelphia restaurant and night spot, that frequently featured big-name performers as entertainers. Palumbo seemed very appreciative of the fact that I often spent time patrolling nearby. One day while off duty, I was driving in the area with my girl friend. As I passed the restaurant, I saw Frank standing outside and decided to test whether his appreciation of my patrol work extended to allowing a black couple to eat in his restaurant. I parked the car at a nearby curb and went over to him and asked if I could bring "my wife"—I thought that sounded more respectable than girlfriend—in for dinner some night.

Palumbo seemed a bit hesitant at first, but then he asked if my wife was with me. I said that she was waiting in my car across the street, and he walked over to the car. I walked over with him, and he put his head in the window to get a good look at my date as I introduced them to each other. When he pulled his head out of the window, he said, "Yes, it will be OK." I suspected that my girl friend's very fair-skinned complexion had a lot to do with it.

A few nights later, we took him up on it. We went to the restaurant for dinner and a show. Palumbo spotted us as we entered, and he seated us personally. He sat with us and ordered drinks for the three of us as we chatted until our food was served. After dinner I asked for the check and was told that Mr. Palumbo had taken care of it.

Although I thought things were going along pretty well in the 33rd, I was totally unprepared for what happened on January 7, 1944. In those days, a number of factories on Washington Avenue paid their employees in cash. Being fearful of hold-ups and robberies, they requested police protection when employees came to the office for their envelopes. The policeman on patrol duty in the area usually was assigned to guard the paymaster at that time.

Each factory gave the policeman who was assigned to this duty a little tip for lunch money. While this too was not officially condoned, no one made a big deal of it. This custom differed from police payoffs to overlook illegal operations in that the businessmen's tips were for services to legitimate operations. Payoffs by people who engaged in illegal operations were for the purpose of aiding and abetting illegal activities.

There was a factory on my beat called England Furniture Makers, and I regularly covered their office during the distribution of pay envelopes. This was considered a good assignment, as the company always gave the officer on duty a two-dollar tip. In comparison, another company that was in the area, Wyche Pharmaceuticals, gave only one dollar. On a day I was scheduled to go to England Furniture Makers, I made my hourly call to the district and was told to go to Wyche Pharmaceutical right away. I protested that Wyche was not on my beat; and, furthermore, I was scheduled to cover payroll at England Furniture Maker's payroll, which was on my beat, at the same time. I was told in no uncertain terms to do as I was told.

While enroute to Wyche's, I met the white policeman who explained to me that he was coming from the beat that included the Wyche assignment to cover the England payroll. The white sergeant had obviously rescheduled him so that he could get the bigger tip. The more I thought about this, the angrier I became. After completing my payroll assignment, I went to a telephone and called the committeeman in my home ward, Charles Preston, who worked in the sheriff's office. I said, "Get me out of this district, I just can't take this." He promised to do what he could.

When I checked into my district two hours later, the house sergeant said, "Reaves, you've been transferred to the 16th District effective at midnight." I suddenly gained far more respect, even if contemptuously, for the power of politicians.

As far as I was concerned, the tip incident was the last of many incidents that I had put up with that I felt were racially motivated. I had been continuously assigned details outside in cold weather without relief and details that required me to carry out hot ashes from the police station's stove. No one else was assigned to sweep and wash the station floors as often as I was.

I could not make arrests of white criminals without fear of retaliation from the sergeant. Three years of controlling my anger and frustrations really pushed me to reach out in desperation to my committeeman. It was better that I leave before I reached my breaking point, I thought.

I loved my new assignment in the 16th District, for I lived only one block from the building, and that made it very convenient going to and from work. I was surprised to find out very early on in my assignment that the supervisors were unusually easy to get along with, and I couldn't understand why. I later learned that most of the supervisors also lived in the 16th district, so that they looked to the same politician—the one who had orchestrated my transfer into the 16th—when they wanted a favor. No one wanted to make waves with a man who had come in with a politician's blessing.

When I was in the 16th District as compared to the 33rd District, one of the first things they did was to make me the number two man on the patrol wagon. I took care of all the paper work, and I rang the bell on the patrol wagon as it traveled to crime scenes. The driver was a pleasant white policeman who empathized with how black policemen were treated in the department.

Although this was in the fourth year that blacks had been assigned to patrol cars in the 23rd District, the 16th District still retained its white-only patrol car operation policy. There were only four patrol cars in the district at that time, and quite often one or more was out of commission. In the district other black officers and I had accepted the fact that we would not be assigned to patrol cars, but I'll never forget an incident that happened one midnight at roll call.

There were very few men on duty and we had a new sergeant in command.

All of the patrol cars were in working order that night, and when the sergeant looked around the room he pronounced loudly, "My God, I don't have enough men to drive the patrol cars tonight," looking past my black partner and myself as if we didn't exist. Neither of us said a word as we marched out of the roll call room to our beats, while the patrol cars sat parked in the rear of the station house. Needless to say, this had a disquieting effect on our morale.

I knew that blacks were not allowed to patrol in patrol cars, but the sergeant's remarks during roll call really upset us. John Smith, the other black policeman with me, agreed it was a slap in the face. "To make a statement like that, he is trying to intimidate us for whatever reason," I remember saying to John. I carried my anger out on the beat. For several nights I did nothing but walk my beat. My usual police behavior would be to shake doors to ensure they were locked and to question suspicious characters. For the next few days, I just put in time near the most secluded sections of my beat, while telling myself that if I ever got the opportunity I would change things in the police department.

When I transferred to the district in 1944, there was a restaurant, the J.P., on the corner of 40th Street and Lancaster Avenue that did not serve blacks. At 41st Street and Lancaster Avenue, the Leader Theater did not let blacks sit on the first floor, and still another at 40th Street and Market Streets that did not even sell tickets to blacks. While working the beat, I often walked into that theater for a few minutes expecting someone to say something to me. Although the workers looked at me with daggers in their eyes, I ignored them and kept coming back to the dump that it was.

Many black people complained to me about discrimination, but I knew I couldn't use my uniform to help them in their fight for equality. The police department would not have kept me around for a second if they thought I was using my uniform in that way. I directed black individuals to the NAACP or the Urban League to handle their complaints. As a member of the NAACP, I knew it was deeply involved in using the legal system to break down the racists' barriers to equality.

In 1945, the 16th District was fast changing to a majority of black residents. In spite of that, however, less than 10 percent of the uniformed policemen in the district, and none of the plainclothesmen, were black. Over the years, I have noticed that there are a lot of white officers who like to work in black neighborhoods. There are also the aggressive ones who have little respect for black people. Far too many use more force than necessary to make arrests. I have found that their overreaction is minimized when black officers are present. The same restraints are operative when the supervisors are black, even if not present at the scene of an arrest.

The 16th District did not have any black policemen in supervisory capacity. Therefore, the supervisors of the 16th District pretty much established that they would treat the black community as an alien community. Their behavior of stopping blacks without cause and beating them with their nightsticks was standard operating procedure for many of the white policemen. The black policemen were cautious in stopping what some of the white policemen were doing, for fear of being charged with interfering with an arrest.

Many black community members made complaints in the station to the sergeant on duty. He treated them with contempt by not looking at them or by pretending that they were not standing in front of him. Another policeman would walk over to the person and in a loud voice would ask, "What do you want in here?"

"I want to talk with somebody about how my father was treated," the person would reply. The policemen would look at one another with smiles on their faces. "You better get on out of here before we lock you up," one of the policemen would routinely say.

Their behavior would really make me angry, but I tried to help that person with the best information that I could give them about their concerns. Other times, some white policemen would bring black prisoners into the station with their heads bleeding. Whenever I was present, I always suggested to the sergeant or lieutenant on duty that those prisoners be sent to the hospital for treatment. Usually, they followed my suggestion.

One night the captain in the 16th told me to work with the plainclothesmen on a special assignment. I reported for duty at the appointed time and was taken to the 4300 block of Reno Street. I thought I had been selected because the captain was impressed with my job performance, but it turned out that this all-white block had been broken by a black family which moved in and promptly opened a speakeasy.

The white officers in the district had tried unsuccessfully to gain admittance to the speakeasy to obtain evidence, and they had decided to bring me along, without telling me why, to get the door opened for them. I rang the doorbell of the house and, when the door opened, the officers rushed in and searched the whole house without a search warrant.

While I took no part in the search, the people in the house castigated me severely for helping the white officers, and I have to say I was sympathetic to them. I never fronted for the white officers again. I recognized that I was being used. It irked me to know how effective black policemen were in plainclothes duty but, other than in cases such as this one, the commanders in the district refused to use them.

Another case of disappointment for me was when I was chosen to make a trip to Atlantic City and I was displaced. In 1945 there had been a terrible storm in Atlantic City, and Philadelphia had been asked to send policemen to assist in public safety. My sergeant told me to go home and get the necessities for an overnight stay. I was pleased and excited to get the assignment, but when I returned with a small carrying bag I was told that there was not room for me in the police car. I was later told by a friendly policeman that I had been replaced by a white policeman who decided he wanted to go in my stead.

My first reaction was to tell my family how I had been shoved aside from taking the Atlantic City trip. They were just as upset as I was. For the next couple of days, I talked with many of the black policemen that I knew. We always agreed that, although these things happened, there wasn't anything we could do against the system if we wanted to keep our jobs.

I did become active with the NAACP, and I informed them about discrimination in the police department. They made it a matter of record, but nothing much was done about it at that time. Dr. Harry Green, a dentist, was the president of the NAACP in Philadelphia. His approach was slow and deliberate through negotiations rather than demonstrations. Actually, the civil rights movement had not yet reached the position of using demonstrations to change segregation.

During this time I talked a great deal to my wife about the pressures of my job. I knew some black policemen under stress that actually beat their wives. She was supportive while I endured the racial discrimination, but at the time I recognized there was very little I could do about it. Five years of my life had been invested in the police department and I felt I wanted to stick it out. I assumed other jobs would have people who didn't accept black people either.

In the 16th district, the captain was nice to me. One of the first things that happened to me after I got there was I got married. I asked him for extra time off to take my wife on a honeymoon. Not only did he allow me to use the vacation time I had earned, but he also gave me a few extra days, for which I was paid. That was really going out on the limb for me. Later on my wife became pregnant, and from time to time he gave me an hour during the day to spend with her during some of her difficult periods. These little things gave me hope that things would change within the department.

Jobs were beginning to open up for blacks in some industries, and the NAACP was becoming increasingly aggressive in taking discrimination cases into court and winning. The NAACP was instrumental in bringing about a lot of changes through persuasion, and by releasing stories to black newspapers.

The main thrust of the NAACP was to fight segregation in employment, housing and overreaction by policemen. One of the most important programs it initiated was conducting a survey of all large businesses in the city to determine the number of blacks they employed. Many blacks were employed by these firms for the first time, or the number employed was increased to an agreed upon percentage, as a result of these programs.

The NAACP also furnished legal aid to many home buyers who had been rebuffed by white real-estate agents when attempting to buy homes in white areas. This resulted in the opening up of areas where home owners often previously banded together to prevent blacks from moving in. The organization also provided legal aid to people who complained that they were illegally arrested, or that undue force had been used by police because of their race.

Probably the most beneficial undertaking of the NAACP was the fight to eliminate the poll tax and other barriers to black people's voting rights. Even the twenty-five cents once levied at the polls kept many people away. The resulting escalation of party registration and strength at the polls signaled an upsurge of black voting strength.

Further, black veterans were returning home from the war with stories about real equality for them in Europe and on the battlefield. My brother, Lawrence, who served in the Army, told me how free he had felt in Europe. He encouraged me to stay in the police department, and to advance myself by using my education and patience. I felt there was hope, even if it seemed dim at times.

CHAPTER FOUR

Many young men were being drafted before the war started—and they generally did not object to this as military service was considered an excellent opportunity to get experience and improve one's lot in life—but the number of men being drafted increased dramatically once the United States entered the war. As a result of this military buildup and the loss of workers on the home front, many jobs opened up to blacks for the first time. I can recall seeing a photographer take the picture of a black man in a gasoline company uniform while he was pumping gasoline into an automobile at 16th and Fitzwater Streets. The photographer considered this a notable event, as it was the first time a black had been employed in that position in Philadelphia.

As draft quotas increased, a lot of policemen left the force to volunteer for military service rather than wait to be drafted. The number of trained policemen in the city began to drop precipitously, and orders soon came from police headquarters for policemen to request deferments from their draft boards. I was placed in the 1-A classification by my draft board three times, and each time an official from police headquarters sent a letter to my draft board and I was deferred.

In addition to my brother, Larry, who served in the armed forces, I had another brother, Walter. Walter worked in the Philadelphia shipyard and did very well there. He had been deferred from military service by the draft board based upon the classification of his job. My mother had two sisters living in Dillon, South Carolina, at the time, and she wanted me to go visit them with her in June of 1944. As she was getting up in age, I agreed to accompany her during her trip, which required all-night travel by train. We were met at the train station in South Carolina by a cousin who told us that D-Day had taken place in Europe. There was a feeling of anxiety among the populace. This continued until V-E Day in Europe. By then, the Allies were island hopping and winning ever so slowly in the Pacific, but, unhappily, at an awesome loss of life.

A lot of police manpower was expended down on the waterfront in Philadelphia to prevent sabotage. With so many men being drafted, there were not many

40

men to fill the vacancies in the police department. I recall on one occasion, the director of public safety wanted to meet the new recruits. There were only four recruits. "My God, is this all you have?" he said to the personnel director. The captain had those men assigned out on the street without any training at the police academy. Seasoned police officers actually gave them their training on the beat.

There were a lot of shortages in consumer goods: cigarettes, whiskey, sugar, gasoline, and butter. Most things were rationed. Each person and family was issued ration books to buy food. Gasoline was also rationed, but it was available on the black market. It cost as much as a dollar per gallon, which was an outrageous price compared to the normal twenty cents per gallon.

The police department cooperated with governmental agencies by trying to enforce the conservation of fuel. Policemen stopped automobiles to find out if the driver was on business or joy riding. Warnings were issued to drivers who couldn't satisfy the police that they were going to, or coming from, work. There were not supposed to be any pleasure rides. When I was in SIS during the war, the police department allowed us ten gallons of gas for our cars for travel to and from the job.

Some Americans dodged the draft by moving to Canada. We were directed to apprehend draft dodgers and absent without leave (AWOL) servicemen. For every AWOL we held for the military, the arresting policeman received fifteen dollars from the military command. The majority of Americans supported the war and their efforts were directed towards patriotic activities to help defeat Hitler. Others were involved in illegal activities, like the two young men we apprehended while they were stealing from the American Stores' supermarket food distribution center.

My partner and I went out there one Sunday afternoon based upon an informant's tip. We stationed ourselves near the warehouse. We weren't there long when we saw a car drive away from the warehouse. The car's springs were so overloaded that its body was bouncing on the axle. We blocked the car to a halt and held the suspects until we searched the car. It had meats, sugar, and other goods that were in short supply. We found out that the men involved were supplying grocery stores and even a barber shop in North Philadelphia. Later, arrest warrants were issued for people who had received the stolen goods.

Finally, on August 6, 1945, the atom bomb was dropped on Hiroshima, Japan, and people hoped that this was the beginning of the end of the war. Preliminary, but unconfirmed, reports of the bombing came to Philadelphia at about 10:00 A.M. on August 7, 1945. I was working on the beat in the 16th District, where everyone along Lancaster Avenue seemed to be jubilant, but there was nothing in the way of mass celebration. People seemed to be numbed and worn out by the war and all the deaths it brought. About 10:30 that morning,

Sergeant Armstrong called me and four other officers in off the street and had us taken into Center City in a patrol wagon. We reported to Captain Krombar at City Hall.

We discovered the situation was quite different downtown. There was a large crowd gathered in the courtyard and all around the building. People were celebrating in a loud but orderly fashion, singing, dancing, throwing paper airplanes, drinking beer as automobile horns blasted continuously. A holiday would have been declared if President Truman had confirmed the reports of the bombing, but he did not go on the radio to speak about it until the celebration had settled down in mid-afternoon, when we returned to our district.

Without television, people at home hadn't really been able to understand the horrors and difficulties of the war; but, once the war was over, the world began to change rapidly. In many ways this was an end to the age of innocence of the early 1940s, and we were about to make a quantum leap into a new age, both in the civilian world and in the police department. Automobiles and radio, which had been in scarce supply in the police department up until this time, were soon to become more readily available, and they would mark the beginning of the end of the neighborhood beat policeman. Improved communications and transportation would enable police to respond to telephone calls for assistance more rapidly, but they would also greatly diminish the routine human contact a beat policeman had with the families in his patrol sector, and relations between police and the citizens they served would never be the same again.

In October of 1945, just after the war was over, Captain Thomas J. Gibbons, who was in command of the Crime Prevention Division, which dealt with youthful offenders, began expanding its activities and personnel. This police unit worked closely with a private citizens' organization called Crime Prevention Association, whose mission was to lower crime in the community. The police personnel in that division all wore plainclothes, and their target became young juveniles. Up until this period, most juveniles arrested for breaking the law where treated like other criminals, and were thrown into overcrowded cells.

But after a number of cases in which youthful offenders were brutalized by adult criminals in the holding cells, there was an outcry. Juveniles were soon placed in separate holding cells while awaiting a hearing, and police officers were instructed to call the crime prevention unit when they were ready to book a juvenile offender. The offender would then be interviewed by a policeman from the Crime Prevention Division.

Over a period of time, the crime prevention division became accepted as a part of the police department. Policemen learned to contact the crime prevention juvenile division whenever a teenager was charged with breaking the law. If the case went to court, a crime prevention officer would testify along with the regular policeman who had made the charge.

Curtis Bock, a judge, was a powerful force behind the crime prevention movement. He was highly respected for educating upper class citizens about the movement. Many influential and powerful white people joined the movement. The old guard within the police department got the message to make the program a success. Captain Gibbons was selected to head the new division. He was a smart and liberal-minded person who was respected within the ranks of the police department.

Assignments to this division were greatly sought after because they involved plainclothes work, and officers had the run of the city. They worked with all different kinds of people and on all different kinds of cases, rather than being restricted to the same small area all the time. Plainclothesmen were given much greater latitude in handling cases. As a patrolman, you had to ask for permission before doing anything out of the ordinary; but, as a plainclothesman you frequently made your own decisions. You got to meet with important people and deal with important organizations, which made you feel more professional. The work was also less regimentated—you didn't have to stand for daily inspection— so an assignment to this squad amounted to a promotion of sorts.

Since these new assignments were so highly prized, the white officers in the police department felt that they should go exclusively to white officers. Black policemen were still definitely considered second-class citizens at this time. White and black policemen were usually pleasant to each other in everyday contact, but when it came down to who was going to get what, the white officers automatically expected to get exclusive access to the best assignments.

Working in patrol cars was considered the ideal assignment by the majority of uniformed officers and, as a result, only those in favor with their captain, or those who had good political connections, received these assignments. The situation was further complicated by the fact that most white officers still refused to ride in patrol cars with black officers. In the years since the first "black" patrol car was assigned in the 23rd District in 1940, the only progress that had been made in the assignment of black officers to patrol cars was that a few additional "black" cars—those intended for use only by pairs of black officers—had been created in three other districts.

Conversely, when undesirable assignments came along, they always went to black officers first. When there was a building or a bridge that needed guarding for whatever reason, or a parade that needed to be worked, or school children who needed to be watched as they crossed the street—that is, boring work that included large doses of exposure to the elements, those assignments always went to black officers first.

Thus, when Captain Gibbons assigned three black officers to his newly expanded squad, there was an outcry among the white officers in the department. Many white police personnel complained to the FOP. "That Gibbons is a nigger lover. He took on three of them and no whites," was the gist of their complaints.

I had been alerted to the expected openings in the division by Edward Payne, a black policeman who had been in the division for over a year. Payne arranged a meeting for me to talk with Mr. Merriweather, chairman of the crime prevention organization. We both met with him in an unused school building at Quince and Pine Streets. The police department's crime prevention unit also had its offices in the building. Merriweather then interviewed me in front of Payne, to my surprise.

A few days later, I met with thirty-five-year-old, tall and wellbuilt Captain Gibbons, a man with an easy smile, in his office. Again, Edward Payne accompanied me. We were in plainclothes. Gibbons was easy to talk with in his office, which was half the size of a regular school classroom. During the interview, he told me my record showed that I had used my gun a few times in the line of duty. "As a member of the juvenile division, I don't expect you to use your gun unless absolutely necessary," Captain Gibbons said in a firm voice.

I received a police department memorandum within several days to report for duty with Captain Gibbons' unit. It lifted my spirits and I told my wife and friends about the nature of the assignment. It was like someone had finally discovered my potential and talent to achieve above the average policeman. Maybe things are beginning to get better in the department for blacks, I remember thinking. I also realized that this would be the second time I was going into plainclothes as a promotion without more money.

During the first day of my orientation by senior policemen, I met two other black policemen who had been selected. Edward Payne took us around for various assignments until we understood what to do. Other policemen would point us out as the new black policemen assigned to the crime prevention division. They nicknamed us "the diaper squad," but my wife didn't care. She was happy I had now mostly normal day hours for a change. There was time for me to be home with my growing family.

Working with children became both interesting and rewarding to me. It was clean work with little or no danger and the children were easy and enjoyable to talk to. They were usually truthful, or easily persuaded to tell the truth. They often volunteered more information than we wanted, frequently revealing information on the illegal activities of their parents and other relatives. Working with them also brought me into contact with school personnel, church officials, and people from other governmental agencies for the first time.

My five years of uniform and plainclothes work had hardened me against the criminal elements of society. I was all charged up, gung-ho, aggressive, fearless and almost insensitive to the feelings of law breakers, even traffic violators. I was really a law and order man, and ever-ready to slay the criminal dragons of society. This first started to change dramatically when I became the father of two boys, and the change continued as I took the special courses in child psychology and sociology that Captain Gibbons made available, but not mandatory, for his men.

In almost every contact I had with a juvenile, I somehow related the case to my two boys, and that made me become more tolerant. I began to become more of a fatherly type and, for the first time, I began to counsel my charges and send them home, rather than strongly rebuking them. This was permitted, even encouraged, by the juvenile courts.

Often while I was doing an investigation, I had to make home visits to talk with parents. All too often, once I got there, I found a one-parent family; even if there was a father on the scene, he just as often was uncooperative or worse, drunk! It was easy to see why the children were going wrong. This had the effect of making me want to do more for my family to ensure a stable environment for my sons.

My wife, Vivienne, showed a lot of interest in my class work and often typed my papers for me. This led to more open discussions about my police work. Vivienne was greatly relieved that my work held little chance for violence. She had heard about all of the shootings that I had been involved in up to that point, usually through third parties. I had tried to shield her from those stories, but some how she always found out.

Violence still played a minor part in my life, though, as was the case in September of 1946. I was off duty and leaving a barber shop at 43rd and Aspen Streets when a man came to me to report that he had been held up in a street craps game by a man who had a gun. He gave me the man's description and pointed to a nearby taproom. I entered the front door and was immediately confronted by a man who pointed a handgun at my midsection. Without a second thought, I impulsively grabbed for the gun and the hand that was holding it, and a struggle for possession of the gun began.

We both landed on the floor as the bar emptied of patrons, some going into the basement while others ran upstairs. Fearing that the man might get the upper hand, I drew my revolver, pointed it at the fleshy part of his upper arm and fired it. The man ceased his struggling, and I took the gun away from him. He was taken to the hospital, treated and discharged. I arrested him, charging him with holdup, robbery, and related firearms violations.

Since I no longer had to do night duty, I had more time to devote to my family. In that my work often dealt with public affairs where large numbers of children would be present, I often took my boys along for the experience. I also became involved with the Boy Scouts and the YMCA, and in both cases I ended up on their boards of directors.

As I look back on it, I'm amazed at the change that occurred in me then. Previously, my family had called me "top sergeant" because of my authoritative demeanor. But after the change, they stopped using that name, and I found that Vivienne and I were getting along much better in our marital relationship.

The creation of this division helped black officers get visibility in the department as solid police professionals. Out of forty-five officers eventually assigned to the unit, there were twelve blacks. In the districts where I worked, most of the teenage prisoners were black. They were placed in separate cells, and many times separated from white teenagers. Most of the time the black teenage prisoners outnumbered the white teenage prisoners, and that led to friction if they were put together. It had nothing to do with segregation as much as it had to do with keeping the hassles down in the city prison. Most of the time, the teenagers were put in guarded rooms until the juvenile officer came on the scene to make a determination of how the case should be handled. Sometimes, there were female offenders who presented special problems, which were handled by policewomen from the division.

In most cases, we sent for the parents of the teenagers. They were turned over to their custody until there was a hearing. In cases of teenagers who had committed a serious crime, or who were out of control, they were housed in the Youth Study Center, which had facilities for males and females. Moreover, the crime prevention organization created community programs for teenagers. There was boxing, track and field, camping, and arts and crafts. The majority of the emphasis was placed on helping teenage boys stay out of trouble.

At the end of World War II, an awful lot of guns were confiscated after they were used in the commission of crimes. Most of the guns were of foreign manufacture, meaning that they had been brought back from overseas by war veterans. This prompted Captain Gibbons to initiate one of the first of many innovative programs in the crime prevention division, one designed to encourage the voluntary surrender of these firearms to the police. I was among a selected group of officers in Gibbon's squad who were given crash courses in public speaking and assigned to visit public and parochial schools. The officers appealed to the students to try to convince their relatives to surrender these firearms at police stations. Even though all schools were included in the program, only two handguns were surrendered in the city.

Gibbons was not deterred, however, and he soon instituted a series of weekly training courses for members of his squad. I attended courses in the Municipal Court Building that were moderated by a succession of college professors, court officers, and child welfare agency workers. In overall charge of these courses was Dr. Jeremiah Shaloo, a professor on the staff at the University of Pennsylvania. I attended related courses at LaSalle College, and the University of Pennsylvania's Fels Institute of State and Local Government.

Nonetheless, despite all my good feelings about my new assignment, I soon found out that some aspects of being a policeman in Philadelphia in the mid-

1940s hadn't changed at all. While pursuing an investigation into a stolen auto one day, I quickly learned that the suspect was a white high school student in the Wynnefield section of the city. I went to Overbrook High School to get the boy out of class, but the principal immediately rebuffed me, saying I couldn't take the kid out of school without his parents being present.

Only a few weeks prior to that, I had gone to the same school to pick up a young black kid, and the principal had given the boy to me instantly. I immediately wondered if there was some racial ugliness going on, but the principal soon informed me that the boy's father was an important magistrate in the area. I knew that, with the connections involved, this was going to be a tough case to prosecute. I also understood the principal's reluctance. His career longevity was highly dependent on support from the governing Republican administration— no public service job in Philadelphia seemed to be immune to politics in those days.

The principal did promise that he would direct the boy I was seeking out a specific door at the end of the day, and I stationed myself there and waited for him, not knowing what would happen. The owner of the car, which had been returned undamaged, intended to press charges, but the magistrate who heard the case could still throw it out of court with impunity if he chose to.

When the boy appeared, I took him to the 19th District at 61st Street and Haverford Avenue. The house sergeant stalled the booking of the boy because he knew his father. The magistrate also knew the father and, having learned my lesson, I agreed with them that, as long as the parents would resolve the matter of the stolen car with the other parties as there wasn't any need to book the youngster. I later found out that the parents did work things out.

The training courses I attended taught me how to respond to juveniles, and how to help them change. In many cases, we had to act like parents towards the juveniles. There were many juveniles who were helped by this approach. One juvenile offender grew up to become a Fairmount Park policeman. He started out breaking and entering into his neighbors' homes for money. The court placed him in the custody of his father. For a while, just about every day, I talked with this teenager about straightening himself out. Eventually, through support from his family and me, he overcame his negative behavior.

One case I worked on gave me a lot of satisfaction. I was called to the Child's Elementary School where a boy had been pointed out as a suspect in taking a teacher's pocketbook the previous day. After denying everything for almost an hour, he finally broke down and told me that he had taken the purse and it was now at his home. I took him home and explained to his mother that he was suspected of the crime. She immediately and adamantly denied that he was involved, insisting that her son would never do anything like that. It was very pitiful and yet satisfying to see her expression and temperament change as the boy left the room and returned with the pocketbook, which he had hidden under his bed.

In yet another case, I worked with William Norman in an effort to prevent boys from loitering around Sulzberger Junior High. We would chase them away if they did not belong there. One rather high-spirited youth had an annoying proclivity for talking back when we ordered him to leave. We gruffly put him into our automobile and threatened to arrest him. He calmed down and pleaded to be released. We did, with a stern warning not to return to the area. Years later that youth, John Tatum, became the director of management and my superior in the Philadelphia Housing Authority.

As a juvenile officer, it was most comforting to be able to counsel and guide young boys and young adults away from antisocial activities and attitudes. This was especially true when the subject mended his ways and went on to greater things, but far too many proved to be lost causes. As I carried out the visits I made to the homes of juvenile subjects, I began to observe a pattern. When the homes appeared to be well kept and the parents cooperative, generally the subject turned out for the good. But, conversely, where the homes were unkempt, the parents were resentful and uncooperative, it also followed that the subject drifted into an unsavory life and become a burden on society. This principle applied whether the families in question were white or black.

One of the more bizarre cases I was involved with during this time concerned the use of children to make bets with an illegal numbers operation. We received a complaint that school children were seen frequenting a cigar store near 25th and Lehigh Streets, and Jack Auerbach, one of our officers, put the store under surveillance for a week. When Auerbach confirmed that the complaint had a basis, and that a bagman could be seen arriving at the store each day in a Cadillac to pick up the receipts, he asked my partner, Thomas Chisholm, and myself to assist him in making the arrests.

We arrived at the location about 2:00 P.M. and awaited the appearance of the Cadillac. The store was a small, unattractive place with cigar advertisements placed in the window in such a manner that it was difficult to look inside. After we had been waiting thirty minutes, the bagman pulled to the curb in front of the store, and we hurried from our cars and entered the store right behind him.

Inside the store we found eight white men who, rather than selling cigars, were standing and sitting around desks and tables covered with paper work and talking on the telephones. The place almost looked like a licensed business operation. Everyone stopped whatever they were doing when we entered and looked at us. Their looks of curiosity were replaced by shock when we identified ourselves and began searching the men and the store. The boss of the operation may have been paying protection money to someone, but I'm sure that it hadn't occurred to him to attempt to bribe the juvenile division which, to the best of my knowledge, was free of graft.

We found paper slips representing over 54,000 numbers plays, and $3,500 in cash—a considerable amount of money at the time—was seized. We conducted a further search of the bagman's automobile and found an additional 2,300 numbers plays. We arrested the men, charging them all with gambling and illegal lottery. We called for a police patrol wagon to transport them to our office at 11th and Winter Streets, where they were held for a hearing at City Hall.

As I got some experience in the division, I became the leading officer in making juvenile arrests, and therefore spent more time in court than anyone else. It was while spending all of that time in court that a second change in my attitude towards juvenile delinquency began to develop. As I sat and watched case after case being processed in the courtroom, the offenders left with smirks and haughtiness for the streets from which they had been apprehended. My new-found tenderness towards young law breakers began to harden. This was especially true when a young man was brought to court for the fourth or fifth offense and he still managed to walk out with little more than a slap on the wrist.

In the schools, the teachers and principals complained that their hands were tied as to dealing with recalcitrant students. They often called juvenile officers in to talk with these persons. They knew that we could talk rough and even slap a few of them around and get results. There were a number of times that I observed schools at the close of day where children were fighting in the school yard and the teachers would walk right through the surrounding crowd, get into their cars, and drive away.

In November of 1947, a storekeeper at 4610 Woodland Avenue complained to me and my partner, Tom Chisholm, that a young black neighborhood bully had broken his store window. The boy often passed the store and taunted the owners by making gestures to indicate that he was the one who had thrown an object through the window. He even returned a few days later and Mrs. Rubin chased him out of the store.

We picked up the 15-year-old boy a few days later on the street. He became very unruly and insolent, and we had to use harsh words and threats with him. We took him home to his mother with the expectation that she would make good for the broken window. She flatly refused, saying that he had caused her too much trouble and that she wanted him put away. We arrested the boy after he used abusive language toward his mother. Enroute to our office, he again became unruly and again we had to physically restrain him.

At his trial in Municipal Court on November 19, 1947, the store owner testified against him, and in spite of the facts that the boy had two prior arrests, and that his mother showed no interest in his being released, the judge put him on report to court officials and released him. I can still see the nonchalant look on his face as he left the court.

A few weeks later, I was assigned with Policeman Charleroi Gray to the Earl Theatre at 11th and Market Streets. Lionel Hampton's band was playing there. As usual, there was an overflow crowd of black juveniles in attendance, with a long line waiting at the ticket box. The longer the line became, the more boisterous the patrons got.

We noticed a teenage boy with a bulging pocket standing in the line. Upon identifying ourselves as policemen, we frisked him and took a hooked, rug-cutters knife with a huge wooden handle from him. When questioned as to why he had it, he became evasive and insolent. We arrested him and took him to the 6th Police District at 11th and Winter Streets.

Upon further questioning, the young man stated that he carried the knife for self-protection. We charged him with carrying a concealed deadly weapon and disorderly conduct. In that there was no telephone at his home, we went there to notify his mother. She met us at the door, and we told her of our mission. She then berated us for arresting her son, saying she had him cutting linoleum for her and that was why he had the knife.

At the young man's trial in Municipal Court, the judge found him not guilty and discharged him, while warning him that his next arrest would result in his going to prison. As he and his mother left the court, both of them looked at us and rolled their eyes. A check of his record revealed that he had been arrested two times before for assault and battery. He was also cutting school that day.

Having come from a family where corporal punishment was administered as a natural part of parenting with successful results, I just felt that this was the way to go with many of these young offenders. I had a good relationship with Judge Millen and often met in his chambers and exchanged opinions. I advocated incarceration for repeat offenders. He agreed with me in a number of cases. I often locked horns with Marshall Tyree, an official in the School District Attendance Office, over the correct method of handling truants. He espoused the conciliatory approach while I favored in-house residential supervision.

Yet, while this hands-off approach to juvenile delinquency continued, I saw example after example in my own work of how beneficial it was to be firm and to set limits. On May Day of 1947, the Nat King Cole Trio performed at the Earle Theater at 11th and Market Streets. The lines were stretched for almost two blocks even after the theater was filled. Juvenile division officers were assigned because the huge number of young people in line were becoming disorderly. The real problem was that the juveniles were staying for two and three performances once they got inside the theatre.

We suggested that no ticket be sold for the run of an entire day's performance, and then we cleared the theater, knowing that everyone had seen at least one show. We had such a problem that we had to call for more manpower. This included the mounted patrol to keep order in the outside lines as we chased everyone from the inside. When ticket sales were resumed, however, all returned to normal.

One case I remember especially well involved Freda C. Dombro, an attendance officer for Shoemaker Junior High, who complained to me about the truancy and defiant attitude of a young man named Roland West. His classroom teacher had requested that he be removed from school because of his disruptive behavior.

I made several trips to the West home for interviews with family members. Mr. West, Roland's father, was a building contractor who wanted Roland to work with him, but he had not had time to secure working papers for him. Mrs. West, the mother, was adamantly against his leaving school before graduation.

I finally was able to get Roland and Mr. West in our office for a conference. The pros and cons of being in school or out were discussed. We asked Roland to give reasons for his noncompliant attitude about school. He stated, "I just don't like school." This was apparent in that his marks were below par.

I explained that he had only a short time until the end of the term, and that he still had time to get a passing grade and graduate. At his mother's insistence, he agreed to complete the term, but he spoke about it in a condescending manner. He was warned that his parents would be brought into court if he failed to keep his word.

Forty years later, I visited the home of Bernard West, Roland's brother, who had become a very successful bank president in Boston, Massachusetts. While I was there, I talked with Roland, who was then a retired building contractor, having successfully taken over his father's business. Roland thanked me over and over again for helping him to turn his life around.

CHAPTER FIVE

When John B. Kelly, the patriarch of a prominent and wealthy Philadelphia family, ran for mayor as a Democrat in 1947, he almost overturned the Republican machine in Philadelphia with the help of the black vote. The Democratic Party was slowly gaining support in the city, thanks to the popularity of President Roosevelt's liberal program. This was especially true among blacks, who had voted Republican since the Emancipation Proclamation.

During the Depression years, there had been few jobs available for either black or white people, and this resulted in thousands of people appealing to the Republican party for jobs and/or favors. The city employed only a small percentage of the unemployed, and many people were unable to pay their taxes. The biggest dispenser of welfare was the Salvation Army, which had long daily lines for giving out food. Bootleggers and numbers bankers did a lot to gain support in the community during these years by frequently sending food and coal to poor families, especially where there were a lot of children.

There were a lot of ward leaders, mostly Republican, who also gave money and assistance to the poor. But, at the same time, politicians also perpetrated a heinous evil when they set up their own constituents and then reported them to the police. An example of this was when a local politician would stake a family with funds to have a pay-house party at which admission was charged. When the house was full of people, the politician would have the police raid the party. Then, the concerned politician would rush down to the station house to spring those arrested from custody, thereby ensuring that the freed voters would be indebted to the politician for life for having "saved" them from the police.

The local Democrats weren't able to make any headway with voters at this time, since they had to rely on the Federal government for favors to be parcelled out to the voters. There were various Federal agencies that offered make-work jobs, usually at low wages. The largest of these was the Civilian Conservation Camps (CCC) for boys and young men.

As the chairman of the city's Democratic Committee in the mid-1940s, Mr. Kelly further endeared himself to the black community by having his black chauffeur sworn in as a state trooper, complete with uniform, badge, and revolver. This made him the state's first black trooper, and it did not sit too well with white policemen in the city. As one white officer, Martin Cosgrove, said to me at the time, "The police did not like him appointing a colored trooper without the man taking an examination. That's why we voted against him."

During that time, I worked a second job with Mrs. Sarah Hubbard, a caterer who did all of the Kelly parties. I worked with her as a waiter when the Kelly's daughter, Grace, who was later to become Princess Grace of Monaco, had a breakfast at the family home for members of her college graduating class. When the breakfast was about over, Mrs. Kelly gave me a $2 tip. Mr. Kelly called me aside afterward and asked how much his wife had given me. When I showed him the tip, he scoffed at it and handed me a $5 bill.

After John B. Kelly, Sr., gave the Republicans a run for their money in the 1947 mayoral election, the possibility for real political reform in the city seemed possible for the first time, and the black community began to be recognized as a political force. If politicians were beginning to show an increased appreciation for the black voter, however, changes in law enforcement came at a slower pace.

I was given a temporary assignment with the postal service in the late 1940s that illustrated that. There were no black postal inspectors in Philadelphia at the time, and postal authorities had been unable to solve a number of cases involving theft of mail in black neighborhoods. Whenever a white postal inspector came into the neighborhood to investigate, people wouldn't cooperate with him. Many black people saw white policemen in their neighborhood as part of an occupying force, and postal authorities were seen as an extension of that.

Finally, George Condit, a white postal inspector, tired of his unsuccessful ordeal of trying to crack the cases, he asked Captain Gibbons if he would assign some black police officers to the cases. Gibbons assigned Thomas Chisholm and myself to him, and we reported to Condit on a Friday afternoon. Condit showed us pictures of three men who had eluded him for months, and filled us in on the background of the cases.

We left the post office and went to 39th Street and Fairmount Avenue, where we immediately recognized one of the suspects on the street. We placed him under arrest without a problem and transported him to the amazed inspector within an hour of our first having left his office. We then drove back to the same area, asked a few questions of people in the area, and followed their suggestions that we look around 37th and Melon Streets. We quickly found the second man and took him in for investigation.

Upon seeing the second suspect in his office, Condit shook his head in disbelief. When we told him that we also had information on the third man, Condit threw up his hand and said, "Don't bring him in today. It'll take me all weekend to process these two."

We left for the day and returned Monday morning. The inspector told us then to take as much time as we needed to find the third suspect. We went to an address we had been given in the 3700 block of Haverford Avenue, knocked on the door, and arrested our final suspect when he answered our knock. We closed out the case before noon.

Inspector Condit was so elated that he wrote a letter of glowing praise for our police work to Captain Gibbons. But, more importantly, it was only a few months later that Samuel Richardson, the first black postal inspector, was assigned to the Philadelphia post office.

When I returned to work on the Crime Prevention squad, which is now known as the Juvenile Aid Division (JAD), my friend, Edward Payne, mentioned that there were elections coming up for representatives to the Fraternal Order of Police (FOP) and The Police Beneficiary Association, which handled police insurance. We knew that Frederick McCallum, the state president of the FOP, who had recently transferred into our division, was going to run for our divisional representative. We also knew that Hugh Belger also wanted to run for the FOP post, or, failing to win that, the Police Beneficiary spot. Payne suggested that I get involved in the election as well.

Edward Payne was a very forward-looking person. He knew that there was a rift between McCallum and Belger and that they would oppose each other. He also reasoned that since both opponents were white, a black candidate that took all of the black votes, and some white support, could possibly slip in.

At the time, blacks were only 15 percent of the JAD personnel. This was a much better percentage than other specialized squads in the police department. It had long been insisted upon by Captain Gibbons that a high percentage of blacks were needed to do juvenile work, since many of the youth we dealt with were black. Nonetheless, the low percentage of black members meant that I would have to win all of their votes.

Payne and I had been friends since we first entered the police department. He knew that I was active in the FOP and attended meetings regularly. He said, "Jim, we can beat them if we try." I didn't particularly want to run, but I thought I had the best chance to win of any of the black officers, and we decided to meet with the other black officers to discuss it.

We called a meeting of the division's six black officers in the only private place that was available to us, the men's room in the building where we were headquartered, the Board of Education. We had a lengthy discussion, which was interrupted several times when men would come in to use the facilities. Payne made his pitch to the men, assuring them that there was a chance to win the representative's spot. One officer, John Smith, questioned the wisdom of voting as a block, stating that this would be segregating ourselves. Officer Charleroi Gray, however, said, "They won't know how we voted because it will be by closed ballot."

It was decided to offer our support to McCallum for FOP director against Belger, if in return he would support me for representative for The Police

Beneficiary Association. It also helped that I had actively supported McCallum when he was elected state president of the FOP. McCallum assured me of his support when I asked for it. "Sure," he said, "I'll support you. We've always got along well, and I don't like that SOB Belger."

The election for FOP director was held and McCallum won handily. The following week at a JAD staff meeting, an election was held for representatives of the Beneficiary Association. Someone nominated Belger and it was seconded. There was a pause and I looked around the room at the four black officers present, none of whom opened his mouth. I was appalled. Since it was so difficult for a black to get into the specialized squads, some of the men who made it guarded their position jealously, and often they were afraid to make waves by speaking up. I concluded that that was what was happening now.

I then looked at McCallum and he spoke up to nominate me. I looked again at the black officers, and they spoke not a word. At that point Captain Gibbons, who knew that I wanted to be elected, said, "I'll second the motion."

The balloting was held and I won 14 votes to Belger's 6. The margin of my victory was a clear sign that McCallum had actively campaigned for me among the white officers, perhaps just to spite Belger.

Whatever the state of racial relations within the department, there were always cases in my work as a cop that gave me a quick reading of what the prevailing public attitude was. One such case involved a long-time friend of mine, D. Wendell Keene. Wendell was a handsome, well-built black man who had been separated from his wife, a very attractive blond white woman, for several years. Wendell wanted to get a divorce, but his wife, whom he was ordered to support, wouldn't give him one. In addition, Pennsylvania divorce laws at the time required that one spouse prove that the other had been guilty of a wrongdoing before a divorce could be granted.

Wendell suspected that his estranged wife had been engaged in an on-going affair with a white theatre manager for some time, and Wendell knew that if he could catch them in the act his problems would be resolved, since adultery was both a crime and grounds for divorce. Wendell asked me to help him, and I agreed after he secured a magistrate's warrant to search his estranged wife's apartment on Larchwood Avenue. He also hired a female private detective and a constable to join in the stakeout and eventual raid on the apartment.

I arrived at the apartment with Wendell one night about 8:00 P.M. The detective and the constable, who had been on the scene since earlier in the evening, told us that they had seen Wendell's wife arrive home, and that they suspected her boyfriend would be along soon. We sat in cars just down the street from the apartment and waited for the action to begin.

At about 11:00 P.M., the boyfriend, who was later identified as Norman Bailey, rang the woman's door bell. She opened the door for him, and both of them looked around outside suspiciously before he entered. Once inside, they periodically looked out the windows as if they suspected we were watching them.

Catching them in bed would be our strongest evidence, so we waited until the lights in the apartment went out at 2:00 A.M. A half hour later, we went to the door and the constable rang the bell. When a voice called out from within to ask who it was, he said, "I have a telegram for you." The woman took her time responding, then said that she wasn't expecting a telegram, and who was it from? We figured the man and woman were getting dressed quickly, so the constable announced that we were the police and moved to force the door open.

The woman suddenly opened the door and admitted us while wearing a nightgown. The man, who came hurrying from another room, had managed to get fully dressed. We arrested both of them on the adultery warrant and took them to the 18th Police District for booking. Because interracial marriage was part of the case, and because both the husband and wife were glamorous and attractive people, the arrest brought sensational headlines in the next morning's newspapers.

The courthouse was full of reporters and onlookers when the case came to a hearing before the magistrate, with everyone obviously anxious to hear the spicy details of our arrest and their affair. The lure of an interracial romance gone sour attracted a lot of attention. Wendell's status as a businessman and his wife's being "a ringer for several of Hollywood's most glamorous motion picture stars," had been mentioned prominently in all the newspapers, as, of course, was their differing races.

Both sides were well represented by attorneys, but the white magistrate treated the wife with open contempt. It was my judgment that his attitude was more related to her having married a black man than to her having committed adultery. The magistrate found that there was sufficient evidence to hold both the estranged wife and her boyfriend on charges of adultery, and required that they post bail before they were released. The next day's newspapers were again filled with scandalous headlines about the case.

The next sign that political corruption and the Republican administration in Philadelphia were coming to an end appeared during the 1949 election campaign. Joseph Clark and Richardson Dilworth, Democratic candidates for controller and treasurer, began hammering away repeatedly about political and police corruption during their campaigns. They also spoke about police brutality and promised to do something about it.

I was assigned by my boss in the Juvenile Aid Division, Captain Gibbons, to attend these campaign speeches and to report back on who the speakers were, what they said, how many people were present, and the response of the crowd to the speakers. I was certain that Captain Gibbon who would be appointed commissioner of the department three years hence under a new Democratic regime was collecting this information under orders from his boss, the superintendent of police, who was a Republican.

A good example of the strenuous opposition to political change by the entrenched administration is the story of what happened to William Nevans. He was a healthy, husky looking, no-nonsense type of policeman. After Richardson Dilworth spoke on a corner of Lancaster Avenue one afternoon, Nevans was so moved that he went to City Hall and changed his registration from Republican to Democrat. This was considered such an act of treason within the department and the Republican party that news of Nevans' actions reached police headquarters—apparently relayed by a City Hall worker who had seen the officer in the voter registration office.

For the next three weeks, two deputy inspectors followed Nevans' every step while he was walking his beat. Nevans knew they were following him in an attempt to spot him doing something he could be fired for, so he did twice as much walking as usual, trying to wear the spies out. And he performed every action exactly according to the book. "I just wanted to walk their tongues out," he told me later. The deputy inspectors finally gave up on him, after having trailed him for all that time without having spoken a word to him.

The signs of this kind of political interference with the police department were everywhere. Only a little over two dozen black policemen were appointed between 1930 and 1950. During this same time, the police department failed to fill numerous ranking-officer positions on a permanent basis. These upper-level jobs were almost always given to people on an "acting" basis, which meant that the department could handpick loyal Republican party followers, who could keep their jobs as long as they remained in line—or as long as they paid up. The word that circulated among the men on the force was that many promotions were purchased on Sunday afternoons in the living rooms of the more powerful Republican ward leaders, at prices rumored to range from $500 up to $5,000.

Politics has always played a major role in law enforcement in Philadelphia. At the beginning of this century, almost every political ward had a police station house located in it. For the most part, their boundaries were coterminous. The ward leaders even chose who they wanted to be the commanders of their local police districts. And, as a result, the commander was beholden to the ward leader for his tenure.

Although many police station houses had disappeared when districts were merged, the ward leaders were still wielders of an awful lot of power. All policemen knew this, and they kept it ever present in their minds when taking police action. Although nothing was written down relative to political do's and don't's, rookie policemen learned quickly. While this was appreciated by the small group of policemen who used it to their own advantage, the vast majority of policemen resented it tremendously.

Policemen take a lot of pride in their work and are always on the alert to make a good arrest. All too often, though, they were frustrated by political interference that resulted in the discharge of a prisoner. This usually happened at the first hearing at the police district, but it could extend into common pleas court cases as well. The only way to avoid being demoralized was to bring the prisoner before the court and to care little about what the outcome was, consoling yourself with the knowledge that you did your job.

Knowing that politicians are a special breed, most policemen tried to keep their distance from them. Many ward leaders tried to extract assessments—i.e., campaign funds pegged to their salaries—from policemen who lived in their wards. The vast majority of policemen strongly resented this. There was a minority, however, who courted this type of relationship because it could, and often did, lead to promotions or opportunities to line their own pockets.

Nonetheless, apparently, Philadelphians were finally ready for a change, for when the votes were counted in the 1949 election, Joseph Clark and Richardson Dilworth had won the two highest offices being contested in that off-year election by 110,000 votes. *The Philadelphia Inquirer* editorialized about the election: "Conditions had become so bad, with heavy thievery and graft and incompetence at every hand, that no right-minded person could stand it any longer. It was not a matter of being a Republican or a Democrat: it was a matter of trying to redeem the city from those who had sunk it in the mire."

A new civil service test for police jobs had been given in 1950, and thousands of men took it, including a higher than usual number of blacks. In that many of the black applicants were returned war veterans, who had military experience and who had bonus points added to their test scores for their military service, it was expected that a goodly number of them would be appointed.

To the amazement of everyone except the highly cynical, however, the first black on the list, Thomas Lambert, was ranked number 312. Black representation on the rest of the list was no better. Officers Chisholm, Norman, and I became highly suspicious, and we went to the city personnel department to examine the list of test results. Imagine the conclusion we drew when we discovered that there were 75 Italian-sounding names among the first 100 on the list, at a time when the president of the city council was named Paul D. D'Ortona.

The fact that politics almost completely overshadowed job performance in the department was not at all appreciated by the many capable policemen who were being denied promotions they deserved. Policemen with years of police experience and good educations were well qualified for promotions, and they just found it completely unacceptable that politics overwhelmed their efforts towards upward mobility. Dedicated policemen accepted this adversity and continued to do their jobs, but others, because of lowered morale, became clock-watchers and did only the minimum they had to do to get by.

In terms of police corruption, there were times when the police department seemed to look the other way when policemen were "on the take." At other times, the department was strict about corruption, but a division or district commander could undercut that by being lax or sometimes even supportive of wrongdoings. This made it easy for policemen to give in. I have often heard shady characters say, "Either you take it or someone else will."

I have also had policemen tell me where I could receive a payoff just for showing up at the given location. My standard answer was, "You take it, I'll pass." Many policemen suggested that I worked too hard, that I could advance further in the department if I played politics. Others came right out and told me that I worked so hard that I made them look bad. They actually resented my enthusiasm for work. I ignored them all, kept my nose clean, and did my job. I knew things had to get better someday.

On September 14, 1950, Senator Estes Kefauver launched a Congressional probe of crime that focused in large part on New York, Chicago, and Philadelphia. On May 1, 1951, the investigators submitted a final report concluding that in Philadelphia the numbers racket, although a big business, was strictly a local industry, controlled by a "politico-gambler-police tie up" that furnished protection and made it impossible for outsiders to break in.

The report further stated that numbers constituted the major gambling activity in the city, and that there was a "casual and cavalier" attitude among Philadelphia judges toward gambling defendants, with light fines and virtually nobody going to jail. It criticized judges for imposing $25 or $50 fines on gamblers instead of the $500 maximum, and said that in the five years before 1950, out of thousands of numbers and bookmaking arrests, only two defendants had gone to jail. The report stated that the city was divided into geographical territories, each with its own numbers bank "affiliated, apparently, with sufficient political connections to be able to operate without too much fear of molestation." The police department was really hit hard when the report stated that from $3,000 to $4,000 a month was paid in each of the thirty-six police districts. One Philadelphia police captain, Vincent Elwell, was said to have received $1,000 a month from gamblers.

With the publication of these findings in May 1951, Judge Edwin O. Lewis ordered a Philadelphia grand jury investigation into the politico-police-gambler connections. Inspectors John T. Murphy and Thomas Gibbons were appointed to head an investigation of the police department. Captain Gibbons, my boss in the Juvenile Aid Division, was considered the city's most honest cop. The investigation focused on the vice and narcotics squads, and it was intended to send out the message that corruption would no longer be tolerated in the police department.

The investigation was a low blow to corrupt policemen, as it cut off unsavory and lavish lifestyles. At least two high ranking officers, Captain Craig Ellis and Inspector Warren Hobson, committed suicide. Many others retired or just quit if they were not eligible to retire, and more than a few were fired. Happily, the majority of policemen welcomed this new departure as an opportunity to bring real reform to the police department.

It was not as one would suspect, that the citizens were in a frenzy about crooked cops. Quite the contrary, people reacted much as the old declaration against Philadelphia went: "Philadelphia is corrupt but contented." Seldom if ever did I hear "the man on the street" mention corruption. As for the policemen, little or no thought was given to it. It was generally thought that members of the vice squad made a lot of money, for so many of them drove new cars and had well-furnished homes, even seashore homes, and boats.

Members of The Juvenile Aid Division were probably the least of all policemen suspected of corruption, primarily because we dealt almost exclusively with juveniles. Some policemen even chided us as being "poor bastards," in the "diaper squad." Generally, we all drove old-model cars that were often out of order. I recall buying a five-year-old automobile for $150 that I drove for about three years. Once, I went to a police station to get gasoline for my car, and the captain took one look at my car and said "My God, we tow better cars to the graveyard than that."

For the most part, the investigators used the federal report to determine who they would question. However, all police department personnel were required to fill out a questionnaire concerning their assets and obligations. When talking with other policemen, I assured them, half in jest, that I welcomed a personal inquiry into my financial standing, adding that the inquiries would prove that I was in such a bad position that the investigators would say that the poor boy needs help, and request a raise for me.

It was very difficult to get incriminating evidence against the suspected policemen because so few people were willing to testify against them. For the most part, the matter was addressed by transferring all of the members of suspect units to different duties. This was particularly true of the vice and narcotics squads.

While this investigation was underway, the campaign for the 1951 mayoral election was in its final days. Joseph Clark and his partner, Richardson Dilworth, who had first broken the Republican stranglehold on city government in 1949, ran for office again, this time for mayor and district attorney.

Clark ran against Reverend Daniel A. Poling, a Republican who was not a politician, but who had made quite a name for himself in his religious broadcast, and by making his own statements against corruption. A lot of people thought that he would make a good mayor, better than any established Republicans in the city, but the Republicans had lost a good number of registrations to the Democrats, especially among blacks. The Republicans were hoping that a clergyman would stem the flow of blacks from the party on religious grounds.

On the other hand, Clark constantly reminded blacks of the changes made by President Roosevelt on their behalf and promised to continue the changes in city government. His extensive campaigning in black neighborhoods was considered a bellwether of things to come.

The street corner campaign rallies really caught on, and people anxiously searched newspapers for locations and times of rallies. They often drew as many as 500 people. In black neighborhoods, the principal speaker always was introduced by a black candidate, who extolled the merits of the mayoral candidate.

I was again assigned to monitor these rallies, and one day I was late for one such meeting where Richardson Dilworth, the candidate for district attorney, was the principal speaker. Dilworth, who remembered me from my monitoring of the 1949 campaign speeches, noticed my absence and said facetiously, "Where is Jim Reaves? I guess it's all right to start without him."

I made no effort to conceal my purpose. I usually went right up front and made notes as the speakers spoke. I really enjoyed what I was doing, because I was hearing things about changes in the city that I liked.

I listened especially closely for any reference to policemen. The promise I liked most was the assurance that an honest merit system would be instituted in civil service. Dilworth spoke loud and clear on appointments and promotions being made fairly. He acknowledged the need for more black policemen, and particularly more black supervisors. That's when he captured my vote, and the votes of all the members of my family.

There were still a lot of old-line black Republicans who found it difficult to vote for any party other than the party of Lincoln. Even though the Democrats had scored big gains in the previous election, people were not sure that they could unseat the city administration, and many blacks voted for incumbent Republicans in local races. In my home division, my brother Lawrence ran for Republican committeeman but lost to the entrenched white Republican committeeman, even though our division was 85 percent black.

In almost all black churches, the pastors were urging a big vote on election day. But the Baptist ministers were more vocal in saying nice things about the Democrats. It must be said for police officials, however, that they almost never took an active part in politics. They never urged you to vote one way or the other.

Election day usually meant that it was a long day for policemen. Every polling place had at least one policeman assigned to it. We were given specific instructions to remain in sight of the polling place, but not within fifty feet until the polls closed. We were to limit our conversation with voters, and under no circumstances were we to tell them how to vote. Our job was to prevent any violence and to enter the polls only at the request of the election judge, which usually meant that he wanted someone ejected.

We were given time off to go home to vote while some other policemen took our places. When the polls closed we were permitted, even encouraged, to enter the polling place while the votes were being counted. We had forms that the judge of elections filled out containing the voting results of the top candidate, and we took these to the station house as flash returns.

The final count in 1951 gave Clark and Dilworth a 122,000 vote majority, and the Republican rule of the city was ended. Few political analyses ever attributed the Democratic victory to the grand jury investigation, although there was no question it had a tremendous impact.

The election results didn't seem to affect the white policemen very much. That is to say, the ones without connections in either party. There is, and always has been, a large number of policemen who do not aspire for promotions, nor do they ask any special favors, they are content just to be policemen.

As for black policemen, the young ones were elated. For the most part, we were much more educated than the older black policemen, who never had a chance at promotions. We knew that our chances with the Republicans had been almost nil, and we reasoned that the Democrats couldn't be much worse. In fact, we had quietly campaigned for the Democrats among family and close friends, for Richardson Dilworth had promised that the new administration would have fair and honest civil service tests. After the election, we often reassured ourselves that "a new broom sweeps clean."

As the investigation of the police department wound down after the election, and a few men were fired, policemen began to take it a bit more seriously. Rumors began to circulate about what was to happen. There were still a lot of old-timers around who recalled the police probe of 1926. In it, a lot of policemen were questioned by the county detectives who were said to have often beat confessions out of policemen.

The worst that Inspectors Gibbons and Murphy did was to discharge a few policemen and transfer those who were operating under a shadow of suspected corruption, although scores of policemen had quietly left the department, ostensibly under their own volition. I only knew two of the discharged policemen well, Reginald Scott and Charles Andrews. They both denied doing "anything other than what other policemen were doing."

The grand jury report was issued a month after the election, in December. Judge Lewis complained in the report that the probe wasn't as effective as it could have been, due to the weakness of the investigation done prior to his ordering the probe. He promised to never order another one until the proper groundwork was completed.

The final report pointed out that over 600 policemen had left the force during the two years the federal investigation had been under way. Those who had left the force included two inspectors, twelve captains and forty-five sergeants—there were no permanent ranks of lieutenants and corporals at the time—and many of them were believed to have left under clouds of suspicion.

Other than the police department, the coroner's office came in for close examination as to illegal ties with funeral directors. Immediately after the report was made public, six men were transferred from the vice squad by Inspector John T. Murphy.

The police probe did not officially conclude until Mayor Clark appointed Inspector Gibbons the new police commissioner. Gibbons then immediately began a new clampdown on vice and corrupt policemen. He made district commanders responsible for vice in their districts, requiring weekly reports on their investigations. If a captain showed little or no action, a special police unit would be dispatched to find out if there were vice operations present. If they were able to make arrests where the uniformed policemen had not, then the captain would be in for disciplinary action.

This policy worked well in increasing vice arrests; but, unfortunately, some few overanxious policemen were apt to plant incriminating evidence to make arrests, which is an abominable miscarriage of justice. Another unfortunate result of this policy was that it put tremendous pressure on police captains to show a high level of vice investigations, and this would inadvertently lead to one of the most painful and difficult incidents in my police career.

CHAPTER SIX

When Captain Gibbons became Commissioner, I was overjoyed, for he had always treated me well. I was a hard worker and processed a large number of juvenile cases. For this, I'm sure he was appreciative. I made it a point to go to him and express my happiness that he was appointed. As for policemen in general, there was an undercurrent of resentment against Gibbons for his part in the grand jury but, at the same time, policemen were pleased that he did far less harm to the department than they expected.

One of Gibbon's early acts as commissioner was to disband the Special Investigation Squad that Dick Anderson had started. The squad had been opposed from its beginning by a small but powerful group of black politicians, headed by a well known lawyer, Austin Norris. While Norris did appreciate its mission, he did not like its being all black. Since he was an ardent Democrat, he did not prevail until the Democrats took over. Commissioner Gibbons was responsive to the black Democrats, as they were in large part responsible for the Democrats prevailing in 1952.

Attorney Austin Norris, and others said they felt that the SIS should be integrated. That rationale does not stand up, however, for it would have been an easy matter for Gibbons to have integrated it without disbanding it. It is my considered opinion that the squad's reputation for roughness was its undoing. While there were a lot of people who praised the work of SIS, there were also the naysayers who stood in fear of its rough tactics.

The new administration also formed the so-called black cabinet consisting of Austin Norris, Rev. E. Luther Cunningham, Rev. Marshall Shepherd, Rev. William Gray, II, and Charles Baker. The appellation of "Black Cabinet" was given unofficially to the black men who were prominent in bringing sizeable numbers of blacks into the Democratic party. They were generally consulted on matters concerning black people. Most of them ended up on city- or state-government payrolls. They, like the vast majority of blacks, had become converts to the party after having been denied positions in the Republican party.

The black community was elated that these men had scored breakthroughs in politics and thought of them in much the same manner that they revered Jackie

Robinson and Roy Campanella. The white community barely took notice of them, although whenever mention was made of them in the white press, it was always positive.

My guardian angel always seemed to protect me during my police career. I took an untold number of knives from suspects, as well as twelve guns, seven of which the suspects had in their hands, with two of them firing at me. I've been involved in six auto accidents while driving almost 100,000 miles doing police work. After all of this, I was only injured once, and very slightly at that.

In October 1952 I was doing juvenile aid work when a problem erupted at the newly built Bartram Village Housing Project. My partner, Samuel Wyche, and I were sent to investigate. We found that the Housing Authority was trying to integrate the project by moving in a black family. The windows in the family's house had been broken out twice, and the man of the house had been threatened while he was on his way to work at 5:30 A.M..

We began going to the man's home early in the morning to escort him to the trolley line, while walking at a distance behind him. On the third or fourth day, we saw two male teenagers throw stones at the man. We took off after them, and they ran in opposite directions. Wyche caught his man and arrested him, but I had problems. The one I went after ran through someone's backyard. As I chased after him, I ran into a nearly invisible rope clothesline that, because of my speed, almost decapitated me. I fell on a protruding stone, ripping a large hole in my pants and scraping up my right knee. The injury didn't even require a physician's treatment, only a large band-aid, and the couple didn't experience any other problems in their new home.

Another change in the police department that accompanied the change of administration was that the FOP became the bargaining agency for labor contracts between the city and policemen. When the Philadelphia FOP lodge was first organized in 1939, it created a stir among the city's political hierarchy. Officials were fearful of the lodge's strength, as they were covertly opposed to policemen banding together. Nonetheless, the lodge became a reality following a series of lively meetings held in homes and church halls, and Louis Zambino was selected as its first president. Membership grew slowly, since many policemen feared repercussions if their superiors learned they were affiliated with such an organization.

Though the FOP grew as the years passed, seldom were there more than one or two black members in attendance at the membership meetings, since the blacks saw the organization as being primarily a white one. Despite this, Ralph Rizzo urged me to run as a delegate to the national FOP conventions in the lodge's election of officers. I was elected on April 2, 1952, as one of Philadelphia's 102 delegates, winning a total of 605 out of 1,082 votes. Fewer than ten black policemen showed up to vote, so apparently I had earned the respect of my white colleagues.

Clouds of fear began churning within me, however, as I prepared to attend my first FOP convention to be held in Miami Beach, Florida. Since I strongly suspected that I might experience some problems with the management of the hotel where we would be staying, I asked chief delegate Harry Price, "Do those people down there know I'm colored?"

Price, apparently surprised at my anticipation of problems, asked, "What difference does it make?"

"It makes a hell of a lot of difference to me," I responded. "I'm not driving 1,200 miles with my wife to be embarrassed."

Price and I went to see Albert Brown, then president of our lodge, who later became police commissioner. Brown, too, thought there would be no difficulties. But, oh, how wrong they were.

At my insistence, a telephone call was placèd to the hotel. Brown asked for some reassurance from the hotel that there would be no difficulties encountered because the Philadelphia group included a black delegate. The hotel clerk, unable to answer Brown's question, consulted with the hotel manager. After some verbal stumbling, the manager finally stated that he was sorry but, "The hotel does not cater to colored."

He added that he would be glad to make reservations for me "at a fine colored hotel in Miami City, where he will be more comfortable with his own."

To Brown's credit, he immediately, without consulting with anyone at the lodge, told the manager to cancel all reservations for the entire Philadelphia delegation of 102 members and their families. Brown was storming mad, and he told the manager that he would follow up the call with a written confirmation. He slammed down the telephone receiver with a curt, "Thank you for nothing."

Brown then called the manager of a second hotel, The Prominade, which was one that he previously had negotiated with, which was located directly across the street from the first hotel. When Brown asked if the hotel could accommodate 102 delegates and their families, the manager said that he most certainly could. When it was pointed out that one of the delegates was a black policeman, the manager replied, "As long as he is in the delegation, we will accept him." While I was not completely satisfied with that answer, I decided not to complicate matters, and to go along with the new accommodations.

The entire situation became even more tolerable when I learned that Pennsylvania FOP president, Frank Topelsky, upon learning of the incident, had cancelled out the reservations of 138 FOP members throughout the state who had planned to stay at the first hotel. In the end, that hotel's segregation stance caused it to lose 240 reservations, costing its management thousands of dollars in income.

My wife, Vivienne, and I drove to Florida for the convention. On our way, we spent one night with relatives in Dillon, South Carolina, and a second night in a flea trap, a hotel designated for black persons, on the outskirts of Jacksonville, Florida. Upon our arrival the next day in front of our hotel in Miami Beach, a bellman opened the door and asked, "Are you Mr. Reaves?" Upon being reassured, the bellman took our luggage inside. At the registrar's desk, the clerk took one look at me and said, "You must be Mr. Reaves."

After settling in our room, we received a call from FOP attorney Sam Gorson, who welcomed us and assured us we would be treated well. Even the hotel bartender had been given instructions not to charge us for any drinks. But there was one incident in particular that served to remind us that we were still black guests. Harry Price apologetically informed us that the hotel management "wished" that we would not use the swimming pool—in accordance with state law. We told Price not to worry, that we preferred the beach anyway.

Apparently, our Miami Beach visit was something of a turning point in race relations in the community. As far as could be determined, we were the first black paying guests in a Miami Beach hotel. For many years prior to this, black entertainers had been permitted to stay in Miami Beach hotels, without charge, as part of their contracts when they were working there. Immediately after the FOP incident, all hotels opened their doors to all guests, provided that their money was green.

The arrest of which I am the proudest occurred on April 4, 1953, not long after we returned from Florida. It involved the robbery of a supermarket at 36th and Market Streets that was part of the American Store chain. I was off duty and in plainclothes, and had stopped at the corner across from the store for a newspaper. While walking back to my car, I observed two men with guns fleeing the store, and I concluded that they must have committed a robbery. I gave chase and engaged the men in a shoot-out when we got to an area where there weren't people around. They ran into a dark alley, and suddenly the men's gunfire stopped.

I ordered the men to come out and marched them to my car, wondering how I was going to handle them both, since I didn't have any handcuffs on me. I decided that the safest thing to do was to get them to the nearest station house as quickly as possible, so I placed the two men in my private automobile and drove them to the 16th District Headquarters, a half-dozen blocks away. I accomplished this by driving with one hand, while keeping the revolver pointed at them with the other.

After I got the men into the building, I started to relax and I realized that, after risking my life like that, I didn't want someone at this district, where I wasn't assigned, to try to take credit for my arrest. To preclude this, I announced in a loud voice within hearing of the district supervisors and the detectives to whom I turned the men over that if anyone tried to get in on my arrest, I would go to police headquarters "and sit on Commissioner Gibbons' desk and yell my heart out."

After the case was held for court, my captain came to me and personally congratulated me for the arrest. He further said he was going to put me in for a commendation. A few months passed and, when I didn't hear any further word, I began to lose hope that I would receive any recognition. Finally, I was officially informed that the commendation had been approved and that it was to be awarded at a special ceremony at Independence Hall on June 3, 1953. I had never heard of such a grand procedure, and I was shouting for joy.

As the time approached, more details unfolded. There was to be a celebration of Policemen's Day with a huge parade of policemen, with school and military units participating. Vivienne and I were full of anxiety and anticipation about the big day. We became even more so when we learned that I would also be given *The Inquirer Award* for bravery. On Policemen's Day we took our boys, Joseph and Alan, having kept Joseph home from school so that they could witness the ceremony. My longtime friend, Charles Hubbard, came to take us to Independence Hall. On arrival, everyone seemed to want to shake hands and offer congratulations.

It was a long wait until the parade finally arrived. We stood on the front steps of Independence Hall as the parade passed in review. Then everyone went to the rear of the building where a temporary stage had been built. There were several speeches by VIPs, and then the presentation. Policeman Norman C. Linwood was given a certificate as the Policeman of the Year for a number of arrests he had made in 1952.

Then the city's Managing Director, Robert K. Sawyer, called me onto the stage and, amid much fanfare, photography, and applause, presented me with the commendation and *The Inquirer's* Hero Award Medal. Commissioner Gibbons presented me with the Hero Award check for $200. As if all of the excitement of Policemen's Day was not enough, I also learned that American Stores had awarded me $500 for the capture of the robbers. The next day, *The Inquirer* had almost a full page of pictures and stories centered around the award presentation. It stated that 50,000 people watched the parade of 16,000 persons. It further stated that I "received warm praise from Sawyer and loud applause from his co-workers and the crowd who appeared in the historic square." All of the black newspapers also carried congratulatory articles about the ceremonies.

It was all a very interesting and satisfying experience. In that I received so many compliments from police officials, co-workers and well wishers, I now felt that I was proud to be a police officer, and that my police career had been the right choice. It also made me more determined to advance as far as possible in the department, although I was certain that would be extremely difficult for a black man to do.

Ironically, it was the president of the Philadelphia FOP, Albert Brown, the man who had changed our hotel reservations in Miami, who also played a role in helping me achieve my dreams. He worked for a change of city policy that was going to change my life far more quickly and far more radically than I ever would have thought possible. Brown was a smooth-talking but no-nonsense guy, and he managed to convince the city's Civil Service Commission to take an unprecedented step.

Brown argued before the board that, given all of the past political corruption involved in police promotional exams, the commission should hold a new series of tests for supervisory positions that were open to all policemen regardless of their current rank. Brown had reasoned that many good men who were capable of performing in these positions had been passed over and that, if given the chance and in-service training at the Police Academy, they could provide the department with a new cadre of leadership.

Shortly afterwards, the city held a series of open competitive examinations for five ranks: sergeant, lieutenant, captain, staff inspector and inspector. Only two lower and three higher ranks were excluded from the schedule. This meant that if a policeman had enough time in the department, he was eligible to take an examination for any or all of the five ranks.

The examinations were a godsend for officers who were competent and had long aspired to be promoted, but had not been because they lacked a powerful sponsor. When the new examinations were given, the results were astounding. Literally overnight, numerous policemen were catapulted to various upper ranks. Albert Brown, himself, even managed to be promoted from policeman to the rank of inspector.

And so ended the system of political "provisional" appointments that had long corrupted the department. It also opened the doors for long-suffering blacks on the force who were justifiably proud of their good showing on the examinations.

I took advantage of this opportunity and took all five examinations. For sergeant, lieutenant, and captain, I passed handily. For staff inspector, I passed the written segment but failed the oral segment. I failed the written exam for inspector and, thereby, was ineligible for the oral. Through discussions with other men who took the orals, we determined that personalities still played some part in the process. We determined that if you were treated warm and friendly during the orals, you did well. If the panelists were cold and acted disinterested, you usually failed.

The coming of the open police examinations for promotion was a joyous occasion for us fellows who felt that, if they were on the level, we would do well. We took Clark and Dilworth at their word that they would insist on honest examinations, and we went into the examinations fully expecting to be promoted to possibly the first two ranks—sergeant and lieutenant—but hardly any of us expected anything more. I expected that men like myself who had finished high school and had at least some college experiences would be promoted. Allen Ballard had assured all of the black members of Juvenile Aid Division that there would be at least five sergeants made among us. At that time, he seemed to be a favorite of both Captain Howard Leary and Commissioner Gibbons.

Test taking didn't excite many policemen, for all had a feeling that only the "in-boys" would make it. This is possibly why only 1,537 of the eligible men took the test. Except for the last two days prior to the tests, I did not even bother to prepare for them. It was my partner Thomas Roselle who told me that I could find a helpful book in the library. I took his suggestions and spent the last two days studying that book on police administration.

As for anticipating the test, I frankly think that I was a bit cocky for I always pass civil service tests, but I had problems getting far enough up on the promotion list to be promoted.

I decided to take the examination for every rank that was available, and the first oral examination given was for captain, which was a long way above my current rank. Commissioner Gibbons was on the examination panel. On entering the room, he greeted me in a very friendly manner. "Hello, Jim, have a seat over here. Relax and have a smoke if you wish." I did not know either of the other two panelists. The questions they asked me mostly had to do with police management. I was aided immeasurably by my readings of the two previous days. Surprisingly, the results were to be publicized within two weeks of the concluding orals on March 7, 1954. They were two very long weeks for me. I didn't volunteer to my friends that I had taken the test, but I didn't deny it if they asked.

When I received the results of my captain's test I was not overly jubilant, for I was twenty-forth on the list. I recalled that in a previous captain's test my friend Milton Smith had been fourteenth, and Hillary Johnston had been twelfth, and both lists had expired just as the men were reaching the top. I recall betting my partner, Vincent Rossi, a dinner that I would not be appointed.

Regardless of my success in passing the exams, I could not be promoted until enough positions opened so that I became the top man on the waiting list for any given rank. In the meantime, I immersed myself in the work of the Juvenile Aid Division, and the increasingly difficult problems we were facing with gang control work.

Policemen have always had a disdain toward gang members, calling them young punks and worse. When gangs assembled in a neighborhood there was often trouble, and policemen tried to disperse the young men from the area as quickly as possible. Juvenile officers worked very closely with civilian social workers who attempted to straighten out the boys' lives through athletic or social activities, often successfully, since the gang members trusted the social workers but not the policemen. Gang workers spend a lot of time with kids while the policemen do not, so they don't have a lot of contact with them. Gang workers often interceded with police on the kid's behalf, and the good ones make a connection with the kids, giving them the kind of leadership that might be lacking at home.

Residents in any given community will report the activities of gangs to police, but only covertly. They are afraid of repercussions, broken windows in homes and automobiles, even Molotov cocktails being tossed into their homes. The growing mechanization of the police force had broken the bond the foot patrol- man had with people in the neighborhoods, and now, rather than people co- operating with the police, residents were frequently afraid to talk to them. In the days when policemen walked the beat and they saw a group of young people congregating, a cop would hit a street pole with his nightstick, holler, and the street would quickly clear of kids. Now, kids were becoming increasingly dis- dainful of police because the breakdown of family life meant that parents didn't care if police brought kids home, and the kids saw themselves as having little to fear.

Gang activities rise and fall from decade to decade. My observations have been that gangs are often formed when young boys in one city block develop a rivalry with those in the next block. This rivalry can originate harmlessly, even in growing out of friendly sports contest. As the boys grow older, they begin to join up with boys from adjoining blocks to make a more powerful team. At times, their numbers grow so large that those who fail to make the regular team join into rival gangs in adjoining communities and declare the gang that rejected them to be the enemy.

As this escalation continues, many boys feel they have to join gangs as a means of survival, since they need protection from rival gangs. If the gangs continue to have sports teams, violence often erupts when one team's supporters challenge the other team's supporters. Just as often, fights break out as one gang member trespasses on another's community or turf. This is especially true if the one trespassing is visiting a girlfriend, one whom the locals have been trying to make time with.

A good example was the Gut and the Schuylkill Rangers, which operated in Philadelphia in the middle decades of the 19th Century. This group of young men were infamous first as street fighters, but they slowly evolved into thieves and then river pirates. Members of the gang lived between South Street and Grays Ferry Avenue in an area just east of the Schuylkill River. The first escalation of their activities away from neighborhood brawls occurred when they began pilfering coal and other valuables from B & O Railroad cars that rode the tracks through their neighborhood. As they grew older, the boys drank a lot of beer at night with groups erupting into fights.

They were at their worst when they began boarding cargo boats on the

Schuylkill River and forcefully looting the materials they were carrying. When they expanded their activities to the much larger Delaware River, they began to specialize in stealing pig iron from boats, which they brazenly sold the next day to local foundries. They also stole sails and riggings from the boats, also for resale. They were finally broken up in the late 1870s. While many were imprisoned as a result of these activities, historians tell us most of them went straight as they grew older. There have been any number of attempts by area youths to reform the Schuylkill Rangers over the years, but none of them ever came to rival the notoriety of the original group.

In contemporary times, as gang members grow older they begin carrying weapons ranging from pocket knives and brass knuckles to zip guns and multiple-firing pistols. Zip guns come in all fashions, often made from radio aerials ripped from automobiles and mounted on a wooden stock with an attached firing pin activated by a rubber band.

To combat that gang problem, as a sergeant, I was placed in charge of three men in the juvenile division, two white officers who had already been assigned to police liquor law violations by juveniles, and a black officer, Samuel Wyche, who had already worked on gangs with me. As gang problems increased, I requested more men and was given William Norman and Leonard "Mack" Gaffney. This was the beginning of the Gang Control Unit.

Although gang fights were a big problem, there were very few homicides then. Gangs that were well known were Tops, centered around 38th and Brown Streets; Bottoms, centered around 50th and Brown Streets; The Syndicate, 57th and Vine Streets; The Villagers, 24th and Cumberland Streets; The Forty Thieves, 22nd Sreet and Columbia Avenue; The Exiles at 12th Street and Fairmount Avenue and The Pandoras, 16th Street and Fairmount Avenue. Many of these areas had younger boys who claimed that they were the juniors of the older gangs.

Gang fights and killings would not reach their peak in Philadelphia until the 1970s, when as many as forty-five boys and young men would be killed annually in gang violence. There was no question, however, that gang activity and juvenile delinquency was on the upswing in Philadelphia in the early 1950s, and there was no denying that the vast majority of the new offenders were black.

In JAD, officers Chisholm, William Norman and I were the leaders in arrests. Our caseloads of investigations, our arrests, and general contacts with the Youth Study Center and courts made us constantly aware of just who the lawbreakers were. At least 80 percent of all juveniles arrested were black. This both embarrassed us and evoked our sympathy for the boys and their families.

We were hard workers trying to improve the lot of our families as well as our race. But to see these youngsters waste their lives away and not doing anything constructive was embarrassing. The vast majority of the offenders came from broken homes, and in many cases their mothers either didn't care or didn't know how to direct their activities.

It was far from unusual to be assigned to cases where as many as six children in one family all had police contacts. In one family, two brothers were charged with two separate cases of homicide. In still another, a father and son were charged with separate cases of homicide.

There were a number of schools where I went to investigate crimes, usually crimes of violence or burglary. When I walked into a classroom, I was unable to understand how the learning process could be effective with all of the noise going on. Often, teachers would say that they were glad to be rid of certain fellows. In one class, I actually had to break up a fight. In another, I threatened to arrest a boy for abusing the teacher. Dealing with this on a day-to-day basis began to disturb me deeply.

I received my first promotion from the open testing in January of 1954, when I was promoted to sergeant. I wasn't impressed very much with being a sergeant because I remained in the plainclothes JAD squad, and I didn't wear a uniform to show off my stripes. Then, too, I continued doing pretty much the same work as I did as a uniformed policeman. About the only difference was that I now had supervisory responsibilities over the same men that I was previously working along with as partners, all of whom were black. Even when I was promoted to lieutenant six months later, there was still little or no change. While I enjoyed my new title and pay scale, I remained in the same division. I had the sneaking suspicion that my superiors were a bit leary of putting me in charge of a uniformed platoon of patrol officers in a district, all of which were at least 75 percent white. The same thing happened to Lieutenant Leonard Jones, another black officer who was promoted after the open testing. He was assigned to the Detectives Division, where he was given so few duties that his supervisor told him to take time off and go fishing, and that he would cover for him.

I continued working with the same men as a lieutenant, with only a few more added. My new men were white officers, and they were given their assignments by the captain, reporting to me only for paper work in the morning and for signing off duty by calling in from a station house that was usually located on the other side of the city. I'm sure the white officers were not keen on reporting to me, for I had also worked with them as uniformed policemen. I had the impression that they were jealous of me. I made no effort to exert strict supervision over them because, in reality, they took their orders from the captain.

My being a lieutenant did not last long; for three months into it, I was suddenly placed on cloud nine when I was promoted to captain.

On the day that my name appeared in the teletype machine ordering me to appear in the Mayor's office on October 22, 1954, I had a Herculean case of mixed emotions. I was overjoyed at the arrival of the time that I would be promoted to captain, but far more filled with uncertainty as to my being qualified for the position. This was because I had never acted in, or trained in, an administrative capacity.

I rushed home to inform Vivienne and other members of my family. Everyone seemed so happy for me and was so certain that I would do a good job. I called John Smith who operated a restaurant at 49th Street and Saybrook Avenue and asked him to prepare lunch for twelve members of my family for the forthcoming promotional day. I truly had difficulty sleeping that night, waking up every half hour or so.

On that most important day, we bundled the boys up and were off to City Hall. On arrival, we found all of my siblings with their spouses, along with my mother and my best friend. I was pleasantly surprised to see Inspector Ballard and Staff Inspector Payne there. I was even more surprised to see Rev. Marshall Shepherd there. He called to me to introduce me to Congressman Arthur Mitchell of Illinois who had come up from Washington to witness the ceremony. He was one of only two blacks in Congress, and Chicago was the only other major city in the country with a black captain.

There were two other men to be sworn in along with me. They were Frederick Dohrman and Brooks Lowe. Commissioner Gibbons swore us in while admonishing us to be ever vigilant against crime and vice in our areas of command. He then shook hands with us as photographers all over the place snapped pictures. It was only after Deputy Commissioner Albert Brown gave us our new badges that I knew where I would be assigned.

After the ceremony was over, we all went out to Smith's Corner where Mr. Smith had a huge streamer in the restaurant proclaiming "Welcome Captain Reaves." There was a delicious lunch prepared for us in the back section of the restaurant on a beautifully set table. There was much joviality during the meal, concluding with everyone drinking water to toast my future success.

After we left, I reported to 55th and Pine Streets where I was introduced to Inspector George Kronbar. He was surprised to know that I had been sworn in. He welcomed me and we had a nice long talk. He gave me the usual precautionary talk about working hard and being honest and fair. He then said for me to meet him in the 16th District at midnight in plainclothes.

At home, I explained to Vivienne that my new position would call for more than eight-hour tours of duty, that I would have to work extra hours at night and weekends. Vivienne was just as proud of my new position as I was, as she often found herself being pointed out as the new captain's wife. She was very supportive. Although the increase in pay was not that much, I did manage to upgrade my automobile by a few years. This pleased her very much, as I taught her how to drive our new car.

I felt that I had finally reached the top. From my first job as a hospital worker at forty-five dollars a month, to a police captain at five hundred dollars a month was an awfully big difference. The road to the top had not always been easy.

There were many anxious moments when I feared for my job, and other times when I feared for my life. I endured my share of discrimination and bad treatment, and occasionally I got pushed around, but I had higher goals in mind, and I just grinned and bore it. Now I knew I was somebody, and I was damn proud of it.

CHAPTER SEVEN

Certainly the greatest transition in my career came from being a policeman in January to becoming a captain, and commanding a busy police district, in October. Excluding my race, most assuredly my case differed from any captain in the history of the police department. I had not previously worked in a police district operations room more than a half dozen days. Even then, all that I had done was to answer the telephone from police call boxes. In those days, black policemen were never assigned to the operations room on a regular basis.

When I reported to Inspector Kronbar that first day, I freely admitted my unfamiliarity with operations and requested his permission to have Lieutenant William Meyers assigned to me to help me learn the routine. The inspector was understanding, and he readily went along with the suggestion. Luckily for me, Meyers had been the acting captain of that district for several months prior to my arrival. I was also fortunate in that he was not only willing to work along, but he also showed me the operations. He was completely loyal in spite of the fact that he had failed the same examination for captain that I passed.

Just as roll call began at midnight, Inspector Kronbar took me before the squad and introduced me as the new captain. Most of the men there remembered me from the time that I was a policeman in that district eight years earlier. I observed roll call and made a short speech to the men, assuring them that we could work together. Inspector Kronbar wished me well and left. I was glad to see Lieutenant John Quinn on duty. We had worked well together, years earlier as policemen, before our promotions.

I was really surprised that the department had made no effort to inform any of the community or civic organizations of my being assigned to the district. I'm sure that the administration wasn't aware that I had practically no experience in administration except from courses taken at the University of Pennsylvania. As a rule, when a promotion is made, the person involved has already spent some time in the new rank in an acting capacity. However, there was another officer, Albert N. Brown, who had been promoted at the same time that I was, who moved all the way from patrolman to inspector in one jump.

In my years as a policeman, I had been most impressed by Captain Gibbons and Captain Howard Leary. I liked their style and decided that I would model myself after them when I made an important decision as a captain. I also made myself a promise that I would always try to say "yes" when one of my men asked a favor of me. I once had a sergeant who would always say "no" before you finished your request, and that had always irritated me.

While I was very happy to have been promoted with all of its trappings, I knew that I would really miss my day-to-day associations with the men I formerly worked with. My new job would take me away from them, and I feared that in some cases my former partners would feel that I had abandoned them. On the other hand, I knew I would develop a new kinship with all of the men who were promoted, and that we would share know-how and experiences with each other.

Within a week of being at my new charge, at least a half dozen white officers came to me with requests for transfers. All of them had plausible reasons, and at least half said that their previous request for transfer had been denied without reason. I complied by granting their request, partly because I wanted to be helpful, but also because I wanted them to leave if they didn't want to work for me.

An immediate problem I had was opening the office safe. No one seemed to know the combination, since the previous captain had retired. I finally sent a request to the Department of City Property to have it opened. When no one arrived for three weeks, a policeman who had been the captain's clerk years earlier came forward. He offered to try to remember the combination. He did and it opened. Months later I received word that he had finally decided that I was not so bad after all and decided to help me. This attitude became more evident among the men as they all increasingly improved their performances.

During my first week as captain in the 16th District, Inspector Kronbar summoned me to his office. I reported there as directed. He said that there was going to be an air raid and he was putting me in charge. He then gave me a long list of verbal orders on how to handle the logistics, and I quickly wrote them down as he spoke. At the sound of the alarm, I was to instruct my men to clear all people and vehicles off Lancaster Avenue from Market to 44th Streets. I took this to include all of the parked cars whose owners could be found.

On the night of the alert, I was at home when the sirens went off about 9:30 P.M. I rushed to the district and began putting the established plan into effect. Our men worked feverishly and moved at least three-fourths of the parked vehicles and all moving traffic off of the street. Just as I was congratulating a sergeant and myself for doing such a good job, we looked up and saw a black automobile approaching that we recognized as a police official's car. It pulled up along the curb by us at 34th & Lancaster. I immediately recognized the operator as a longtime police friend of mine, Chief Inspector Albert Trimmer. We had once worked together in the 33rd District.

It was obvious that he was disturbed as he walked within six feet of me and stood at attention. I did the same and gave him a salute. He said in a most official voice, "Captain Reaves, why did you move all of these parked cars?" I replied that it was done on orders of the inspector.

"That's all wrong," he said, "you were only supposed to eliminate all moving traffic." "What should I do?" I asked. He said to do nothing until the all clear sounded. He turned and quickly walked away. It was the most embarrassing and depressing moment of my life. After having my bars for only five days, I was afraid I was going to lose them. We waited for about fifteen minutes to see what would happen, when from around the corner came Inspector Trimmer. He approached us in a more relaxed way and smiled. He said, "Jim, I just finished talking with Inspector Kronbar, and he has taken full responsibility for the foul up." I gave a deep, obvious sigh of relief. He smiled again and left.

My new status brought on friends I did not know that I had. Many even said that they had made contacts that helped to get me appointed. I thanked them all, while being certain that they had nothing to do with it. I accepted all social and civic invitations. I was a favorite at men's breakfasts. Ward leaders called or came in for favors, all of which I granted, providing they were legitimate, reasonable, and did not disrupt my programs.

From the beginning I was aware that, as a ranking black officer, I would be subject to more scrutiny and criticism than my white counterparts. I knew that I would have to conduct myself and make decisions in a manner that would withstand any inspection. Bearing in mind that I had three-fourths white officers and one-fourth black officers under my command, I had to constantly be alert to not appear to favor one group over the other.

I inherited two plainclothesmen, one white, one black. I was glad to see that they worked so well together. I retained them for almost a year, until they became recognizable on sight and lost their effectiveness as vice investigators. When I replaced them, I continued the policy of having a mixed racial pair doing plainclothes work. Good reasoning dictated that two black investigators would have been more effective in working in black communities, but that wasn't the only factor to consider. I found this policy to be very effective in enhancing the morale of the white policemen in the district, the majority of whom hoped to be used in plainclothes work at sometime. I also found that a mixed plainclothes squad was less inclined to socialize, rather than work, during work hours.

My difficulties with the white officers were that I had to appear to be lenient to obtain their loyalty and cooperation. With the black officers, they expected favoritism because of our mutual color. To the contrary, I found that in many cases I was compelled to take severe action against black officers to demonstrate my impartiality.

When I was promoted to captain, two black lieutenants were sent to my district, Leonard Jones and Richard Edwards. Both had been in plainclothes in the Detective Bureau, and influential blacks at the time had requested the transfers as a means of getting them into lieutenant uniforms. It was also taken for granted that I would take care of them and keep them out of trouble.

Both were good officers and got along well with the men. However, I had to discipline each of them once. Lieutenant Jones manhandled a woman once and pushed her around. She complained to police headquarters, and staff inspectors made an investigation. I had to prefer charges of conduct unbecoming an officer against him. He was reprimanded by the Police Trial Board. I don't think he held it against me, as we are still good friends.

Lieutenant Edwards' case was for laxity. When he was working for me, he became increasingly less inclined to obey orders. I assigned him to investigate a commissioner's complaint against one of his men for harassing a businessman. After two days, I asked how he was making out with the case. He said he had been too busy to get to it. The next day he gave me the same answer. This was on a Friday. I then told him that I must have the completed case on my desk by Monday morning or that I would report him to my inspector. He threw up his arms in a huff and walked off.

On Monday morning I called him at home and asked for the completed case. He said he still had not completed it. I then wrote out a complaint against him and took it to the inspector. He instructed me to send Edwards to see him, which I did. When Edwards returned he came storming into my office wanting to know why I had reported him. I responded that it was simply for disobedience of orders. He was furious and said, "I never thought one of my own kind would do that to me." He appeared to be absolutely livid. I told him that race had nothing to do with it, that I was acting only as his commander. No further action was taken, and his attitude seemed to improve.

On the other hand, I was in a position whereby I could make sure that black officers received fair treatment and special little bits of training and information that would advance their careers. Many present and former high-ranking officers in the department freely admit that I was the catalyst that made the difference between success and failure in their careers.

When I heard that a police unit, the Community Relations Division, was being formed, I sensed that this was a chance to help some black officers. Historically, such units have always been difficult for blacks to get assigned to. Each district was required to send three men for screening, with one to be chosen from each. To assure that my district had a black representative, I selected three black officers and sent them. All three were well qualified and would have done a good job. The one chosen ended up advancing the least in the department. Of the other two, one became a sergeant and president of a black policemen's organization, the Guardian Civic League, and the other became a deputy police commissioner and vice president of Temple University.

I am proud to say that my reputation among the white officers was such that they all respected me, and in many cases they requested transfers into my district. There was, however, something that took place far too often to have been happenstance, and it caused me no small amount of anxiety. When the formerly high-ranking white, provisional, and acting officers were reduced in rank after failing to pass their promotional exams, they were often sent to my district, and I feared this was happening as a punishment to them. I made certain that they were treated fairly, and within no time at all they made it known that they were pleased with the change.

I seized upon another opportunity to appear to be objective in my actions, and that was the increasing number of commendations that I requested for the men who performed good police work. In one City Hall ceremony where a commendation for one of my men was being read, an important city official said within my hearing that it was not so much good police work as the way the commendation was written that had gotten the award, and that the writer should have received the commendation.

There was one aspect of my promotion that made me uncomfortable. More than a few of my former partners and associates, both black and white, and even some civilians, seemed to resent my progress. They just seemed to shy away from me. A couple of my longtime partners never congratulated me, nor did they even come around for months thereafter.

From the very beginning of my captaincy, I made an effort to conduct roll call at least two times a day in order to see as many of the men as possible. Even if I was out on social occasions at night, I tried to stop in for the midnight roll call. In order to not be too pretentious, I merely observed roll calls without uniform during the early days.

During these times it seemed to me that I was living a make-believe life. It was hard for me to believe that I had made it to the top after having been a policeman for so long. I even found it difficult to respond when someone suddenly tried to get my attention by calling "captain." At home, Vivienne and the boys fell right into the spirit of the moment, and they were less demanding of my time. Vivienne did more and more of the chores at home that were mine. The boys began calling me "chief" instead of dad, and for a while they took to saluting me facetiously.

While I always tried to make sure that I was fair to all of my officers, there were a number on inequities in the way black officers were treated that I immediately set out to correct. I was serving as a captain in an almost all-black area of the city, but my staff was overwhelmingly white, and the black officers that were in the district were still walking the beat. There was, however, one car in the district known as the "colored car" that was reserved for the black police-men. If there weren't enough blacks to man the car, it just didn't get used that tour of duty. The only integration in the district was the one white and one black plainclothesmen who specialized in raiding homes that were black homes 99 percent of the time.

Although the department had initially created a patrol car for black officers in the 23rd District in 1940, only a few other districts followed suit, and there were no integrated patrol cars on regular duty. I took the initiative to change that. At a staff meeting, I told my lieutenants that I wanted them to fill the next patrol car vacancy with a black. I explained that this would lessen harassment complaints against our men by community residents, thereby creating less work for the department in making investigations and writing reports.

The lieutenants all seemed against the idea, saying things like: "The men will rebel, they already say that they spend more time with their partners than they do with their wives." "Our men work well together, it would be harmful to their morale to separate them." "The men all would want to transfer out." They said these things in all seriousness, but I stuck to my guns telling them that we were going to try it. A couple of them barely spoke to me for a few days. I had left them with the option to select whomever they wanted, but it must be a black and that I was holding them responsible for the car crews' performance.

The first vacancy was on a patrol wagon, and Joseph Dangerfield was assigned to it. He was a tall, handsome officer with a winning personality. He proved to be an excellent choice for he and Harry Slider, the white officer on the vehicle, hit it off very well. After a few days, I asked each man separately how it was going, and each said that it was fine and that he wanted to continue. The lieutenant seemed pleased that I was pleased and later, in an aside statement to me, agreed that, "It should have been done a long time ago."

In that I walked the business areas of my district in uniform daily, I was often stopped and congratulated for squad car integration by people in the neighborhood. Some of the youth referred to the mixed crew in a flippant manner as "salt and pepper." There really didn't seem to be an unusual number of requests for transfers among the men in the district. In fact, as time passed, more and more men transferred in at their own request.

I also found that contrary to predictions by the lieutenants, job performances among the men picked up. This was aided in part by my giving extra hours off as a reward to officers who made special efforts in the line of duty. The result of the policy that I was most pleased with was the decrease in police brutality complaints.

I don't think that it was just by chance that Deputy Commissioner Leary and Chief Inspector Albert Trimmer came to my district unannounced. During our conversation they seemed awfully interested in the reason for the decrease in brutality complaints. Even if it were not true, I attributed it to the mixed cars. Inspector Ballard then instructed the captains in the North Central District to affect the same change. Within a short time, all districts that had a sizeable number of black officers also fell in line.

I used the same rationale for integrating the operations room, insisting that a black be in the room at all times. I often pointed out to my subordinate officers the statistics indicating a sharp decline in citizen complaints when black officers dealt with members of the black community.

Shortly after my promotion to the rank of captain, Jean Barrett, a reporter for the *Philadelphia Evening Bulletin* requested permission from Commissioner Gibbons to interview me. Chief Inspector Trimmer called me prior to the interview and said that it was okay to do it, but that I should be careful about how I answered her questions.

The reporter came to my district for the interview, and we talked for about an hour. While the questions dealt mainly with juveniles—she knew that I had spent a number of years in the Juvenile Aid Division—there were a number of other questions, and the answers I gave ruffled a lot more feathers than I expected. I must give credit to the interviewer, for in spite of our conversing in my office, I was ill at ease until she made herself appear to be much like an old friend.

She had a very pleasing personality, was about twenty-five-years old and white. I noticed that the more we talked the more both of us loosened up, which made both questions and answers flow more easily. I'm certain that neither of us realized what a sensational story it would make.

I had welcomed the interview because, based on my long police experience, I had something to say about crime and criminals, and I thought that people would listen to me now because of my new rank. From my experience and statistics that I have seen, I knew that blacks commit far more crime proportionately than whites. Certainly the reasons for this are most unfortunate, mainly economics and broken homes. But I also felt that one must not disregard a lack of discipline in the home by parents as a cause of juvenile delinquency, and I told the reporter this.

I felt the same went for a lack of support by parents for upholding discipline by school authorities. I said that school officials should be permitted to use corporal punishment on unruly students, and that a more aggressive approach should be taken by attendance officers in physically taking truants to school. I also said that I thought the courts should bring more severe punishments to bear on young offenders, and that black newspapers should not be so fast to glamorize and defend all blacks accused of crimes, regardless of their guilt or innocence. I spoke of how the papers, in their efforts to sell more papers, put so much emphasis on crime stories, but that this only appealed to many criminals who wanted the publicity.

As a board member of the local NAACP, I had once suggested that the branch pick out a few obviously guilty black criminals and actively pursue their prosecution. In this manner, the courts would give the organization more credence when it defends others. This did not go over too well with the members, and it

Police Captains - sworn in by Commissioner Thomas J. Gibbons
L to R: James N. Reaves, Brooks Lowe, and Fredrick Doherman - October 22, 1954

Housing Policemen graduate from Police Academy
L to R: (front row) James N. Reaves, Gilbert Stein, Dir., PHA, and Peter Shovelin, Dir., Housing
Mgt.

Dr. Martin Luther King, Jr.
L to R: Dr. King, Det. Karl Von Lipsey, Det. Adolphus Woods, Captain James N. Reaves, and Dr. Thomas V. Hawkins - 1962 (photo - courtesy of Fletcher Brodie)

Philadelphia Inquirer Award to James N. Reaves for bravery
L to R: (seated) Samuel Gorson Esq., Managing Director, John J. Lohrman, James N. Reaves and Commissioner Thomas J. Gibbons - June 3rd 1953.

was rejected with the statement, "We're not in the business of prosecuting anyone."

The article appeared on November 14, 1954, with the headline *"Top Authority on Juvenile Gangs."* My criticism of the black newspapers brought on a series of weekly criticisms of me and my actions as a police captain in their publications. The papers attested to my honesty, but they questioned my knowledge of sociology.

It did not take long for other reactions to surface. The following week, the *Philadelphia Evening Bulletin* published a Jean Barrett interview with Robert C. Taber, the school board's director of pupil personnel and counseling. It was forty inches of newspaper columns, plus a 5" x 6" picture of Taber with a chart. All of this in an effort to refute my criticisms of the school system's actions regarding delinquents.

It began by saying "The old-fashioned 'hooky-cop'is through, and his strong-arm tactics were dropped by the Board of Education because the board had decided they didn't work." Further in the article, Taber pointed out that statistics of the Board of Education show an increasing emphasis upon law enforcement. He also stated that "no one agency has the answer or is alone sufficient to deal with juvenile delinquency."

This article was followed by one in the *Catholic Standard* and *Times* the next Sunday, praising me for "such a forthright article on conditions as [I] saw them." It also republished the entire *Bulletin* article as it appeared originally.

Happily, the Pennsylvania FOP State Bulletin for December 1954 did much the same by running the entire *Bulletin* article. It stated in part: "It took a lot of courage to face inevitable criticism from a half dozen fronts for a Philadelphia Police Captain to lay the facts on the line in the public press."

Among numerous letters to the editor of the *Bulletin* was one from a teacher that read, "I completely accept the validity of the criticism of our school system by Captain Reaves, and I truly endorse his recommendations."

When I read the article in the *Bulletin*, I had some concerns about the newspaper publicity, but I knew that I had spoken the truth, and that I had been given permission officially to do so. Whatever trepidations I may have had were quickly dispensed with by a telephone call from Chief Inspector Trimmer. He said that he liked the article and that he stood behind me. His assurances put me at peace with myself, but the piece de resistance came a few days later when Commissioner Gibbons himself called to tell me that he too thought that I had done well in the interview. From then on I heard nothing but compliments from police officials. The whole matter just seemed to fade away with the passage of time. At no time was I required to write explanations or be questioned by police officials. I think that the resultant publicity enhanced my image in the police department immediately and in the community eventually.

Any negativism or doubts surrounding my promotion were quickly and completely overshadowed by positiveness and good will. I received many letters of congratulations and invitations to speak or make appearances in uniform. People came from far and near just to see me in uniform. My first speaking engagement was at the Rawnhurst Presbyterian Church in the all-white Northeast, where I was given a plaque.

The church's men's club had extended the invitation to speak at their club meeting at the church. They had read the controversial article in the *Bulletin* in which I was so outspoken, and they wanted to hear more. Upon receipt of the invitation, I had some reservations about accepting it until I discussed it with Lieutenant Meyers. He assured me that there would be no problems, and he even volunteered to accompany me for moral support.

On December 3, 1954, Lieutenant Meyers and I went to the church in full uniform. We were escorted to a community room where there were about fifty men. I felt fairly comfortable in that I had my notes to a well-thought-out and practiced speech. It helped to know that Meyers was a good talker and was willing to do so if asked. Mr. Lewis A. Oechlin, the president, introduced me by reading a brief resume that I had sent to him as well as adding some of his own concerns about my subject.

I spoke for about twenty minutes, rehashing some of the subjects mentioned in the article, but clarifying many points that they might be concerned with. I was careful to let them know that the criticism mentioned in the article did not pertain to blacks only. I was speaking of all races. There was a question and answer session in which Lieutenant Meyers amply assisted me. At least a dozen questions were asked and responded to. All were very cordial except one chap who said he was given a hard time by a policeman when he was given a ticket.

Their main concern was the quality of education and the failure to enforce discipline in the school system. I concluded by assuring them that the recent reorganizing of the police department would mean better crime prevention and improved overall law enforcement.

Shortly after this engagement, I was invited by Reverend Marshall Shephard of Mt. Olivet Baptist Church to be a speaker. During my talk, just to add a little humor, I told the black audience about the time that I was in the 16th District as a policeman, and that a few of the men, including a sergeant, held me in contempt for what I assumed was my race. Upon my return as commanding officer nine years later, however, they were singing a different tune. Many of the formerly contemptuous officers were singing my praises, and the sergeant often brought me coffee unsolicited. The story went over well with the congregation. They loved it, but unfortunately it also reached the daily papers.

I sensed afterwards, that there was some tension in the district that I was unable to account for. Later in the week, one of the men came to me in confidence and told me that word of my statements at church had come back to the men at the district. At the next staff meeting with my lieutenants, I apologized for anything I said that they might have been uncomfortable with, arguing that my statements had been taken out of context.

Many people that I encountered on the street during my walking tours related unhappy experiences with policemen to me. As nice as it was to have people stop me for conversation, it was disconcerting for so many of them to have negative impressions and experiences relative to policemen. I listened attentively as they related personal contacts wherein policemen overreacted or failed to react. The most recurring plaint was that of having their homes entered without a warrant, with the doors often being kicked in during the process. Others complained of receiving traffic tickets unjustified. Almost as common a complaint was that they received little or no satisfaction when they tried to reach police officials. I assured them that my office door was always open to them, and that any and all of their complaints would be investigated and proper action taken where deemed justified.

My experiences in JAD had taught me that the best remedy to complaints was just to listen to the complainers. Often you didn't have to promise to do anything to have people say, "I feel so much better now that I've talked with you." I knew that expressing my personal concern to my policemen would cause them to be more cautious in the way they conducted themselves with the public.

The first professional police organization for ranking officers I became aware of was the International Association of Chiefs of Police. At the behest of my mentor, Staff Inspector Payne, I joined in 1954. He and I were the first blacks to be admitted nationwide. We were both well treated and attended monthly meetings and annual conferences. Our first conference was in 1955 in Chicago. We drove out and back. We were the toast of the few black police officials in Chicago. They insisted on taking us to *Ebony* magazine's offices, where we were interviewed and photographed. Pictures and writings also appeared in *Jet* magazine.

It was, by far, a different reception that my application for membership in the Delaware Valley Police Chiefs Association received a number of years later. I was given an application by Inspector Dennis Rooney of Philadelphia. I filled it out and mailed it in with the required membership fee. Within a week it was returned by mail with the explanation that the membership campaign had closed. It was signed by the secretary, whom I knew very well since we were both captains in the same division.

The next time I saw Inspector Rooney, he bawled me out for not joining. I showed him the rejection letter. He became angry and said, "Give that to me. I'll straighten them guys out." Apparently, he did, for within two weeks I received approval for membership. I'm almost certain that I became the first black member. Thirty-five years later I'm still an active member. They have treated me splendidly as a member and I've enjoyed it.

CHAPTER EIGHT

Police raids on private homes and business establishments have been an accepted practice of law enforcement for many years. In the era of Prohibition, illegal liquor was the main object of search, and it became a common practice to seize paraphernalia related to the making of liquor and the operation of a speakeasy. It was normal to see open-bodied police trucks transporting tables, chairs, dishes, glasses, and even stoves from suspected locations. Some raiders, not wanting to bother removing the items, would break them up with an ax and just leave them there. Unfortunately, these practices were often continued after the end of Prohibition, when the search was just as likely to be for stolen property or a wanted person, as it was to be for illegal liquor, drugs, and numbers.

Another excessive practice during a raid was that everyone on the property at the time of the raid was taken into custody, often necessitating the use of two or more patrol wagons. In almost every case, only the operator of the establishment was held or fined. Everyone else was discharged. On the suggestion of one of my lieutenants, I ordered my men to arrest only the principles and chase everyone else away. I also prohibited the destruction of property at the site.

This worked well, and we continued it once we were not upbraided by our superiors. All the other districts soon found out about it and followed suit. I received a lot of compliments from the citizens for the innovation, although usually not from the people who were arrested. I often went on weekend raids with my plainclothesmen, Priston Scott and Edwin Mosley. We raided a gambling game at 36th and Filbert Streets at a time when we were still taking in all of the participants. While in the house, one of the men being arrested accused me of not being racially conscious, and asked why I was not giving "a brother" a break. I countered by taking out my membership card to The NAACP, showed it to him, and said "You show me one and I'll let you go." He did not have one, but word got out that I would release all NAACP members in raids. All of a sudden there was a rash of new NAACP members.

We raided a gambling house at 41st and Girard Avenue so often that one night we went there, rang the bell and were admitted by the obviously drowsy male owner. He went back to his living room bed, and back to sleep, while we searched the house. After finding nothing illegal in the house for once, we didn't even bother to wake the man up as we locked the door and left.

Another time near, 36th and Melon Streets, we came upon two subteen boys walking the street at 3:00 A.M. When we asked why they were out, they said they were waiting for their uncle to take them on a fishing trip. I sent my plainclothesmen, Scott and Mosley, further down the street to check out a regular gambling spot. Meanwhile, I took the two boys to their home and rang the doorbell. A man opened the door, but only very reluctantly—and I'm sure he wouldn't have opened it at all if I had been in uniform. As he was admitting that he knew the boys were outside, I could hear loud noises coming from a group of people inside the house. I pushed by the man at the door, entered the room, and saw about fifteen men around a table shooting craps.

I yelled "police" as I scooped up the dice and money from the table and put them into my pocket. I reached for my badge to identify myself, only to find I didn't have it with me. I reached for my gun to protect myself, only to discover that I had no gun. I knew that I just had to have my blackjack but, when I reached for it, it wasn't there either. I just wanted to drop through the floor.

I began talking very loudly and authoritatively, trying to cover myself. I asked who the owner was and a lot of other questions, hoping all the while that my plainclothesmen were going to come looking for me any second. They did arrive in a short time, and they never looked better than when they walked in that door.

Within six months of my being assigned to the 16th District, Inspector Kronbar made me the acting inspector in his absence, which included his three-week vacation. I asked why I had been chosen instead of one of the other three captains. He said that they were old and not likely to be active commanders. During a time when I was serving in this capacity, I received word that a television personality, Bishop Fulton Sheen, would be visiting and holding services at St. Ignatius Parish at 43rd and Wallace Streets on Good Friday. I was to clear all parked cars in the immediate area to make way for his motorcade. On the day before his arrival, our men cleared the streets as ordered.

A delegation of black clergymen came to the office to complain that the 16th District captain had removed all automobiles from in front of their churches just so that the Catholics could use the spaces for their cars. The secretary heard their complaint and referred them to the acting inspector. She led them to my office where I invited them in. They appeared to be flabbergasted when they saw me.

I explained to them that I had the area cleared on orders from Police Head-quarters, that it was not my idea. They seemed to understand, and said that they were elated to see that I was the chosen one for the acting position. They thanked me for my time and left. When Bishop Sheen arrived he sent for me to personally thank me for the cooperation. We posed for pictures together and he blessed me.

I caused an embarrassment to the Police Department when I raided a health center at 41st Street and Haverford Avenue for gambling. On January 26, 1955, my plainclothesmen came to me to say that a big gambling game was in progress at 603 North 41st Street. I joined them and went to the location at about 1:00 A.M. The door opened for a patron and we entered with him. We went to the third floor where we found a pool table being used as a craps table with about twenty men taking part. A Mrs. Gladys Weathers was selling whiskey and beer in bottles to the patrons.

While several men escaped over rooftops, we arrested Mrs. Weathers and charged her with running a gambling house, keeping a disorderly house, and selling untaxed whisky. She had personal business cards which read "Gladys and Jimmy's, 301 N. 41st St." The hearing was held at 50th Street and Lancaster Avenue before Magistrate Elias Myers. During the hearing, officer Scott recognized James Weather in the courtroom. He arrested him, taking him before the magistrate who held both of the Weathers on $800 bail each.

The next day, Inspector Trimmer called to say that he wanted a report on the raid and arrests, and asked why I did not notify the Health Department prior to the raid. I explained that at the time of the raid we entered the building on the 41st Street side and that I did not realize that this was the health center, which has its front door on Haverford Ave. at 4077. He explained to me that James Weather was the building's custodian and lived on the third floor. He complimented me on the arrest and said he would explain the operations to Dr. Norman Ingraham, the Deputy Commissioner of Health and apologized for the police action while excluding Health Department officials.

"Too Tight" was the nickname for Ralph Carden who had a reputation for being brutal. It became more intense after he killed a man who had accused Ralph of being sexually involved with the man's wife. I received a complaint from a white woman who said that he had slapped her while giving her a traffic ticket. The details are that Ralph, who was black, stopped her for a traffic violation and gave her a ticket. During the time she said something to him that he objected to. When he handed her the ticket, he slapped her. She came to my office to make the complaint. I sent for him and spoke to him privately, asking what had happened. He related the story as told by her, adding that she had disregarded him as an officer and insulted him.

I explained to him that he must go into my office and apologize. He became highly upset, calling her a bitch. I gave him a stern warning that she would be going to Police Headquarters to complain if she received no satisfaction from us. I then ordered him to apologize or I would prefer charges against him.

He then entered the office and halfheartedly said that he was sorry for his actions. I then insisted that he offer to shake her hand. He did, but I'm sure his heart was not in it. She thanked me and left. I heard no more about it, except that Ralph accused me of being "too soft." He retired shortly after that.

In the latter part of 1956 I was invited by the Lancaster Avenue Businessmen's Association to a dinner at Palumbo's Restaurant. It was an annual affair in which they used to both socialize and express their appreciation to community leaders. They requested that I appear in uniform so that "everyone will know that we have a black captain of whom we're proud." It must be noted that they were 80 percent Jewish.

At the end of the dinner they asked me to pronounce the benediction. I quickly recalled an Episcopal blessing that I used, making a slight change so as to not offend the Jewish present. "May the peace of God which passeth all understanding, keep your hearts and minds in the love of God, deleting "and of his son Jesus Christ." Afterward several persons congratulated me on such a nice prayer.

It did not take too long for my men to get to know me and what I stood for. I firmly believe that this is a major reason why brutality complaints always decreased under my commands. I'm just as certain that fewer of my men became involved in corrupt practices than in like districts.

I always tried to be fair in dealing with people, especially my policemen. Whenever possible I went out of my way to grant favors to them. I was most generous with commendations. In making out disciplinary charges, I listed just those necessary to close the case, which meant I could have added more. The men soon realized this, and they soon came to respect and like me. Conversely, I soon came to know my men and know their attitudes toward work as well as toward race. If I found a man who was potentially a source of racial problems, I soon requested his transfer out of the district.

My wife says that I never miss an opportunity to make a speech and it's true. I received many requests to speak at churches, schools, and even the Lions Club, which was all white. My door was always open to visitors and complainers. I was told that I received more visitors and complainers in one week than previous captains did in a month.

One day late in December of 1957, I heard someone crying in one of the prisoners' cells. Upon entering, I saw a teenage boy who was quite upset. When I asked him what was wrong, he said that a policeman had kicked him on the shin. I looked at the boy's leg, and it was indeed bleeding.

I ordered the turnkey to put the boy in the detectives' room to await the arrival of a juvenile officer. A few minutes later, a highway patrolman—a squad with a reputation for roughness—came storming into my office, accusing me of taking his prisoner, while shaking his finger in my face. I immediately slapped his hand down and reminded him that I was the commanding officer of the district and, therefore, responsible for everything in it. Then I ordered him out of my office. Within a few minutes, the patrolman returned with his captain, Frank Nolan, a man I had worked with in Juvenile Aid Division. Nolan asked what had happened, and I explained it to him. He said that he was satisfied that I had acted properly, and said he wanted to bring charges against his man. I declined to do so, saying that I considered the case closed. The case was reported to Commissioner Gibbons, and he also closed it out. Not too long after that, however, I received the shock of my life. I was transferred out of the 16th District. It felt like the walls had tumbled down upon me.

It happened a few days after New Years of 1958. I was in my office when the telephone rang. It was the captain of the 31st District, asking if I had seen the orders which came over the teletype machine. I said I hadn't. He said, "You'd better look at it. You've been transferred." Sure enough, that's what it said.

I thought what a cold way to inform someone of a matter of such extreme importance. I freely admit, I cried for the first time in twenty years. I knew that there had been a lot of racial problems in the district that I was being transferred to, but I never gave a thought to my being transferred there to solve them.

I took the teletype message to my office and read and reread it. There was no margin for error, it meant just what it said. My first thought was to ask why *me*? As I recalled the years of hard work I had put into the 16th District trying to professionalize it, and the programs I had initiated, I thought it almost a crime to take me away from it.

Although Police Commissioner Gibbons denied it, I think that there were two reasons for my transfer. First, and probably the foremost, was the need to deal with the police brutality in the 31st District. Second, and the "smoking gun," was my encounter with the highway patrolman.

The resulting newspaper article on the highway patrolman that appeared in *The Philadelphia Independent* on January 1, 1958, a black-oriented newspaper, made it appear that I was weak in dealing with white policemen. It also hinted at lingering animosity that they harbored as a result of *The Bulletin* article where I criticized them on November 14, 1954.

Whenever one is transferred in this manner, there is always some speculation by police personnel as to what the reason was. No matter what the reason, policemen are prone to think negatively toward the transfer. What would my wife say, or what could I say to her and other family members?

At the four o'clock roll call, I announced the transfer and made a short speech to the men thanking them for their cooperation and wishing them well. My voice broke before I concluded my statements. I attempted to hide my face by dropping it and turning my back as I wiped my eyes. I'm certain that my crying came because I felt that the transfer was an injustice, and that I should remain there as long as I was doing a reasonable job. I'm also sure that somewhere in my thoughts I felt a wee bit insecure about going to an unknown district, especially because I knew that there were racial problems there.

Immediately after roll call, I went for a ride in the park and just sat in my automobile to think matters over and settle my nerves. Then I returned to the district and cleaned out my desk. I had accumulated so many personal items and records that I just packed them in boxes to be picked up later.

At home, I talked it over with Vivienne. She was shocked much the same as I had been; however, she was very supportive as usual, saying everything would turn out all right. When questioned by family and friends as to why I was being transferred, I speculated to them that I was being used to straighten out the 31st District. This made it appear that I was being complimented by the administration in this move.

At home, I gave the move a lot of thought as to how I would handle it. I checked a Human Relations Department map and found that the district was 60 percent black as to residents. A telephone call to Policeman George Morse, a former SIS man who worked there, assured me that about 20 percent of the policemen there were black, but that the number seemed to be increasing. I was told that there were no blacks in patrol cars, nor in the operations room. This was shades of the 16th District prior to my arrival as commander.

I arrived at the district on the first day with a box full of personal belongings, including my uniform. I introduced myself around to the ranking officers, policemen in the operations room, and the clerk, a white man who arrived late. I had made up my mind that I would use the same tact in administration as I did in the 16th District. Nothing beats success like success.

From my past dealings with the public, I knew I had to get involved in the community affairs of my new district. Speaking engagements was a good place to start. I accepted all of them but, unlike my boastful speech about the coffee-bringing sergeant, I was low-key about my personal gains to the public.

I felt that in order for police brutality to exist it would have to be either condoned or ignored by the top command. While focusing in on it, I solicited the aid of Inspector Ballard, to not only issue weekly orders against it but actually asking him to speak at my roll calls against it. I further required my lieutenants to make in-depth investigations of each complaint. By involving them in the process, I gained their support for preventing and eliminating police brutality.

I had been told of numerous white policemen in the 31st District who used racial slurs towards and even beat blacks they arrested. It helped to know that the racial makeup of the police and the community were practically the same in the 31st as in the 16th. Therefore, I had the feeling that I could use the same approach on the 31st as I did on the 16th District. There was one very important difference in the two. The 31st seemed to have more organizations that were involved in police/community relations. I hoped I could work positively with them.

Brutality is more than injury which requires medical treatment. It also comes into play when one abuses another by word and wanton destruction of one's property. Blacks, when confronted by policemen for crimes or other improper actions, often accuse the policeman, especially if he is white, of abuse by the use of racial slurs. This has happened to me in cases where I was the arresting officer, and words were attributed to me that I never use, even in all-male company.

I was of the opinion that the complaints about the 31st district were basically true on many of the complaints that I heard. The problem in dealing with this type of complaint is that, all too often, it is one person's word against the other's. There are no witnesses to the incident and, therefore, no action can be taken. It must be noted that complaints are brought against black policemen at about the same rate as against whites. Some people have said that black policemen are even worse.

I decided that whenever possible I would attempt to adjust complaints without taking disciplinary action. Usually, by bringing the complainant and officer together to discuss the problem, it can be resolved without further action. When the complainant is satisfied that the supervisor will handle discipline in his own way, the case can be closed.

I had also found that it was helpful to keep a private record, if not an official statement of fact, in the policeman's personnel file. The policeman was told that if no more complaints were received against him, the fact sheet would be destroyed. If more complaints were brought against the same policeman, then more severe disciplinary action was called for.

During my first day at my new district, I met the lieutenant and sergeant on duty. They gave me a normal welcome. Not too warm, not too cold. I called a staff meeting for the following day. At that meeting, I briefed them on my usual program of integrating the patrol cars and the operations room. They didn't seem to mind the cars being changed, but spoke out for retaining their operations workers. I agreed that they could retain their operations personnel until a vacancy occurred by attrition, then a black would have to fill that vacancy.

As in the 16th District, there were a few men who wanted to transfer out. This was approved without prejudice. There was, however, an important transfer at my request. The captain's clerk was a longtime employee who came to work late daily, took long lunches, and left early. When I removed him, two women were sent to select a replacement from. I chose Shirley Carolina, who later married one of the officers, and who remained in that district for thirty-two years.

Prior to my arrival at the 31st District, I was not told what to expect. The prevailing theory is that a captain should be knowledgeable enough as an administrator to quickly find his way around. In fact, most district commanders resent suggestions from their predecessors. They prefer to find their own way around. You do this by having meetings with your lieutenants and sergeants in separate groups, then by having individual talks with each of them. From there on you talk with your policemen one at a time, this gives you a fairly good idea of what is going on.

I had heard so much about brutality in the 31st District that I concentrated on it so much that I didn't give much thought to police corruption. The first alarm should have gone off when a black officer, for whom I had overruled a lieutenant to give him a day off, came to me with a nervy request. He wanted to be my "pickup man." I was shocked and told him so. He was very charismatic and I could not bring myself to prefer charges against him.

I did, however, use him to get information that no one else would volunteer. He was the one who first explained to me what the "bankers' car" was. He explained that this was the patrol car that collected the most money. From then on, I frequently changed the crews on that car.

I had often heard that there were some captains "on the take." I didn't give it much thought, for it was widely believed that Commissioner Gibbons had cleaned up the department. In order to satisfy myself, I began asking questions about the other captains. I found that many of them had homes costing two and three or more times what I paid for mine. Many of them had seashore homes, homes in the mountains, and at least two had yachts. At the same time, I was struggling to pay my mortgage and personal loans.

I always knew that as the lone black captain, I was constantly watched, not only by the police administration but by the community at large. For that reason, I made every effort to be beyond reproach. I would not submit to temptations that were constantly beckoning to me. My philosophy was that all temptations had strings attached.

I refused to let it bother me that there were other policemen who were doing so much better than I was. I felt that I was well blessed to be in my comfortable position. My philosophy was strengthened ever so often when I observed others who had fallen victim to greed suffer the consequences. My reputation as one who was not "on the take" preceded me to the 31st District, and as a result no one attempted to entwine me.

During my time in the 31st, I made a concerted effort to bring the policemen and community leaders together to discuss problems and just to get to know each other. One of the first bits of public relations I initiated was on March 27, 1958, to invite the Police Sanitation Squad to meet with clean-block captains in the 31st District station house. As a result of this contact, the block captains promised full cooperation to the police, even to the extent of appearing as witnesses when needed.

As I continued to harp to my men about being professional rather than irrational, one lieutenant and two sergeants along with about six or eight police-men transferred out. Within a very short time, a more open and friendly atmosphere prevailed with the men.

I also established a pleasant rapport with a community weekly newspaper, *The North Penn News*. We kept in constant contact, and I gave them the news and clarified information. Often, while I was walking along the business strip, people would stop me for conversation. All of them, both black and white, would say complimentary things about the news articles and offer their support.

On April 5, 1960, a teletype message came over the machine listing the names of ten police captains who were shifted to other districts. My name was on it, indicating my transfer to the 9th District at 20th & Buttonwood Streets. I was in my office at the time that a lieutenant brought the teletyped message to me. At first I was shocked to see my name on it, for I thought that all was well in my district. There had been no outstanding problems for over a year and a half.

There is always suspicion when a commander is transferred, but it is not necessarily true that the transfer is for disciplinary purposes. I accepted it as routine, since so many others were involved. I had been in the 31st for more than two years, which is about the average tenure of a district commander. I immediately cleaned out my desk and went home. I didn't even wait to meet the oncoming shift at 4:00 P.M. to say goodby. The lieutenant and sergeants on duty all expressed their displeasure at seeing me go. At home, I informed Vivienne of the transfer. She said, "Here we go again" and accepted it as a matter of fact. Neither of us thought of it as a disciplinary measure.

Two weeks after my transfer, three policemen from my former district, the 31st, were arrested, charged with taking protection money from a numbers writer. As a district commander, one has to make a weekly report of vice and gambling conditions in the district. One has to relate what attempts have been made to correct the condition. The information submitted on the weekly vice report is for special headquarters squads to work on. Problems arise for the district com-mander when the special headquarters squad make arrests in his district that his men have not been able to make.

Divisional inspectors hold weekly conferences with captains, at which time vice conditions are discussed. Arrests are compared from week to week, and district versus district. The statistics are derisively referred to as fever charts. Captains are reluctant to make too many arrests one week for fear that they will have to do the same every week. There are times when some arrests are not reported on the weekly charge for fear of escalating numbers that have to be fought later.

At the end of the reporting week, if vice arrests are not high enough, pressure is put on the sergeants and lieutenants to do everything possible to increase the count. This is dangerous, for some policemen will use improper or even un-

Staff Inspector Edward M. Payne's leave-of-absence luncheon
L to R: Payne, Inspector Allen B. Ballard, and James N. Reaves observes - December 4, 1956
(photo - courtesy of Fletcher Brodie)

Top-level Black Police - 1955 in Philadelphia
L to R: Sgt. William Lindsey, Lt. Leonard Jones, Capt. James N. Reaves, Insp. Allen B. Ballard,
Staff Insp. Edward M. Payne, Lt. Richard Edwards, Sgt. John S. Smith and Sgt. Frank Winfrey -
June 1955 (photo - courtesy of Fletcher Brodie)

Inspector John Driscoll and James N. Reaves presenting commendations for good police work to the police of the 31st District - July 26, 1958

Inspection time - 16th District - James N. Reaves with Lionel Hampton and Lt. William Brooks - May 16, 1957 (photo, courtesy of Fletcher Brodie)

scrupulous means of making arrests. In addition, because of the extreme pressure within the department to make vice arrests, some districts pull regular patrolmen from their normal assignments and assign them to plainclothes vice work to pump up their vice arrest numbers, even though this is against department regulations. Although I knew that it was not regulation to have squad leaders use men this way for vice work, I pretended not to notice when I learned that this was being done in the 31st District.

It was just this practice that led a squad leader to use Policeman Edward J. O'Kinsky as a plainclothesman on April 20, 1960. His mission was to arrest adults who were buying alcoholic beverages from liquor stores for minors. But instead of making these arrests, Patrolman O'Kinsky began using his time to solicit payoffs when he discovered that the operator of the candy store was also a numbers writer.

Staff Inspector William Meers and Joseph O'Neill, from department head-quarters, eventually arrested O'Kinsky, Policeman William Cook, and Walter J. Szczepaniak—two other policemen with whom O'Kinsky split the payoff money. They also arrested John Williams, a black man who operated the candy store. The three officers implicated three other officers who were also arrested: William Modell, Phillip Walls, and Alfred Frierson. All of the officers arrested were white, except Frierson who was black. These men were questioned extensively, and they implicated eight other policemen, with whom they had split the payoff. All eleven men were suspended, pending further investigation. At a hearing, the three officers were held on $500 bail each for grand jury action.

I was awakened by the telephone ringing at 5:30 A.M. the morning after the first three officers were arrested. When I picked up the receiver, I heard the voice of the policeman who had volunteered to be my pickup man. He said "Well, what do you think about your plainclothesmen now?" He went on to explain that one of them had been picked up by a staff inspector, and that the man had "spilled his guts to them," telling them that he was the pickup man for his platoon, and that he distributed the money to the men individually.

I told him I was tired and sleepy and hung up the telephone without thanking him for the information. I knew that he was gloating over the breaking of this case. I was angry at him for calling me so early in the morning and disturbing my sleep, but I was also glad for the information that would allow me to put myself on the offensive. I could not understand why I had not been informed of the case and brought in during the initial questioning of the policeman. That could only mean that I was suspected of complicity. I knew that there would be repercussions, possibly something in excess of the routine transfer I had already received.

Later that day, Inspector Ballard and I were told to report to City Hall. Ballard had called me in my office to give me the information. My mental reaction was about five times that of when, as a school boy, I was told to report to the principal's office. I went to Ballard's office and we rode together to City Hall. He drove at normal speed as we attempted to anticipate questions. There were far more questions than we could think of answers to.

Both Ballard and I had followed this case and were aware that we would be brought in for questioning. We spoke of how these men were allowed to run rampant in search of legitimate arrests. Although I had not discussed their plainclothes assignments with him, somehow I knew that he was aware of their being in plainclothes.

We both agreed that we would tell all that we knew and accept whatever followed. We each agreed that the men involved did a very stupid thing to get into such action and to act as agents for the other policemen working that area.

Instead of the plainclothesmen working as their lieutenants had assigned them, they went around to known numbers men and to men who sold illegal liquor and received payoffs. The routine was for a man to approach an operator and identify himself as representing the lieutenant or captain or inspector, and to demand money and threaten that the operation would be shut down and an arrest made if necessary. Usually a list of former arrests would be shown to the operator, while implying that "This could and will happen to you if you don't act right." Usually the payoff was made and the money split, often with the lieutenant and sergeant as well as other officers who worked that area.

If the payoff was too steep or the operator decided not to payoff for whatever reason, he would contact police headquarters and complain—often not giving his own name. Undercover men would be sent to keep the location under surveillance. More often, operators would arrange for officials or undercover men to be at a location at a given time so that the action could be observed.

Ballard was possibly more upset than I was, for he had no way of knowing whether or not I was involved. He kept shaking his head and sucking air through his teeth. Neither of us felt that we were deliberately set up, for we both thought that we had a good relationship with our superiors. I don't think Ballard was angry at me, he just accepted it as the danger that went along with the territory. I felt sorry for the both of us as we were highly respected in the community, the police department, and by our families.

We were met in the commissioner's office by the staff inspector who took us to a small room on the second floor that was used as a storage room. It was a dingy place that I surmised was used by elite squads to question prisoners. I looked around for the legendary drop light and rubber hose, but none were present. We were questioned separately first, then together. They wanted to know what we knew about vice in the district, what we knew about the plainclothes-men, who the numbers banker were, where their locations were, what we had done about them in the past, and whether or not we had reported them on any vice reports. They further wanted to know how we got the plainclothesmen, who recommended them, and if we had confidence in them.

They began the questioning in a calm, even friendly, manner but as time went on and it was obvious that either we didn't know anything about the case or that we weren't talking, they became more serious, even indicating that they would recommend our dismissal from the force.

The whole case revolved around a man, John Williams, at 22nd and Norris Streets. He had been arrested on a warrant charging him with bribery, conspiracy, corrupt solicitation, and illegal lottery. He, too, was held under $500 bail for grand jury. The inspectors said that the department had received information that two policemen from 26th & York Streets were taking protection money from a numbers bank. Even though I had been in the district for over two years, I had never been in that store, nor had I known of its reputation.

I was very bewildered in that I had not been so much as suspected of wrong-doing in my fourteen years on the force. I also disliked the persistence of the two investigators, both with whom I had formerly worked and shared secrets with. I knew that I was not involved in the payoffs, but I felt that the suspicions and resulting publicity would cast aspersion on my good reputation.

I was also teed off at the department for permitting the staff inspectors to treat us the same as common criminals, and I especially disliked the way that they handled Inspector Ballard, since he outranked them. I even got irked at Ballard for not protesting the rank of our interrogators. In spite of it all, we cooperated with them in the fullest. At one point during an intermission in the interrogation, Ballard suggested that I use my political influence if I had any. I said no, that I wouldn't because I had nothing to be afraid of.

This went on for three days, about two hours a day. They were attempting to establish a nonexistent link between the two of us and the payoffs. Finally, Chief Inspector Frank Rizzo told them to call it off, that they had put us through too much already.

The police Trial Board finally held a hearing for the eleven men who were charged. Five were found not guilty and were returned to duty without loss of pay. The board recommended the firing of the other six, three of whom were held for court.

Two days after our interrogation, I was out with the tour lieutenant riding in a patrol car checking on the men who were assigned to traffic duties on Broad Street. The police radio directed us to contact the district office. Instead of calling, we went into the district where the house sergeant said that I was to call Deputy Commissioner Leary. I called and his secretary immediately put me through to him. He spoke very calmly, almost apologetically. He said that I was suspended for ten days, effective at midnight. I asked him if this was the extent of the discipline. He said that it was. I knew that I could handle the ten-day suspension; but I also knew if I was threatened with termination, I would fight it.

Commissioner Gibbons released information to the press giving his reasons for my suspension on April 29, 1960: "Contrary to regulations of the police department, Reaves gave verbal orders to policeman O'Kinsky to use his private automobile while investigating vice in the district. Reaves failed to notify his superior, Inspector Allen B. Ballard, in charge of North Central Division, that he was doing this. Reaves assigned O'Kinsky to investigate vice despite the fact that he never requested permission to assign him to these duties, and despite the fact that he had two regular men assigned for this work."

All of the aforementioned charges were true, but there was a good reason for it. There was so much pressure on captains to make vice arrests that we were under constant threats of disciplinary action if the vice numbers dropped. All captains were resorting to extra measures, contrary to orders, in order to build up their expected weekly vice statistics. The problem in my case was that Edward O'Kinsky was not only making vice arrests, but he was also accepting payoffs and was caught at it.

The newspapers had a field day with such headlines as: "Three Policemen Arrested on Extortion Charge," "Ten Police Shifted in Shakeup," "Captain Reaves Suspended for Neglect of Duty," "Six Fired by Gibbons In Police Graft Probe."

Not being too sure what would happen when I returned from my suspension, I cleared out my desk and left for home with a heavy heart. All the way home I agonized as to how to break the news to Vivienne and the boys. One of my most fearful thoughts over the years was that I might do something or be accused of doing something wrong and have it headlined in the newspapers. The affect it would have on the family would be devastating, such as Vivienne being ashamed to face her family and friends. Worst of all, the boys might suffer unrelenting taunts from schoolmates.

I was pleasantly surprised at Vivienne's attitude after I explained it to her. She took it calmly at first, but later she accused the department of not appreciating my hard work and long hours. She suggested that I go away on a long trip to relax and forget it all. I said "That's a good idea, I think I will."

Early the next morning, I packed my belongings, borrowed $100 from a friend, and left town. I was on my way to the Carolinas to visit relatives and friends. I quickly forgot my problems and had a relaxing trip. There was just one event that I was not prepared for. While driving through Durham, North Carolina, I stopped at a one-room roadside ice cream stand. There were two people in line at an open service window. After the two people were served, the attendant walked away.

When it was obvious that he would not serve me, I asked for an ice cream cone. He came to the window and said in a very deep southern drawl, "We don't wait on colored people." I found this hard to believe, since I had planned to take the ice cream cone along and eat as I drove. And this was in 1960, seven years after Vivienne and I and the FOP had helped to desegregate Miami Beach.

I returned from my self-imposed exile after two weeks, physically strong, mentally awake, and morally straight. I was anxious to get back to duty as I climbed the granite spiral steps of City Hall to report to Chief Inspector Albert Trimmer. He was very gracious and hoped that I had a good rest. He said I would be put on the 4 to 12 midnight shift working citywide as night commander, and that I was to be on call from midnight to 8:00 A.M.

I later found out how close I had come to having my police career destroyed by this incident. I was at police headquarters one day when Deputy Commissioner David Malone called me into his private office. He showed me a copy of the staff inspector's report on Ballard and me. The first thing I noticed was a long diagonal red line through it, along with the word "disapproved." The report recommended that Inspector Ballard be busted in rank to a sergeant, and that I be reduced in rank to a policeman. The rejection of this was signed in red ink by Mayor Richardson Dilworth.

As I review the whole episode of my suspension, I can reach just one conclusion. Commissioner Gibbons had completely turned the department around over a period of ten years. Almost all of his ranking officers were new, after he cleaned house of the old-line corrupt commanders. He was the toast of the town, with bids coming in from all over the country from cities wanting him to head their departments.

Just before my case developed, there had been rumors of organized crime wanting to take over the numbers business in the city. Gibbons had to do something to dispel those rumors. My case was ideal for sending the word out that he was still in charge, and that he would not tolerate the underworld moving in. The firing of the five officers and my suspension were just what he needed at that time. I felt that I had been the sacrificial lamb.

On my new assignment, I was given a patrol car and told to respond to any and all calls that had a potential for a lot of needed manpower. I thought this would work very well for me, and I had the feeling that, since I was the top-ranking police official on duty, I was the chief of police. This did not last long, for one of my first calls was a police shooting in the far Northeast part of the city, some distance from the center of town. I lost my way, stopped, and got out of the car in full uniform. I must have appeared to be puzzled, for a little old woman came up and asked if I was looking for the police district. Feeling very ashamed, I said "Yes." She proceeded to direct me, with a smile of amusement.

For as much as I enjoyed the assignment, I found that it soon became boring. By the time I arrived on a police scene, the action was usually over. I relayed this information to Inspector Trimmer, and he agreed it wasn't such a good idea. He then began using me as a replacement for vacationing captains, and for special assignments, one of which was a circus detail.

The circus detail was enlightening. It was held in the far Northeast, a section of the city that wasn't integrated. I had no policemen working with me, and I felt like a square peg in a round hole. As I walked around, I soon noticed that there were a couple of so-called skilled games that very seldom paid off. I examined them carefully and found that it was next to impossible for a customer to win. On one game, customers were supposed to knock a doll through a hole to win a prize. It turned out, however, that the hole was too narrow for the dolls to pass through, and it was impossible for anyone to win. I quickly closed the game down.

I then found a baseball toss game in which the baseballs were weighted off center, also making it impossible for people to win. I closed that game down too. Within an hour of closing the last one, I received a call from Chief Inspector Trimmer telling me that I had been pulled off the circus detail, and that I was to go to the 16th Police District and relieve the captain who was off duty.

I was then continually shifted from district to district as a fill-in, usually for two weeks at a time. The 37th, 6th, 9th, and 17th. I spent two weeks at the 37th at 4th Street and Snyder Avenue. It was the quietest and most boring of them all. The captain's phone rang only about three times a day. After riding around the district twice a day, I filled in my time playing a pinball machine across the street from my office.

On August 2, 1960, on my first day of temporary duty at the 17th District, I was watching a magistrate's hearing. I saw Mr. Eugene Rhodes, the publisher of *The Philadelphia Tribune*, a major black newspaper. He wanted to know why I was there. I explained that I was "on the bench" and being sent here and there. The next day, there was an article in *The Philadelphia Tribune* captioned "Quo Vadis Reaves?" that detailed what I had been going through.

The day after the article appeared, Chief Trimmer sent for me. He wanted to know why the article was in the paper. I explained the circumstances. He didn't seem too pleased. Four days after the article appeared, I was transferred to the 23rd District on permanent assignment.

CHAPTER NINE

Increasing unemployment, increasing crime, and increasing complaints of police brutality were facts of life in North-Central Philadelphia in late 1960. In early 1961, a coalition of fifty black preachers called for a meeting with Mayor Dilworth, which was held in the mayor's office. Commissioner Albert Brown ordered Inspector Ballard, Staff Inspector Payne and myself to be present. I'm sure it was meant to show off the highest-ranking blacks in the police department to those who may not have known of our existence.

The clergymen who were present complained about police conduct in North-Central Philadelphia and demanded more police presence in the area—especially by black police officers. The meeting lasted for several hours, not even breaking for lunch. It was chaired by Commissioner Brown, with Mayor Dilworth coming in and going out from time to time. While no specific promises were made, a general promise was given that improvements would be forthcoming. The immediate results were that more policemen were hired, many of whom were black, with a goodly number being transferred to North-Central Philadelphia.

It was also partly as result of this meeting that I was transferred to the 23rd District, which was a twin of the 22nd District in North-Central Philadelphia, for they were about the same size in area as well as in population. Like the 22nd, the 23rd had about 85 percent black residents and 15 percent white. With 75 percent of the police being white, the residents often complained about being mishandled by the white police officers. While many complaints were justified, I also found that there were a sizeable number of contrived complaints.

There were a large number of business and commercial establishments in the area, and there were also the accompanying crimes of shoplifting, burglary, and holdups. We had our share of black-on-black crime, with a disproportionate number of homicides by gang killings. We constantly pleaded with Gang Control supervisors to have their men increase the amount of time they spent in the district.

I encountered an early sign of the racial conflict that was later to plague the area when, on February 14, 1961, I received a call alerting me to the possibility of trouble at 16th and Girard Avenue. I quickly drove to the scene where I saw

101

a crowd gathered around a group of policemen who were talking to a white lady who had a sign on her car that read: "The worse criminals are niggers."

The policemen on the scene were holding the sign, while trying to persuade her to leave the area. She was adamant about staying, standing on her civil rights. I talked to her for a few minutes as the crowd moved even closer and became louder. She finally got the message and left, but not before a news reporter appeared. The subsequent article and photograph that appeared in the newspaper only served to increase tension in the area.

On June 6, 1963, Inspector Morton Solomon informed me of a complaint against two officers in my district, James McTague and Ernest Trotter. The complaint had been filed by Sheila Robinson, a twenty-year-old black female who alleged that she had been threatened, assaulted, and raped by the two policeman the previous day.

Inspector Solomon instructed me to take all pertinent records to Inspector Joseph O'Neill at staff headquarters. I knew from the sweeping nature of the orders that the department was taking this case seriously. In addition, Solomon was a straight shooter. He called the shots as he saw them. He would insist on a full investigation and let the chips fall where they may.

This case also frightened me for two reasons: I was afraid that it might reflect unfavorably on my leadership, and two white cops being accused of raping a defenseless black woman had the potential to disrupt the black community. Sheila and her mother, Princola Robinson, had originally made their complaint to The NAACP. Although I was not in on any of the top-level police meetings, I'm sure that the case was being carefully orchestrated by the top police command. Civil rights were very much in the forefront by this time, and riots were erupting all over the country to such an extent that it was a legitimate concern for all law enforcement professionals.

As a former member of the board of directors of the NAACP, I was also fully aware of the tenacity of the board in prosecuting similar cases. The knowledge that the NAACP was interested in this case most assuredly had a bearing on the amount of attention given to it by top police administrators.

On arrival at headquarters that day, I found Detective Captain Joseph Bonner, Sheila Robinson, and her mother. Sheila Robinson told us that she had been with friends in a restaurant until 3:10 A.M. on the night in question. She then proceeded to Broad Street and Columbia Avenue to catch a southbound bus home. After waiting for a bus for about a half hour, she went into the subway and waited for a train for another half hour. When no train arrived, she went back up to the street.

While standing on the corner, a white man stopped in a car and asked her if she wanted a lift. She said yes and got in. When they had traveled a few blocks, they were stopped by Patrolman Trotter and Sergeant McTague in their police car. The policeman had observed Robinson talking to and being picked up by the man in the car, and they suspected Robinson of prostitution. The policemen questioned the driver of the car and let him go, but they put Robinson into the police car and took her to the station for questioning.

At the station house, they placed her in a room while they looked up her record. Discovering that she had no prior record for prostitution, the officers said that they would take Robinson back to Broad Street and Columbia Avenue to catch the bus. While traveling east on Columbia Avenue, Robinson said in her complaint, the officers continued across Broad Street to 9th Street, then parked their car under a Reading Railroad bridge. Robinson said that Sergeant McTague got into the back seat with her, tried to have intercourse with her, but could not. She stated that when she protested he slapped her and threatened to lock her up.

She said that McTague then put his penis in her mouth and discharged, and that Trotter then got in the back seat of the car and had intercourse with her. They then took her back to Broad Street and Columbia Avenue and put her on a bus. She got on the bus and went to spend the night with a friend.

Sheila Robinson was shown the photographs of six sergeants from the 23rd District. Out of these, she picked Sergeant McTague. She was then shown sixteen photographs of policemen, and she identified Trotter. Robinson then submitted to a polygraph examination conducted by Captain J. M. Brophy, whose resulting opinion was that Robinson had made no attempt at deception in her complaint to the police.

The woman Robinson stayed with that night also gave a written statement, saying that the young woman came in at 5:30 A.M. and, while in tears, told the story of what had happened to her. The man who had picked up Robinson in his car also gave a written statement confirming Robinson's story. Sheila Robinson's mother also gave a statement, saying that her daughter had called her from her friend's house that morning, but had been unable to say more than, "Mom, Mom." Sheila Robinson's friend had then gotten on the phone and told Sheila's mother what had happened.

A policewoman took Sheila to the Philadelphia General Hospital where she was given a physical examination by Dr. Campbell. The police laboratory examined the clothing worn by Robinson at the time of the rape, but was unable to detect any seminal stains, nor were any residues from police uniforms found under Robinson's fingernails.

Later that day Captain Bonner and I took the accused officers to police headquarters for questioning. It was obvious that the men harbored intense resentment towards us for our actions. Sergeant McTague gave a written statement. He admitted having met Trotter at Broad Street and Columbia Avenue where they observed Sheila as she got into Mr. Grandinetti's car. They stopped the car, questioned the driver, and released him. They took Sheila to the district and checked her out. Then they took her back to Broad Street and Columbia Avenue and placed her aboard a bus and told the driver to accept her pass, as the subway train was not operating. He stoutly denied taking Sheila to 8th Street and Columbia Avenue and having illicit sex relations with her. Policeman Trotter gave a similar written statement.

Following the written statements that both Sergeant McTague and Policeman Trotter signed, both submitted to polygraph examinations. The results of these examinations showed that "specific reaction to questions asked relative to the matter under investigation indicate attempts at deception," according to the examiner who administered the test.

A few days later, Inspector O'Neill interviewed Mr. John Knauf, the driver of the bus that Sheila Robinson had boarded. He stated that he arrived at Broad Street and Columbia Avenue at about 4:40 A.M. on June 5, 1963. He recalled that a policeman put a colored girl on the bus at the time, saying that he had given her a pass, and that she had been detained for an investigation.

On instructions from Inspector O'Neill, I informed Sergeant McTague and Policeman Trotter that they were suspended, and that they faced criminal charges. They were taken home by detectives to change out of and surrender their police uniforms. Magistrate Lane signed a warrant for the arrest of Sergeant McTague and Policeman Trotter, charging them with rape, sodomy, assault with intent to ravish, threats to kill, and conspiracy. The charges placed against Policeman Trotter were rape and assault with intent to ravish. Both men were later released on $1,000 bail.

I was totally surprised that these two particular men were involved, for I had considered them above this type of bestial behavior. The more I thought about it, the angrier I became at them for the ill repute that they brought on my district in particular, and law enforcement in general. I also seriously questioned whether or not they would have behaved that way if the woman in question had been white. I think not, for I'm aware that white policemen took far more liberties with black women than black policemen would even think of taking with white women. Nonetheless, if there was anything good about the case it was that if it had occurred a decade earlier, it would not have engendered anywhere near as much official attention. In spite of the men's despicable conduct, however, many other policemen were anxious for them to get off. The FOP had no problem furnishing legal aid for them, giving them one of the best criminal lawyers in the city, Bernard Lemish.

The black policemen who spoke to me were not at all supportive of the men. Some even went so far as to say that they had long suspected these men of this type of conduct, and that they totally discounted any possibility that the victim had set the policemen up. Setting a policeman up is not unusual, especially by criminals making untrue assertions that they were mistreated by the policeman after being arrested. In cases where the arresting officer was of a different racial group to that of the arrestee, the arrestee often accused the officer of using racial epithets. In this case, however, facts seemed much more clear-cut.

As incidents like this continued to occur, and as racial riots erupted in other cities around the nation, it became obvious that a better method had to be developed to enable the police to cope with racial problems. The black community, unfortunately, had come to look upon white policemen as an occupying force, and in many cases for good reasons.

As an experiment, the police department had established a new division, the Police Community Relations (PCR) Division. Word circulated in the black community that the real reason PCR was established was to have a place to assign Inspector Ballard, a black officer who was ranked number three on the promotion list for chief inspector.

Ballard was promoted to chief inspector and placed in command of PCR. Of the twenty-five men he commanded, he had one lieutenant and two policemen who were black. The presence of this division was felt almost immediately in that they quickly moved into areas where there was potential for unrest. They were, in fact, so successful that other cities sent representatives to Philadelphia to study their methods of operations.

The Community Relations men all wore uniforms with distinctive arm patches. They were, for the most part, a problem-prevention force, usually moving in before physical violence developed. They sought out church and civic leaders, held meetings, and discussed community problems with them. They attended special programs in schools where they spoke to the children in the auditoriums. If there was a problem of a racial nature with a merchant, they made every effort to reconcile it.

Where there was an actual physical confrontation in a neighborhood, they let it be handled by the regular patrolmen, then became involved immediately after hostilities subsided. Their prior knowledge of who the leaders in a neighborhood were was a great plus in bringing about a lessening of tension. The police supervisors from the area were also brought in to meet and establish good relationships with the leaders.

Unfortunately, Chief Inspector Ballard did not live long enough to appreciate the fruits of his own work in creating the PCR squad. He died on December 26, 1962, after a lingering illness. Lieutenant Chester Gathers was placed in command of the squad on an interim basis. He did quite well until he had to leave the job to meet military obligations.

At the time that Gathers left the squad, I was still assigned to the 23rd District. I received a telephone call from Commissioner Leary's clerk one day to report to his office. Leary met me with a big smile when I arrived and invited me to have a chair at his desk. "Jim, I have to place someone in permanent command of PCR," he said. "Would you like to have it?"

I asked if a promotion went along with it. He said, "Not at present, but maybe later." I said that I would like to try it. He stood up, shook my hand and said, "You'll do just fine, your transfer will become effective at midnight."

I left the office with mixed emotions. I had been in the 23rd District long enough to get it the way I wanted it. I got along well with the policemen and the community, but the possibility of a promotion was far into the future, if at all, if I remained in the district. In PCR there would be city-wide exposure with top police and city officials as well as with business and civic leaders. When I told Vivienne of the transfer, she was glad. She referred to it as being "a safer and cleaner job."

The more I thought about the new job the more challenging and interesting I hoped it would be. I was also pleased to realize that I would be following in the footsteps of Chief Inspector Ballard, a man of such great accomplishments, and a man who was so well thought of by both police and civilians. I felt that I must have been doing something right to be chosen for the position.

I realized that the job called for someone who would be sensitive to the community. Other cities had already had their share of riots, and there were possibilities of even worse problems after the upcoming March on Washington, especially if there were property damage or bloodshed as a result of it.

In my new job I had an office in the police administration building called the "round house," and a private parking space in the police yard for the city owned car assigned to me. Although it was not required, I wore full uniform every day and on all speaking occasions. I usually started my day off with speaking at roll call to the men, giving them general orders and inspecting them. The lieutenant handled the scheduling and personal supervision.

I knew that an important aspect of the job would be investigating police disciplinary cases brought before the Police Advisory Board. The board had been established in 1958 at the request of a group of black ministers who felt that complaints of police abuse were not investigated properly. The board was composed of eight members who were appointed by the mayor. The Advisory Board's findings were reported directly to the mayor, with copies also sent to the managing director and the police commissioner, with the commissioner having final authority on the extent of disciplinary action taken.

The board was opposed from its inception by the Fraternal Order of Police. Members of the lodge contended that civilians did not understand police work, and therefore they were incapable of rendering fair decisions for policemen. In spite of the lodge's contention, the police commissioner put a lot of stock in the board's findings and usually followed its recommendations.

In all of the cases I handled, I attempted to rationalize the policemen's conduct, giving them the benefit of the doubt until evidence proved otherwise. But in far too many cases, the evidence was such that I had to call it as I saw it. This meant that the policemen were to receive disciplinary action, and I had no say in how severe it would be. As a policeman, I had first-hand experiences with handling suspects and prisoners, and I knew how they reacted toward police-men. Many of the subjects would purposely do and say things in order to infuriate the policeman and to gain the sympathy of the crowd if one gathered. I also know that policemen often did and said things to upset subjects for the same reason, but usually when no witnesses were present, thereby giving the policeman oppor-tunity to abuse the subject. While making investigations of cases, I would look at both sides. If there seemed to be equal arguments on each side, I usually sided with the policemen. The morale of the policemen had to be taken into consid-eration in order to assure their future dedication to their duty.

Most complaints against policemen involved illegal arrests, unnecessary rough-ness, use of racial slurs or profane language. I was amazed at my own attitude toward the policemen who were being complained about. I just wanted to choke them until I heard their side of the story, then I wanted to choke the complainant. Then, somewhere in between the two sides, I had to make a decision, and it often wasn't easy.

A man, James W. Wyatt, once complained of police brutality. He was at a bar at 23rd Street and Columbia Avenue at 2:15 A.M., apparently acting as a bouncer. Three men entered the bar, which was closing, and an altercation developed when one man seized the owner by the collar of his shirt. James Wyatt stated in his complaint that he tried to break up the attack, and in doing so knocked one of the men out.

At this point, Officer Dante Liberi, who was white, entered the bar. When James Wyatt asked Liberi to arrest the attacker, Liberi refused, saying that Wyatt would have to get a warrant since Liberi had not witnessed the attack. Wyatt then used abusive and provocative language toward the officer. At this point, Officer Benjamin Richardson arrived, and Liberi and Richardson placed Wyatt under arrest. Liberi placed Wyatt in the rear seat of the patrol car without handcuffing him, and then got into the front seat.

Wyatt complained that Liberi then turned around and struck him repeatedly with a nightstick without provocation. Liberi countered that Wyatt had provoked the attack by trying to throttle him by grabbing hold of his collar. Liberi admitted striking Wyatt "once or twice on the head in order to make him release his grasp." Officer Richardson said he was too occupied to see who did what. Wyatt was subsequently taken to Graduate Hospital and treated for head lacerations that required several stitches.

My opinion was that Liberi had used excessive force, in that there were two officers and one civilian, and that Liberi should have sat in the back seat with Wyatt, since there were no handcuffs available.

Another case I handled involved a complaint by Gary D. Berg, an eighteen-year-old black man. Berg complained that he was arrested for trying to "thumb a ride," and that he was then taken to the 14th Police District in Germantown, where he was beaten. He accused Sergeant John Park of punching him in the abdomen, after two unidentified policemen struck him on the back and legs. Berg's brother John testified that there were marks from the beating that he could see the next day. The secretary of the Advisory Board saw marks three days later.

In his statement, Officer William Norton said that he made the arrest when he observed Berg crying and trembling in the street. He said the young man obviously had emotional problems of long standing, which Berg admitted to. Sergeant Park denied even being in the building at the time of the arrest. The lieutenant on duty, Lawrence Love, denied seeing any beating, as did Officer Norton.

In that the only evidence, other than Berg's word, were the physical marks, which could have been inflicted elsewhere, I was unable to make a finding for or against the police sergeant, and the case was dropped.

In a third case, James I. Williams was stopped by Officer William Girrard at Broad and Christian Streets at 5:30 A.M. for driving his automobile with the lights off. During their conversation, Williams said Girrard said, "You guys are always having trouble and getting into accidents." Williams resented the statement, considering it a reflection upon his race. The officer countercharged that Williams used obscenity and generally became loud and boisterous. This caused a crowd to gather, so Girrard called for a police wagon and arrested Williams for disorderly conduct.

At the police station, reported Williams, Lieutenant Slack handled him roughly and accused him of "smelling like a distillery." A search of Williams' automobile, without a warrant, revealed a chance book, for which Williams was additionally charged with operating a lottery. The grand jury threw out the lottery charge.

Lieutenant Slack denied having handled Williams roughly, and no one testified against him. The officer who rode to the police station with Williams thought Williams was capable of operating a vehicle, which belied the lieutenant's statement that Williams smelled like a distillery.

It was my opinion that there was not enough of a case against either the complainant or the officers, and that the case should be dismissed by the Board of Inquiry.

I was assisted in my investigation of these cases by Sergeant John S. Smith, who did most of the legwork. We studied each case, and I included a lot of his suggestions in my final recommendations. Other than that, no one pressured me. One thing that disturbed me was that in almost every case where the complainant was of a different race than the officer, somehow the race problem erupted. Even in cases of black complainants and black officers, the officer was often referred to as being "a white folk's nigger." The vast majority of police disciplinary cases were not reported to the press. This probably accounts for the low percentage of penalties (4 percent) being recommended out of the 501 cases handled by the Board between September 1963 to November 1966.

While I was head of the Police Community Relations Division, I worked many demonstrations with George Fencl. I had first met Fencl in 1958, when he was a sergeant and the chauffeur for Commissioner Gibbons. He was a tall, handsome, well-built man with a constant smile who always had a good word for you. After his promotion to lieutenant, he was put in charge of the civil affairs unit. I often worked with him on civilian demonstrations, especially if the demonstrators were black. After Commissioner Leary became head of the police department I was called into these problems more and more. I was told from a number of sources that his first order when told about a disturbance in the black community was "Get Jim Reaves."

I was always glad to see Fencl at a demonstration, for between the two of us we had established a good rapport with either white or black demonstrators. As time went on, he seemed to know the demonstrators wherever we went, whether they were black or white. This made him very valuable, for he was often able to settle a problem before it developed. In many cases the demonstrators would insist on seeing him before they set up barricades or picket lines.

Fencl had a very outgoing and pleasing personality, a back-slapper and hail-fellow-well-met. He'd pick out the leaders and go and talk to them. His attitude in a demonstration was: What do you demonstrators have in mind, what do you want, what will you settle for, how can we work this out? The demonstrators trusted him more than other policemen because he treated everyone decently and tried to avoid manhandling whenever possible. This was his professional demeanor, his job was to keep peace, and he didn't particularly care what the demonstration was about.

To this day, retired Police Lieutenant Leonard T. Jones and I feel honored to have been an integral part of historic events in Washington, D.C., on August 28, 1963. No doubt, that feeling has been shared by the other men who accompanied Jones as part of a contingent of black policemen from Philadelphia.

Jones was the only commanding officer among the members of the Guardian Civic League (GCL), an organization of black Philadelphia policemen, who made the trip to Washington. I went as a representative of Police Commissioner Howard R. Leary, in that I was head of the Police Community Relations Division.

In a one-on-one conference with Commissioner Leary, he instructed me to go alone and to submit a written account of my observations. I didn't attended any meetings where the march was discussed, nor was I given instructions on just what I was to be on the lookout for, but I had a fairly good idea of what should be included in such a report. In fact, I was surprised that the commissioner thought so little of the march that I was the only official representative of the police department that was going.

Years earlier during the Franklin D. Roosevelt administration, a number of nationally known black leaders had let it be known that they were planning a march on Washington. One of their leaders, A. Phillip Randolph, a labor organizer, was summoned to Washington by President Roosevelt. As a result of that meeting, the president's executive order #8802 was signed. It stated that "there shall be no discrimination in the employment of workers in the defense industries or government because of race, creed, color, or national origin." Randolph was satisfied and the march was immediately called off. He later admitted that it had been only a threat in order to pressure the president into signing the order. That is why so many people regarded preparations for the 1963 March as only a threat.

At first I was hesitant to attend for fear of trouble, but when the commissioner gave me instructions to go, I had no problem carrying out the order. I think that everyone expected that there would be some amount of trouble, and for that reason much effort was expended trying to keep the peace. Riots and demonstrations were the order of the day in many urban communities, and the expression "long hot summer" was well understood. Therefore, any information on the subject was anxiously sought.

In June 1963, at a meeting of the Guardian Civic League, it was announced that what had been regarded by many blacks as an empty threat was now a promise: There was to be a Freedom March on Washington on August 28. The invitation to participate was open to everyone, especially blacks.

Alphonso Deal, president of GCL, suggested that the Guardians volunteer to participate as a group, and serve in whatever capacity the Freedom March organizers requested. It was later suggested by march organizers that the Guardians serve as "keepers of the peace" in Washington.

During the next two months, the Guardians were busy making preparations for the big day. Special meetings were held at St. Paul's Baptist Church at 10th and Wallace Streets. Enthusiasm among league members intensified as they began a steady buildup of preparations. In the city's black areas, there was an extensive amount of publicity, including streamers and placards urging everyone to "Join the March for Freedom in Washington, D.C., on August 28, 1963."

Many civic groups financed the chartering of buses to take those who wished to make the trip to the nation's capital. These groups had been fired up by a procession of speakers from New York, principally the NAACP. This was easy to do, in that minorities had been denied so many of their rights, and shut out of jobs. As the date grew nearer for the march people, both black and white, became more euphoric in anticipation of a positive outcome of the march.

The Guardians welcomed the opportunity to get into the act and be a prominent part of the action. Although I welcomed the opportunity to go, I still had mixed emotions as to what the outcome would be. I had the feeling that if violence broke out, or if governmental officials boycotted it, our status would suffer a setback of enormous proportions.

On the appointed day, the Guardians assembled at St. Paul's Church at about 1:00 A.M. Alfonso Deal informed them that they were to be sworn in collectively as U.S. Marshals for the day. Yellow arm bands were issued to the Guardians, for identification. They felt as if they were wearing badges of honor as they boarded the bus at about 2:00 A.M. Fifty-four of Philadelphia's finest headed southward, far, far into the night. Yet few realized that they were an integral part of the greatest demonstration for racial equality in the history of this nation.

The Guardians arrived in Washington about 5:00 A.M. and proceeded to Constitution Avenue with the other buses. After a briefing by Washington police, they moved to their assigned area near the Washington Monument. Daylight came and with it the realization that there were considerably more buses than had been obvious in the dark of night. As the daylight increased, so did the traffic. Buses by the hundreds, station wagons, cars, vans, and trucks kept up a steady stream into the capitol. All vehicles were directed by various law enforcement personnel to designated areas.

I traveled by train to Washington, arriving at 8:00 A.M. Inside the station, I was impressed with the actions of police in keeping an open corridor for the exit of train passengers through the milling crowd in Washington. The policing seemed to be done by metropolitan, military, and reserve policemen, plus some firemen armed only with nightsticks. Uniformed policewomen were also assigned to the station and were particularly in evidence near a temporary first-aid station. I spoke to Lewis Magruder, a black detective sergeant who later retired as a lieutenant, in the station, and he told me his men were on the alert for pickpockets.

A group of people tried to hold an impromptu rally in front of the railroad station, but police broke it up. No automobiles or taxi cabs were allowed directly in front of the station. Only shuttle buses were permitted there and, upon being loaded, they proceeded directly to the Washington Monument area. I walked the mile and a half from the station to the Washington Monument with streams of people. All intersections were staffed by uniformed personnel.

The Guardians knew that they would be an integral part of a mass movement—both physically and spiritually—but none could have envisioned the outcome in terms of the achievement of enhanced civil rights and the historical impact it would make worldwide, highlighted by Dr. Martin Luther King's speech.

As I walked along with the mass of people, I was just elated that I was witnessing such an overwhelming event. Everyone was so pleasant and agreeable. But what impressed me more than anything was the tremendous number of white people, many of whom were carrying banners, placards, and flags. I felt somewhat let down that I was not a part of the security. Unlike in Philadelphia, where so many policemen recognized me on sight, to the D.C. policemen I was just another person that they were urging to move on, move on.

By mid-morning, what might earlier have been described as a "crowd" had swollen into a multitude, numbering in the tens of thousands. Moving in an awesome continuum, this surge of humanity pressed toward their goal: to give America the message that the time had arrived for equal opportunity for all peoples. It has been estimated that about 300,000 people of all races, and many ethnic groups and religions, gathered that day. By 10:00 A.M., the crowd on all sides of The Washington Monument was so thick that it resembled the inside of an athletic stadium during a sold-out event.

A permanent pavilion near the monument was used by about 100 radio and television reporters, and it was here that I came across Philadelphia civil rights leader Cecil B. Moore, who was drinking a cup of water. I asked him why he was not with the people preparing to lead the parade, and he said, "Not me, that's for the big boys." I was disappointed by his answer as, given his impact in Philadelphia, I had considered him to be just as important as they were. I said good-bye to him and moved on, taking notes all the while for my report, and growing increasingly uncomfortable in my coat and tie in the summer heat.

A temporary stage was set up at the monument where musicians entertained prior to the march. Loudspeakers were placed all around the monument grounds. Huge tractor-trailer trucks were used to hold public telephones, while three lines of people waited their turn to place calls. U.S. Army water wagons provided water taps, and lines formed there as well. Some fire hydrants were fitted with temporary fountains for additional drinking water. Temporary toilets, with ever-lengthening lines, were placed strategically around the site. All adjacent public buildings were guarded, but the public was admitted to restrooms in those buildings too. All vendors had to be authorized, and they were only allowed to sell hot dogs and ice cream from their trucks. The sale of alcoholic beverages was prohibited for the day.

The security plans that had been made were highly effective, and the day's events proceeded without disorder. No parking was permitted on either side of the street from the railroad station to the Washington Monument. There also was no parking from the monument to Lincoln Memorial on Constitution Avenue. On intersecting streets, parking was restricted to buses only—hundreds of them.

Police personnel were furnished with box lunches and dinners, financed by the City of Washington. Policing in the immediate area surrounding the memorial was done primarily by National Park Service guards. These were augmented by military and metropolitan police, whose captain and an aide were highly visible. Also in evidence that day were representatives of the Secret Service, Federal Bureau of Investigation, U.S. Marshals, the U.S. Army and, almost assuredly, the Central Intelligence Agency—all actively assisting in keeping the peace.

The only possible threat to the peace and security of the demonstration was posed by the leader of the American Nazi Party, the infamous George Lincoln Rockwell. He and sixteen of his uniformed followers showed up at the Washington Monument. They were immediately surrounded by units of the metropolitan police and Army personnel, who remained with the Neo-Nazis for the entire day.

The march from The Washington Monument to The Lincoln Memorial began about 10:30 A.M., though smaller groups had marched earlier. This made it difficult to determine exactly who was leading the parade. Many well-known Philadelphians, both black and white, were among the parade leaders. My personal estimate is that the crowd was composed of 20 percent white and 80 percent non-whites. About one out of every six persons carried a sign, most of them calling for full civil rights and employment opportunities for minorities.

At the memorial, I identified myself as a policeman and was able to get through police lines to reach the top of the memorial steps, where the speakers were assembled. The restraining lines consisted primarily of police barricades, though at some places only snow fences were used. In spite of the number of people being held back, a few policemen were sufficient to prevent the crowd from overrunning the barricades and snow fences, given the cooperative spirit of the day. In some other areas hedges were effectively used as barricades. About every fifteen minutes someone had to be placed on a stretcher by army personnel and taken to a first aid station, having been overcome by the heat.

In my position at the top of the stairs, I was within a few feet of the famous assemblage that was to address the crowd. Although I was in awe of them, I was even more struck at seeing Lena Horne being interviewed by a reporter. She was dressed comfortably, and she just radiated exuberance—a real African-American beauty. Then I looked down and saw a real American—or should I say, French?—legend bounding up the stairs, Josephine Baker. She had some type of uniform on, possibly from some French cultural or charitable organization. She and Lena embraced like long-lost friends. As I watched, I tried to think of some pretext to engage them in conversation, but to no avail.

As the day moved into the afternoon, there was great anticipation of the main event, which was the call to action by civil rights leaders. Hundreds of thousands converged upon the Lincoln Memorial, where the podium was located. Many well-known civil rights leaders were introduced, prior to singing by Mahalia Jackson and Marian Anderson. Among those who spoke were A.P. Randolph, one of the architects of the march, and Roy Wilkins of the NAACP.

The speaker's stand was set up on a landing of the Memorial's steps, with about 100 chairs for other dignitaries arranged behind the podium. The loudspeakers apparently were very effective, since the crowd made no special efforts to get up closer after all seats were taken. The applause was thunderous at times during the speakers' presentations, and I was thrilled to be witnessing this spectacle.

The task of policing the area designated for speakers and other dignitaries was assigned to black policemen in plainclothes, and they were termed "marshals." They wore arm bands with a big "M," plus white sailor's caps for easy identification. Nearly all these policemen were from outside of Washington, and they had volunteered their services, and in most cases paid their own expenses, included in their ranks were numerous Philadelphia policemen. I was very proud of Al Deal, who was one of the most active supervisors of the marshals.

Finally, the climax of the day came when the Reverend Martin Luther King, Jr. began speaking. At first his manner was gentle but, as he warmed to his subject, he began the powerful delivery for which he was so famous. "I Have a Dream" was to become the most impressive and persuasive speech in the annals of the civil rights movement. There is little doubt that it was a powerful influence in the subsequent choice of Doctor King as a Nobel laureate in 1964.

After Doctor King's address, all remaining speeches were anticlimactic. Finally, the program ended and the crowds began to leave the city. Moving the crowds out of the area peacefully required as much attention as the inbound movement had earlier in the day. The direction may have been reversed, but traffic problems and crowd control were relatively the same.

Shuttle buses transported people back to the railroad station, while hundreds of regular rental buses set out on other routes. Taxi cabs were the only automobiles allowed in the area. The railroad station was a mass of human movement. However, surprisingly, everyone seemed calm. Again, the policemen opened up corridors in the crowd so passengers could board the trains.

It was close to 8:00 P.M. before the mass of visitors appeared to be thinning out in the city. Included in this exodus were police groups from throughout the Eastern Seaboard and as far west as Chicago, who had answered the call for volunteers. I boarded a train and was lucky to find a seat quickly. My luck continued, as the person I sat next to was one of the grandames of the Philadelphia court system, attorney Sadie T. M. Alexander. We had known each other both socially and in the courts, and we began a long conversation about the march as the train departed the station.

Mrs. Alexander was a very charismatic lady who knew how to put one at ease. We both shared the excitement of the day, telling each other of our observations and opinions of what it all meant. She was most impressed with the congressional speakers and what their promises were. I spoke on my appreciations for the wide range of speakers and the most efficient job the security people did. Both of us were trying to outdo each other in expressing our joy at the attitude of the people and that there were no embarrassing incidents to mar the events of the day. As I showed her my notes for my report, she said she would probably sit up all night writing in her diary. We both related to each other how far we had come and the second-class citizenship we had endured.

As for me, the whole world had taken on a new image. Everyone seemed to be so friendly, especially the white police official who was so helpful in getting me up on the speaking area. He was a long way from the white sergeant who had looked at me on my first day on the job and said, "My God, it gets worse." I thought surely that tremendous good would come out of that day. It was a highlight in my life, one that I would enjoy telling my children and grandchildren about.

I sensed that conditions would most certainly change and that the attitude of white people was such that there would be no opposition to minorities asserting their moral, if not their legal rights.

The Guardians did not leave Washington until about 9:00 P.M. On boarding the bus, the men quickly settled down in comfortable positions, since they had been on their feet since early in the morning. The bus headed northbound on Route 40, then stopped at a roadside restaurant in Delaware so that the men could get something to eat.

Lieutenant Leonard Jones was the only supervisory officer on the trip, but until that moment rank had not been important. Jones decided to remain in his comfortable position on the bus, and get a good nap while the men ate. Suddenly, he was awakened by one of the other Guardians, who told him there was trouble in the restaurant. Jones left the bus, entered the restaurant, and tried to find out what the problem was.

Jones learned that one of the Guardians had requested service from a white waitress. She had replied that he should wait his turn, and then proceeded to wait on two white men who had entered after the Guardians. The Guardian protested that she was serving out of turn. The waitress had replied that "If you characters can't wait, you can get the hell out of here."

At that point, all of the men had voiced their dissatisfaction in rather vivid terms. The waitress then spoke to a man in a back room, telling him to call the sheriff or the state police. She yelled, "Tell them to come and lock these damn niggers up. I don't have to take nothing off of these black bastards."

Within very short order, word of the confrontation drifted to the kitchen, to a nearby service station and to various other persons in the area. Some appeared with weapons of all types that were only partially concealed. Fortunately, no attempt was made by either side to get physical.

Route 40, stretching about 70 miles from Baltimore, Maryland, to Route 13 near New Castle, Delaware, had the reputation among blacks of being the most inhospitable highway in America. Black people were stopped and arrested on the slightest provocation, and more often than not were then subject to what some termed "cruel and unusual punishment" at the hands of the authorities. But despite the reputation of this highway, some of the Guardians declared that they intended to wait for the local police to arrive. Somehow, Jones was able to persuade them that the hassle was not worth the trouble, and they boarded the bus and proceeded home.

There had been no reported incidents involving the 300,000 persons who had marched in Washington that day. It would have been the cruelest of ironies if the day's activities had been marred by, of all people, the fifty-four police officers from Philadelphia whose duty it was to help keep the peace. Given the reputation of law enforcement on Route 40, it was probably just as well that they didn't wait around.

Later, I-95 was built parallel to Route 40, offering integrated restrooms, and food and service stops. This was a godsend to blacks who had long been discriminated against and denied all of the common courtesies normally afforded travelers on Route 40. Blacks had no sympathy for the many segregated businesses on Route 40 which subsequently folded after the new highway opened and times continued to change.

Upon returning to duty, I reported directly to Commissioner Leary with my written report. In it I gave a detailed account of how the security was handled throughout the day, putting a lot of emphasis on the benefits of the volunteer policemen, especially those from Philadelphia. However, he seemed more interested in who was there, who spoke, and the attitude of the speakers as well as the crowd. He was so impressed that he had me give a verbal report at the following inspectors' meeting in his office.

CHAPTER TEN

I found myself with a new boss on January 6, 1964, when Lieutenant Richard Edwards, a black officer, was promoted over me to deputy commissioner, and he was assigned to PCR, where he took command. This came as a shock to me, for I didn't think that the department would skip an officer from lieutenant to deputy commissioner. I thought those days were over with after the open civil service examinations of 1953.

After the death of Chief Inspector Ballard on, December 26, 1962, I was left as the highest ranking black policeman in the department. Although I was deeply grieved at Ballard's death, I also felt that I had inherited some of his stature. I thought that now as blacks gained empowerment in the city, I would rise in a matter of due course and continue as the top black police official. However, I made no attempt to court the power structure, either black or white.

This was probably my undoing, for I learned later that I should have, as Lieutenant Edwards was leaving no stone unturned to get the deputy commissioner appointment. I knew that he had good Republican ties, through the late Judge Herbert E. Millen with whom he had a family relationship. But what I didn't know was his ties with a city councilman, Thomas McIntosh, who was a good friend of the new mayor, James H. J. Tate.

I later learned that the police commissioner had the authority to make interim appointments until such time as an examination was given. The interim appointee and all other eligible applicants would have to take competitive examinations for the position. Edwards received the interim promotion, much to my chagrin.

During the early part of May, 1965, I met with Police Commissioner Howard R. Leary. I informed him that I wanted to retire and to take a position with the Philadelphia Housing Authority's management training program. He was shocked and surprised. Moments passed between us as he hesitated to accept my retirement papers, but he sensed that my mind had been set on my retirement and starting a new career. With a warm handshake, he let me know that I had

117

served the police department to the utmost of my professional abilities and he deeply felt also I would be hard to replace.

On Monday June 14, 1965, I reported to Mr. Beckett at the PHA personnel office, and he sent me to the Harrison Plaza project at 10th and Master Streets, where I reported to Robert Loving, a longtime friend who was the manager. For the first two years I worked as Bob's assistant, managing four different projects. I had chosen this direction because at the time I was anxious to get away from police work, but I didn't find working as a housing manager much of a challenge or very exciting.

So much of the work consisted of desk work with record keeping and supervision of clerical and maintenance workers. I did, however, find it interesting in my dealing with tenants. The big problem with them was getting them to pay their rent on time. This entailed listening to a lot of hard luck stories. In extreme cases we had to use threats and, finally, eviction proceedings.

One day I went to visit a woman who was three months in arrears with her rent after she refused to come to the office to talk about the situation. She reluctantly let me into her apartment after I made it obvious that I was entering one way or another. Upon going on an impromptu inspection, which I was not authorized to do, I found an awful lot of evidence that a man was living there.

Although no man was listed in the contract, I didn't chastise her. Instead, I took the opportunity to suggest that since there was a man living there she should make him pay at least part of the rent. She became all upset saying, "What do you mean? Do you think that I'm a whore?" Realizing I was treading on thin ice, I bowed out gracefully, but she did catch up with the rent a short time later.

Housekeeping can sometimes be a major problem in low-income housing. While the majority of tenants are good housekeepers, far too many are not. One tenant at Mill Creek Apartments came to the office to request a larger apartment because she had another baby. I went to her place and inspected it, only to find that she had a two-bedroom unit with one of the rooms given over entirely to her dog. There was only one bed in the room with dog waste all over it. I gave her two days to clean it up or face eviction. On reinspection she had complied. I left without even discussing her original request. I never heard any more about it.

At Champlost Homes, I checked the records of a family that had three bedrooms with eight children. It just happened that the adjacent apartment was an empty four-bedroom unit with two baths. I went to the family and suggested that they move to the vacant unit for their enlarged family. The man of the house said he did not feel like moving, saying he was satisfied where they were. I became so enraged that I momentarily forgot that I was not a policeman, and began berating him for his lackadaisical attitude and threatened to evict him for overcrowding. He moved the next day.

At Hawthorne Plaza the tenants once complained of a foul odor coming from an apartment, and I went to inspect. I found that there was an old lady living there alone. In the living room was a huge oil drum used as a trash receptacle. It was full to overflowing. She said it was too heavy for her to handle. I scolded her mildly and had the maintenance men remove it. I then sent her a small wastebasket.

One of the worse cases of insensitivity to family problems I saw was also at Hawthorne Plaza. I received another tenant's complaints of foul odors coming from an apartment. I entered with a passkey and found the decomposing body of the elderly female tenant. I called the police and had the body sent to the city morgue.

Upon checking for the next of kin, I found that the woman had two sons living in Kansas. I notified them and they arrived within two days. When they came to the office soon after we opened and identified themselves, I turned the key over to them. Late that afternoon they returned the key saying that they were returning to Kansas and that we could dispose of the remaining contents of the apartment. When asked what they were going to do about their mother, one said "Nothing. Let the city handle it." With that, they turned and left. A reinspection of the apartment revealed that it had been thoroughly searched and left in a topsy-turvy condition.

The one incident that I'll always remember was the time I caught a couple, man and wife, taking mail from another person's mailbox at Mill Creek Apartments. I spoke to them in a loud, authoritative voice as I saw a housing policeman on patrol nearby. I said "Give me that mail and stand against the wall." The man complied, but his wife said, "Who's he?" The husband said, "He's a policeman". She said, "Show us your identification."

I ignored her while waiting for the housing policeman to come after I waved to him. When she insisted on seeing my badge, I knew that I could not say that I was a policeman for I'd be impersonating an officer. So I said, "I'm the manager."

"A what? A what? You ain't shit," she said in a most disdainful voice. With that they both walked off.

Another Hawthorne Plaza tenant, a rather attractive lady, invited me to her apartment to see how well she kept it. Fearing she had ulterior motives, I took a female office worker with me on the "inspection tour." Upon entering we found the most lavishly furnished and decorated apartment I had ever seen in a public housing project. We praised her and took pictures of it, which we displayed on the public bulletin board at the office.

But the most exasperating experience I had as a housing manager was when another attractive woman called the office. She asked me to come to her apartment at the Queen Lane Apartments, that she had a problem that she wanted to discuss with me. Unsuspecting and trusting as I was, I went alone, only to be met at the door by the lady in a housecoat. A red flag went up immediately as she invited me on in.

She began to ramble on about family problems, her sisters and brothers all "looking down on me for living in public housing." She even offered me "something cold to drink," which I refused. She then came right out and said she wanted to have a baby by me. I excoriated her harshly, informing her that I was a happily married man with a family. I then beat a hasty retreat, only to be told about seven months later that she had given birth. A classic case of attempted entrapment.

Living in a housing project is just a way of life that many people accept as normal, for they have always lived there. We had cases where there were three generations who had lived in the same apartment. The residents learned to accept conditions as they were, and complained only when they were physically attacked. For the most part, they knew everyone around them, and in turn they were known by everyone. This makes for a system of mutual protection and assistance.

The concept of public housing, from its inception, was to house people on a temporary basis, until private housing could be obtained. Unfortunately, this has not been the case, for many people came to view it as a comfortable, permanent way of living. Others mismanaged their budgets to the extent that they were asked to leave or were evicted. Fortunately, there are a fair number of people who lift themselves up by their bootstraps and go on to a better way of living. A classic example of this is TV's Bill Cosby, who lived in the Richard Allen Homes in Philadelphia as a child.

I have observed public housing since its beginning. The first tenants were well screened for family structure and temperament. Only reputable families were allowed in. The prospective tenant's former housing had to be visited and be judged as being well kept before the tenant was allowed to move into a new project. Once in, their units were inspected on a regular basis, and disruptive and criminal tenants were evicted.

With the rise of the tenant rights groups in the 1960s, these policies were quickly replaced. Screening became almost nonexistent, and inspections were made only by appointments. Evictions were effected only after a time-consuming process, through legal channels. Some tenants learned how to beat the system to the extent that, when they finally left, they owed thousands of dollars.

In my dealings with tenants, I found that I had to learn to be more friendly and to deal with them more as an advisor than as an authority figure. Many tenants were rebellious and resented any attempt to make them conform to the rules and regulations. However, there were those who readily accepted direction and often sought advice. Usually those were the ones who eventually bettered themselves and went on to improved private housing.

My previous experiences in the police department made it easy for me to get police action whenever it was necessary. Mr. Loving, my boss, was particularly impressed with the ease with which I was able to get abandoned automobiles removed by the police tow squad.

Mr. Loving often spoke of the difficulty he had getting abandoned cars removed. It was usually done by contract tow trucks, paid for by the housing authority. Policemen as well as their top supervisors usually thought of housing projects as being totally the province of the federal government and, therefore, not entitled to municipal services other then fire fighting.

My observations over the years were that, other than actions through tenants' organizations, the tenants did very little in the way of improving the physical conditions of the projects. There were some cases where certain well-meaning tenants would sweep the hallways on their floor of the building, even in some cases washing graffiti from walls outside their apartments, but not many.

The housing authority organized a task force to review problems at the Richard Allen Homes at 10th and Parrish Streets early in my tenure. Mr. Alton C. Berry suggested my name for the group. Two other managers and I were selected. We investigated all phases of management problems, including maintenance and security. Our report was submitted on February 1, 1967, after three weeks' work.

Although I never heard any official reason for the task force, unofficially I heard that, because the project was close to center city, management hoped to rehabilitate it to the extent that better-class, higher-income tenants—yes, even white tenants—would want to live there. It had been one of the first projects in the city, and was in dire need of painting, altering, repairing, and landscaping. And even then, drugs were beginning to be a problem for the police. It's very possible that the authority wanted to keep in step with other urban renewal projects in the area.

In that my expertise was in law enforcement, my contribution was concerned primarily with project security. While investigating, my initial observations were that there were not enough guards assigned there. They were untrained except for what the manager taught them, and they were poorly uniformed. Some of them had no uniform, no revolvers, no commissions, and no supervision. Except for a very few retired city policemen, all others were hired right off the street. They did very little patrolling, and travelled in groups of three or four.

My suggestions were: double the manpower, take supervisory responsibility for the guards from the manager, establish means of training the guards in modern police tactics, establish new ranks of corporal and sergeant for improved on-site supervision and better effectiveness, and hire a director of security. The recommendations of the sergeant rank were the only ones put into place at once. The others required much longer.

When we submitted the task force recommendations, the changes we suggested were so massive that it was financially unfeasible to handle them all at the same time. Over the next five years, most of them were acted upon with the help of concerned politicians, who insisted on government funding to improve living conditions.

On August 1, 1967, I was appointed a full manager in charge of the Morton Homes complex in Germantown. I remained there until the death of Martin Luther King, Jr., on April 4, 1968. The Housing Director said that he expected trouble in South Philadelphia and needed a stronger man at Hawthorne Plaza, which was later renamed after Dr. King. I got the call with instructions to maintain a hands-on supervision at all times.

The news of Martin Luther King's assassination came while I was conducting a tenants' meeting at Queen Lane Apartments. It was so devastating that several women cried out in grief, while others walked out of the meeting. Seeing that it was useless to try to continue, I called for a motion to adjourn. In that it was a night meeting, I went directly home, fearing disturbances enroute, and for the safety of my family at home. The city was still cautiously geared up for "a long hot summer" as a result of unrest in other cities.

I had much the same feeling as when President Kennedy was killed. It was like losing a member of the family. Grieving for someone cut down so young, and reviewing all of the good he had done, and the loss of his potential for the future. I wondered what would happen next? Would there be more race riots, more burning, more killing? Or worse still, would civil rights suffer a setback after so many gains over the past twenty-five years?

The next day, the housing director called a meeting of managers to discuss the problems. Except for some minor vandalism, conditions were surprisingly quiet. We were given instructions to keep in close touch with the projects, keep the guards on patrol constantly, report all untoward actions or acts of vandalism, and have the local police captain's phone number handy. All leaves were cancelled, and we were told to make frequent project checks at night.

The city had extensive preparations for any anticipated problems. There were always two busloads of policemen ready to be dispatched to any problem area. The Community Relations Division was still active in preventing problems from arising and ameliorating tensions wherever they occurred. On the whole, calmness prevailed in Philadelphia at the time of Dr. King's death, but other cities erupted as soon as his death was announced.

Hawthorne Plaza is only eight blocks from City Hall. It is composed of four high-rise buildings of all poor black people. Most were long-term residents, but a goodly number were newly arrived, and many of those were thought to be troublemakers. The Housing Authority, in anticipation of trouble, hired private guards. They were instructed to patrol in quartets. It was believed that this would have a sobering effect on any potential troublemaker.

But there was a fatal flaw with the "rent-a-cop" operation. The guards were not properly supervised. I discovered this during my first week on the job at Hawthorne Plaza. On returning to the project on two different occasions, I found as many as twelve guards in the maintenance office, some lounging around while others played cards. The sergeant on duty tried to explain their presence there, but no explanation was acceptable to me. My report to the PHA administration caused the whole group to be replaced.

There was a constant fear that hostilities would break out in the projects. If properly organized, this would have a devastating effect in a high-rise building where sharpshooters could hole up and take an enormous toll in life and property damage. In my contact with tenants and the public in general, I had no problem dealing with this, for I had a well-developed buttress against fear.

As housing manager, I always maintained a good relationship with the local police district captain to the extent that we were on a first name basis. Therefore, I was never reticent about asking for police favors. As a former Police Community Relations official, I knew that I had to establish a good relationship with the community-minded tenants. I maintained an open-door policy at all times. This served me well for I was often made aware of potential trouble long before it was to have occurred.

My experience in the police department was that whenever you wanted to draw a crowd, you brought in conspicuous numbers of policemen. Therefore, I maintained an open line with the tenant group, trying to minimize the appearance of trouble by keeping large numbers of police out of the project whenever it was avoidable.

In hindsight, Philadelphia was fortunate that there were no large demonstrations or large public memorial services for Dr. King. However, practically all black churches included some type of memorial in their usual Sunday services. It was a credit to the black leadership that tensions were maintained at a manageable level. The black community was grieved as we recounted Dr. King's death and the potential loss of advances in civil rights that might be caused by the loss of his irreplaceable leadership.

In the various group discussions in the black community in which I was a participant, I often heard the expression, "We have been set back a generation by Dr. King's death." There was a feeling that conditions would retrogress with his passing from the scene, and there was some fear of infighting for black leadership positions. Surprisingly, there were those who maintained that his death would accelerate civil rights, thinking that the conscience of the nation would dictate the righting of long-standing wrongs to black citizens in honor of Dr. King's death.

The director of management for the housing authority called me in for a consultation not long after Dr. King's death. It was becoming obvious that the administrators were giving more credence to my police experience. My words to him were, "These men must be trained and led by a dedicated professional of proven ability." In a sense, I was paving the way for my becoming their chief, albeit not intentionally.

While I was working at the Philadelphia Housing Authority, I managed to maintain some official contact with the police department after Mayor James H.J. Tate appointed two former police officers, James A. Ippoliti, a former sergeant, and myself, a former captain, to vacancies on the Police Advisory Board. This was a panel that reviewed citizen misconduct complaints against the police and, by appointing us, Tate sought to give police department members some semblance of input into deliberations and decisions affecting policemen. This was done upon the insistence of Clarence Farmer, who was executive director of the Advisory Board.

The appointment of two former police officers to the board did not set too well with the Fraternal Order of Police membership, despite the fact that I tried to justify my board membership with the contention that the police needed "a friend in the enemies' camp." Nonetheless, the FOP demanded that we resign from the board. Ippoliti resigned immediately, but I did not.

FOP President John Harrington then brought charges against me of "Violation of His Oath of Obligation as a member of the Fraternal Order of Police." Harrington further charged that, "The national, state, and local lodges have mandated that the FOP is unalterably opposed to any and all civilian review boards, or any similar boards or agencies. Despite these mandates, Reaves became a member of the Philadelphia Advisory Board."

I appealed to the lodge for reconsideration, citing my many years of loyalty to the FOP. At a hearing before the Grievance Committee of the lodge on August 29, 1968, the committee recommended my expulsion if I failed to resign from the board within thirty days.

At a general membership meeting of the Guardian Civic League, composed of the city's black policemen, on September 24, 1968, I requested support for my case before the general membership of the FOP. The Guardians, acting on a recommendation made by Lieutenant Donald Gravatt, voted unanimously to support me.

The FOP meeting was held on September 26, 1968, in the spacious ballroom of the Philadelphia Athletic Club at Broad and Race Streets. Even though the Guardians attended the meeting en masse, they were far outnumbered by the more than 500 white policemen who arrived at the meeting in special buses. It was the largest outpouring of members I have ever seen at a regular FOP meeting.

A special resolution was put on the floor to give President Harrington a vote of confidence in his charges against me. Guardian President Al Deal, in a most effective stentorian voice, called for a defeat of the motion. Surprisingly, he was joined by two white policemen who didn't want to see the lodge split, but they were promptly shouted down.

I then took the floor on my own behalf with voluminous statistics to show my effectiveness as a member of the Advisory Board. I cautioned them that if the Advisory Board continued to exist, policemen in general would be far better off having one of their own adjudicating their cases. When the motion was put to a vote, the results showed that the membership was divided entirely along racial lines, and I lost my case by a wide margin. Consequently, I was given thirty days to either resign from the Advisory Board or be expelled from the lodge.

Though I never officially resigned from the board, my name was never stricken from the FOP membership rolls. Eventually, the entire case became moot when Mayor Tate officially disbanded the Police Advisory Board on December 22, 1969. Tate said the department "should not be impeded in its mission by a controversial agency which has shown its inadequacy after more than a decade of existence."

This incident was far from the first time—or the last one, either—that the Guardian Civic League found itself in conflict with the Fraternal Order of Police. The first attempt to organize the Guardians took place in the spring of 1954. Edward Payne, who would become an inspector, was the person who first advanced the idea of organizing black police officers in the 1950s. He had been teaching in the Police Academy, and was an ardent student of law enforcement. Although serving as an instructor, his rank and pay grade was that of an acting sergeant. He was highly respected for his police knowledge, which served him well as he lectured to ranking police officers who were much his senior in rank.

Payne, Inspector Ballard and I chanced to meet at a community meeting in West Philadelphia while on duty. Payne mentioned the fact that there were several ethnic organizations in the department, and that there should be one for "colored policemen." The underlying idea was to gain status to the extent that we could be of mutual assistance when problems occurred. Ballard and I immediately agreed that we would do it. We discussed the fact that the administration might not look kindly on the idea of an all-black organization, and we decided that we would organize as a social and civic organization to avert this problem.

Ballard, Payne, and myself, a sergeant at the time, sent written notices of our intentions to all of the black members of the department. We invited them to a meeting at the YMCA at 1724 Christian Street, for the purpose of organizing a social and civic group. The first meeting was attended by about fifteen men, including Deal, Tommie Frye, Thomas Brown, Frank Winfrey, Ballard, Payne, and myself. Inspector Ballard acted as temporary chairman, explaining the purposes of the group, while I acted as secretary. After a brief discussion, the meeting was adjourned.

There had been an unusually large number of black policemen appointed recently, and I met a few at our initial meeting. One of them was Alfonso Deal. I was impressed with him from the beginning. He was very talkative and asked a lot of questions for a rookie policeman. Deal had been born in a small town near Jacksonville, Florida. He was educated in the public schools of Jacksonville, a community to which he would be awarded the Key to the City in 1981.

At the beginning of World War II, Deal entered the Army. After recruit training, he rose to the rank of sergeant in an all-black military police unit. He protested racial segregation in the Army, and he was honorably discharged at the close of the war in 1945 after four years of loyal service.

Back in civilian life, he put down stakes in Philadelphia, where he met his wife, Ruth, and they raised two daughters and a son. His first job was with an auto body manufacturing company, Edward G. Budd and Company. Deal soon became active in the union movement, and was the local's first black official. Within a very short time, he was made chairman of several committees in United Auto Workers Local #813, including the first fair-employment committee.

Deal became active in the NAACP in 1948, heading boycotts, voter registration drives, and civil rights demonstrations. He served as vice president and, later, president of the North Philadelphia Action Branch. Under his administration, it became the largest branch in the state. The branch was particularly successful in raising funds for the NAACP in Mississippi after that state's government lifted the organization's charter. The Action Branch raised $52,000 to fight the decertification action.

In 1954, Deal was appointed to the police department, where he would spend twenty-four years as an honest and sincere officer. Deal was to become the most highly controversial police officer in the history of the Philadelphia Police Department, but he also was the most highly respected for his ideals and his tenacity in adhering to them. He would steadfastly hold his course, knowing full well that retribution would be taken against him.

The second meeting of the Guardians brought out an even larger group of men for discussions and socializing. The name "Guardians" was my suggestion. I borrowed the idea from the City Guardians Credit Union. Later, after the Guardian Civic League was formed permanently, the credit union changed its name to the present Philadelphia Police and Fire Federal Credit Union.

Within a few days after the second GCL meeting, Payne received a call from a city official of high political standing who told him in no uncertain terms to withdraw from the group. Payne had a friendly relationship with the official, who was an insider in the city administration. The caller warned Payne that he had had a conversation with other officials in City Hall, and that those men had made veiled threats against the organizers of the Guardians.

Payne relayed the message to Ballard and me. We discussed it pro and con, and we all agreed that it was best to disassociate ourselves from the organization. The other black officers to whom we spoke all agreed that, because the department was in the early stages of reorganization and the subsequent promotions of blacks, this was not the time to make waves, and the organization died aborning.

Some time after this, Alfonso Deal became active with the FOP. This was a natural for him, given his background as an active union official at the Budd Company. Deal attempted to get FOP backing for a special committee within the lodge to handle racial problems within the department, but he was quickly and resoundingly rebuffed. Because of this reaction, he and other black officers resurrected the idea of the Guardian Civic League to address their concerns about the treatment of black officers within the department.

Deal was as aggressive as he was articulate, and these characteristics alienated him from those members of the FOP who thought that he should be docile. I was always treated well at lodge meetings and conventions, and there was tolerance between blacks and whites in the lodge, but blacks had little if any clout. The real problem then, as it has always been, was that not enough black policemen attended FOP meetings regularly to create an effective voting block.

Virtually all black policemen belong to the FOP, and have monthly dues withheld from their paychecks. This also applies to black pensioners. This means that the FOP benefits handsomely from the over 1,500 plus blacks who pay dues. Other than a few convention delegates and a token vice president, however, blacks wield almost no power in the lodge.

Deal's intentions for the resurrected Guardians was an idea that was long overdue. As an entry-level policeman, he had no rank to fear losing for speaking out on racial issues. This same philosophy guided him throughout his police career.

In the second round of GCL meetings, the time was spent in gripe sessions, and in discussion of the mechanics of getting organized. Typical complaints were aired about black officers not being assigned to patrol cars, about not being assigned to special units, about being assigned to distasteful details, about being charged with offenses more often than white policemen who commit the same violation, and about receiving more severe discipline than white officers.

Many discussions were concerned with the effect such an organization might have in pressuring the new "black cabinet" of advisors to the mayor to take more of an interest in the plight of black policemen. Black policemen have complained historically that black politicians expended little or no effort in their behalf. Because of this, many black officers aligned themselves with white politicians from whom they could exact a favor.

In the process of organizing the Guardians, the members were mindful of the pressure exerted on Payne, Ballard, and myself to cease and desist our activities.

For this reason, there was a hesitancy on the part of some prospective members to join. Then, too, there were still a few of the old-timers around who remembered the problems that the FOP had had with the police administration in its initial stages, and who urged the organizers to keep at it.

A small group of men continued to meet at Officer Jerome Berry's home at 5634 Morton Street, and permanently formed the Guardian Civic League during the spring of 1956. They retained the name, Guardians, since, as police officers, they thought of themselves as guardians or protectors of the community. They not only were concerned with their problems as policemen, but also with the problems of the community as well. Although the initial meetings were sparsely attended, usually by only eight to ten men, the overall membership grew steadily. They soon outgrew Berry's home and moved their meeting place to St. Paul's Church at 10th and Wallace Streets.

As the GCL grew over the years, their meeting place changed, to Richard's Lounge at 62nd and Walnut Streets and, two years later, they negotiated the purchase of their own building at 1516 West Girard Avenue, moving in after extensive renovations in 1973. The new home and the new spirited attitude apparently were strong magnets, and new members joined by the droves. The general attitude was, "We finally have something of our own and we are going to be more outspoken." Nothing provided more evidence of the renewed spirit than the fact that the Guardians were able to pay off the mortgage on the Girard Avenue site within less than four years.

In 1979, a proposal was presented to the city's Office of Housing and Community Development for funds to reconstruct and refurbish the new home, a three-story structure. In 1983, a proposal also was made to the U.S. Department of Housing and Urban Development, for funds to complete the rehabilitation. Both agencies approved grants totalling $210,000. The grants were given with the express purpose of providing offices and meeting rooms that would be available for use by the community.

As their membership grew, so did their programs. Over the years, they have focused their attention on the needs of the community, along with their social functions. Because of the changing social climate within the black community in the late 1960s and early 1970s, the Guardians' approach toward attaining its goals took on a more aggressive role.

When Alfonso Deal decided in 1972 to run for president of the Fraternal Order of Police, he was the first black to seek that post of the predominantly white organization. Never before had his qualities of strength and courage shown more markedly than in his determination to continue his campaign for the presidency even though, immediately after he announced his candidacy, he was transferred from his post on the Labor Squad to a foot patrol. He did not gain the presidency, but was successful in stimulating the interest of other blacks to participate and become involved.

Deal always has been an outspoken critic of any improper police action, especially when it involved brutality. He would take on all comers, regardless of rank or station in life. The first time Deal attended an FOP meeting, he stood up and challenged the chair on a point of order. The chairman, who had to concede the point, obviously was embarrassed. When Deal sat back down, he found that his shirt had been set afire by a lodge member. Of course, no one admitted doing it, though the chairman did apologize.

Years later, as a result of the widely publicized police confrontation that broke out with members of the controversial organization MOVE on August 8, 1978, Deal did the unpardonable. He publicly criticized the actions of a white police-man, who was filmed by the news media while kicking a MOVE member as the man lay prostrate—and weaponless—on the ground.

On September 19, 1978, while Deal was speaking about the incident before a grievance committee inside the FOP Hall at Broad and Spring Garden Streets, about 100 people met in front of the building and held a prayer vigil in his support. For violating the unwritten police code, "We take care of our own," Deal was suspended from the FOP for two years. He also was fined $1,000, and instructed to apologize to the officer he had accused and to the FOP. Instead, Deal took the FOP to court and succeeded in having the FOP's punitive actions lifted.

Deal's final months on the force were marked with scorn and harassment. For more than two weeks, members of the Guardians followed Deal either on foot or in automobiles while he patrolled his beat, to give him some form of security.

Although he never was promoted, Deal was eminently qualified for any rank, possibly including that of police commissioner. His outspoken protestations against any and all forms of segregation, discrimination and police abuse un-doubtedly constructed barriers to any of his attempts at upward mobility.

When James "Big Jim" Holley negotiated for a cause, he liked to go one-on-one with the powers that be, with no holds barred. As a general rule, he had done his homework and presented irrefutable facts. He sought fairness, not favors. His statuesque physique and stentorian voice lent added strength to his position. As a member of the GCL, he often spoke out about the inequalities faced by minorities. This culminated in his election to the League's presidency in 1971. As their new leader, he came out swinging.

A cornerstone event in black police history was a 13-year lawsuit initiated by seven unsuccessful black police candidates who charged the city with discrimi-nation. Holley persuaded the Guardians to join the litigation in 1972. It was well worth the effort; the black police eventually won the suit.

But much to his distress, Holley found he not only had to fight the admin-istration regarding the lawsuit, but he also had to fight the Fraternal Order of Police. The FOP attempted to oust him from its membership, charging him with "Conduct Unbecoming a Member." They were eventually dissuaded, how-ever, from ousting Holley by the intercession of a federal judge.

Once, an incident occurred involving a group of black officers and their wives, who attempted to but were not permitted to enter an FOP hall late one night. The doorman claimed it was too late. Some pushing and shoving began, and one of the wives was struck in the face. The police night command was called and the confrontation subsided. The GCL sought official redress from the FOP, but was rebuffed.

Holley called for the GCL to put a picket line in front of the FOP building and GCL members showed up ready to march. At about the same time, a group of staff inspectors and other officials showed up, in helmets and with riot sticks. Fortunately, trouble was averted just in time as FOP President Thomas McCary contacted Holley and promised to negotiate the complaint. The pickets were called off and tensions abated.

Holley continued his fearless leadership of the GCL in spite of the personal harassment he had to endure as president. He once said, "You just wouldn't believe the number of submarine jobs (traffic tickets written but not given) I got." He found himself constantly being sent to the 17th, the 16th, the 6th, the 1st, the 26th, the 12th, and then back to the 26th again. And he usually was given the most undesirable work hours, from 7 P.M. to 3 A.M.

He was constantly followed by police officials. Commissioner Joseph O'Neill admitted it was being done. The last straw was police harassment of his son. At last he went to see Mayor Rizzo to seek relief from intolerable working conditions. He cited the hardships his family had been forced to endure. The Mayor agreed that he had been penalized enough, and ordered his transfer to the Police Court Liaison Unit.

The suit was originally filed in 1970 as a class action suit when the Justice Department joined in a federal antidiscrimination suit with five blacks, four men and a woman who had been thwarted in efforts to join the force. The suit argued that tests and background investigations used to screen candidates discriminated against blacks and other minorities who are more likely to have minor arrest records as well as "ideas or beliefs contrary to an undefined moral code of the Police Department."

The GCL claimed that as Mayor, Rizzo "stonewalled like mad" to prevent implementation of federal court orders. In 1972, the GCL joined the plaintiffs in prosecuting the case. On April 10, 1973, after the federal judge agreed with the black plaintiffs and the state attorney general that the written test for entry to the Police Academy discriminated against minorities, the city scrapped its written examination. Educational Testing Services of Princeton was hired to devise a new test that would be more job related and less racially biased.

In 1979, the GCL decided to support William Green's mayoral candidacy on his promise to increase the number of black officers in the department. By January 15, 1982, Mayor Green still had not followed through on that promise. It was at this point that GCL President John Green called for black organizations and important political figures to boycott Mayor Green's breakfast given in honor of Dr. Martin L. King Jr.'s birthday.

It is generally conceded that the boycott was successful in that on August 13, 1983, Mayor Green issued an executive order that provided for the hiring of 293 black police officers and the promotion of two black police sergeants.

CHAPTER ELEVEN

On January 5, 1970, as a result of a change in organizational structure, I was transferred to Mill Creek Apartments in West Philadelphia by the Housing Authority. There had been a great deal of tenant unrest, and a firm but fair leadership was needed. There had been two types of problems at this location. Juvenile gang fights were erupting, and graffiti and vandalism was proliferating. The second problem was a near tenant rent rebellion on the part of high-rise tenants who wanted out of the building and into the low-rise buildings. In both cases, I appealed to level-headed tenant leadership for calmness. As for the gangs, I appealed to the Police Gang Control Division for attention. Within short order, peace reigned.

The problems at Mill Creek had escalated over a period of years because of the recalcitrant attitude of an elderly manager who had long outlived his usefulness. My new policy of filling all vacancies in low-rise buildings with tenants from high-rise buildings was a mitigating factor in quelling the rent rebellion.

I spent a little more than a year at Mill Creek. After the initial problems were solved, there was not much of a challenge there as manager. Then, the managing director requested a report from all managers of their conception of the duties of a housing manager and how they related to employees, tenants, the surrounding community, and to management. Fortunately for me, I had been required to do the same type of reports when I was a police captain. I pretty much used the same script for the managers' survey. The answers were found almost entirely in methods of good relationships, good communications, and accountability. When I submitted a proposal to the managing director, Mr. Marion Scott, he was so impressed with it that he utilized many of my suggestions.

He followed that up with a personal visit to my project and stated that he wanted me to take over the housing police and reorganize them. He wanted me to do this job as a captain, as the previous supervisor had been a captain. I rejected the role of captain, in that it would not give me enough discretion to do the job properly.

Scott said that there would be an increase in salary, naming the amount. I rejected it on the spot, saying that the reorganization he wanted required an administrator on the level of a director, with an equivalent salary. He said "no" and left.

He called a week later wanting to know if I had changed my mind. I said "no." He said he could not meet my price, and I told him I was not interested. Still, another week later, he called me to his office. He said that the board of directors had agreed that the position was needed and that they would make me the director of security. I agreed to the move.

Mr. Scott seemed pleased with my acceptance, and gave me sufficient time to close out the loose ends of my managerial duties. The more I thought of the new challenge, the more pleased I was. Now, I thought to myself, I was at the top of the department, in the vocation in which I had spent the major portion of my life. I tried to envision what it was going to be like being the top policy maker, and how I would direct the operation. In effect, I would be the Chief of Police. This, I decided, would be even better than being inspector in the city's police department.

On March 1, 1971, I was transferred to the central office, and given carte blanche in handling housing guards all over the city. It was not an auspicious beginning. My desk was in the far rear part of the PHA administration building, where I shared a secretary with the building superintendent. I had no locker or closet in which to put my personal belongings. I only had a shared clothes pole. The only supervisors I had were two sergeants, and one of them went off duty on sick leave.

I soon made a personal on-site survey of almost all projects in the city, and I set out to get a first-hand knowledge of the total PHA security operation. I found that a few, but not all, of the high-rise buildings had contract guards on duty. None of them seemed to be interested in what they were about. They were mostly unsupervised. The PHA guards worked out of the projects management office and took their directions from the manager. They spent most of their time in the manager's office, ostensibly guarding the manager and rent collections. Many of the smaller projects didn't have steady guards. Once or twice a day, shared guards would drive through. They were ill-prepared and ill-equipped to do guard duty. Many had allowed their watchman's commission to expire. Few had ever made arrests, just being content to chase troublemakers away, even for serious offenses.

I then wrote a proposal to the director of management, Mr. Scott, asking that we double the number of guards, that we have them trained at the police academy, and that we outfit every man in a uniform and a service revolver. I further suggested that their classification be changed from guards to private patrolmen, with supervision by corporals, sergeants, lieutenants, and captains. Finally, I suggested the purchase of walkie-talkie radios for more effective communication between the men, and between the men and the office.

From all that I had observed in my survey, it was apparent to me that major changes would be necessary to assure effectiveness. Since my experience as a law enforcement officer had been in the Philadelphia Police Department, recognized as one of the best in the nation, I naturally wanted to model the PHA guards after the proven effectiveness of the city police. It was my desire to create a police force on a par with the city policemen, to train, equip, and supervise in such a manner that even the city policemen would be proud to work with them. I wanted to make policemen out of them, and get away from the guard concept. I wanted them constantly on patrol, with all of the police authority necessary to get the job done.

One of my first tasks was to choose the best-qualified ones as supervisors and train them. This was to be done at our newly established Housing Police Office in the West Park Project at 46th and Market Streets. I was anxious to instill in them the work ethic and a desire for upward mobility. Much emphasis would be placed on treating people properly, being polite, and preventing any hint of corruption, I fully realized that whatever the department became would reflect my leadership. I utilized my own training in management at the University of Pennsylvania to be a constant teacher in every personal contact with my men.

Recognizing that 90 percent of public housing residents were black, I attempted to have the guards reflect the residents. This was a far cry from the composition of the city police, where only about 15 percent of the force was black at that time. For some reason, we had a problem recruiting white officers. They would be willing to do office work, but not to patrol the projects.

I was not too happy with what appeared to be all black officers on the force. I even made concessions, giving some white recruits favorable positions, working mostly in the quiet projects of senior citizens, and those in the mostly white northeast section of the city. I wanted to reverse the treatment that I had received on my entry into the Philadelphia Police Department. I welcomed the few white policemen we had, and saw to it that they were properly treated by the black officers.

In my staff meetings I always instructed our men in the necessity of being fair, honest, loyal, and a student of law enforcement. I was determined to make respected policemen out of them. Many of our men were just marking time, as they wanted to join the Philadelphia Police Department. As time went on many of them did, thanks to the training and experience they received with the Housing Authority Police.

Through my contact with Commissioner Rizzo, Police Academy instructors came to West Park and gave all of our men a one-week training course. This worked out so well that we were able to extend the training so that they were sent to the Academy for the full training course. This was a great step forward for us, for it meant that they were now qualified to be private patrolmen with full powers of arrest.

These powers were not only effective on PHA property, but also anywhere in the city. This meant that our men would no longer be subject to arrest for carrying a firearm off PHA property. Because of this, their morale was raised to the sky. In an effort to make this more official, we held a ceremony at the Police Academy on October 3, 1972. This marked the graduation of the first Philadelphia Housing Authority Police-trained class. We were so proud as Police Commissioner Joseph O'Neill and Mr. Gilbert Stein spoke in praise of the new training that our men received. Captain Henry Anderson and I presented the Academy with a plaque of appreciation as we all posed for a "class picture."

This was a real highlight for me as I was now recognized as a full inspector, which in police terms carries more weight than director of security. I prominently displayed my oak leaf on the shoulders and clusters on the cap bill of my uniform. All of this gold made for an impressive-looking police official.

I'm sure that our men also had a far better impression of themselves. In my tours of inspection following the graduation, our men had almost no resemblance to the guards that I had been hired to supervise. They looked better, walked better, and spoke more authoritatively than ever.

At the March housing board meeting all of my proposals were approved, and we began interviewing and hiring men and a few women. In my desire to emulate the Philadelphia Police, it was only fitting that we hired women. This was not new to me, as I had worked with policewomen for the entire nine years I spent in JAD. Policewomen were especially good for working around the housing projects. Our work consisted largely of dealing with women. We found it far safer to enter housing units with policewomen. This prevented any false charges being brought against our men. We made no special effort to hire women, but neither did we try to discourage applicants. We generally averaged about three percent women in our department, which was almost consistent with Philadelphia Police percentages. We were so impressed with one policewoman, Annie Fripps, that within a year of her appointment she was promoted to corporal.

It was only a matter of days before it was decided to establish a working security office away from housing authority headquarters. Space was found at West Park Project at 46th and Market Streets. It was immediately named Security Operations Center, which made for a catchy acronym S.O.C. This relocation was welcomed by housing authority headquarter employees who disdained seeing so many young black men entering and leaving the housing authority office building. It didn't take long for this word to reach my ears.

While the vast majority of housing employees in the projects were black, the vast majority of central office employees were white. Politics play an important part in obtaining employment in the authority. Thus, job tenure depends on the employee's City Hall connections. I had quickly made friends with one of the Jewish office workers at the PHA administration building. It did not take us long before we were comfortable discussing racial issues.

It was in such a discussion that she volunteered information that white workers were making these racial remarks. This information irked me at first, for it revealed the racial attitudes existing in the central office. But then I gave it more thought and decided to put it to my advantage in requesting more space for security operations.

When I brought this to Mr. Scott's attention (a black man) he said, "That does it, we'll find a place for you to relocate." Within a few days, space was found at West Park Project and we swiftly moved in. I never revealed to the men what the deciding factor was for the relocation, other than more comfortable space. They were well pleased with the new headquarters.

The new location was ideal with plenty of office space and parking area for both police and private vehicles. I particularly liked the extra room in which to hold roll calls. The only problem was that officials, VIPs, and even regular citizens were reluctant to visit us when they discovered that our location was in a project. I would hastily assure them that the office was in a safe location and that housing policemen and adequate lighting were always present. I could understand their squeamishness in not wanting to visit a project, for to the average person all projects are places to be avoided.

Francis Bickett, the director of personnel, worked very closely with me in interviewing new recruits. We then announced and placed into effect promotional examinations. Our immediate need was for corporals and sergeants. On April 17, 1971, we held examinations at the Locke School for these two positions. About 80 percent of the men took the tests which were monitored by personnel office employees. We worked feverishly marking the papers and published the results in a short period of time.

I had worked with the central office in putting the examination together, and I felt that the people with whom I worked were honest. Except for Mr. Beckett and myself, all personnel employees who worked on the tests were white. Therefore I had no reason to believe that there would be prior contact between Mr. Beckett's people and the men who took the test. I put a lot of confidence in Mr. Beckett, and I never had reason to regret it.

In order to build the men's morale and give a lot of credence to the promotions, we took the men to the City Hall chambers of Judge Robert Williams. He very ceremoniously swore them in as sergeants, giving them the proper admonitions. We did much the same with the corporals. The difference was that Judge Robert

N.C. Nix came to West Park and performed the ceremony in a beautiful tree-arched area of the project. Being in complete uniforms with new badges, and being sworn in by a judge, gave our men a feeling of exaltation.

Our first group activity was to take part with the Guardian Civic League in going to New York City on September 12, 1971, to march in the annual Veterans Day Parade. We sent the biggest Philadelphia contingent ever. With the Guardians, there were three busloads of Philadelphia policemen, six police cars, six motorcycles, and two police trucks. This was a far cry from the two motorcycles we first asked for and were initially refused.

On our initial request about the trip to New York, contact had been made at a low level of police officials for the police equipment. Without knowing all of the facts, it was easy for the official to say "no." We were, however, able to get the decision reversed and the parade went on. The results were so successful that when the news reached top-level officials, there were no longer objections to our having taken the equipment.

Our men were so impressed with being with the Guardians that they formed their own group of Housing Police Guardians on October 12, 1971, and they eventually received a charter forming a lodge of The Fraternal Order of Police. The housing authority officials were so impressed that we received several commendatory letters.

All of this new activity prompted the men to insist on being called policemen. We even got new badges and patches designating them as such. This also caused a change in the thinking of the tenants, who could no longer refer to them as "just guards." They were now full-fledged policemen.

At this point an interesting if not comical event took place. It seems that things were going so well that apparently someone within our department became envious and desired to cause trouble for me. In our attempt to have our men stand out in their uniforms, we permitted them to purchase special Ike jackets. They paid for them in advance with their own money.

Around mid-1973, the directors of management and personnel came to my office unannounced and demanded to audit my records on the jackets to ensure that the men had paid for them. I was both embarrassed and insulted by this, for I knew everything was in order. But the part that bothered me the most was that I had thought that I was well respected and trusted.

We went into my office, giving strict orders that we were not to be disturbed. Just as we were about to open the files, a clerk began knocking on the door continuously until I opened it with an unhappy expression on my face. The clerk apologized and said that Mayor Rizzo was on the telephone.

I picked up the receiver and began a very friendly conversation, including asking about each other's families. We talked for a good ten minutes. By the time we finished talking, the two directors had gathered up their effects and left.

They had obviously been intimidated by my friendly conversation with the mayor, for they did not get to see my records. I never heard any more about the audit.

Another sign of maturity of the housing police was that I was able to persuade the administration to buy us three jeeps for patrol supervisors, and for transporting men to their assignments when additional coverage was needed.

As a means of demonstrating our appreciation to Mayor Rizzo for his interest and the doors that he opened for us, I suggested that our men contribute to the Police Athletic League (PAL). We were able to raise $500. In order to get the most mileage out of it, I contacted the Mayor's office and made arrangements to bring a group of our men to his office to make the presentation.

On March 27, 1973, two city police buses took seventy of our men, led by Captain Harry Anderson and me in full uniform, to City Hall. We marched into the Mayor's office. Mayor Rizzo and PAL officials reviewed us and a number of speeches were made with an unending string of superlatives as we presented the check and posed for pictures.

Even though I had been retired from the police department for some time, I still remained an active member of the Guardians. In October of 1973, they invited me to attend the National Conference of Black Police Associations in Atlanta, Georgia. I attended as their guest, taking Vivienne with me. At their banquet, I was chosen as one of the ten men honored for "Outstanding Dedication Towards the Goals of National Black Police Associations." With that I was presented with a handsome silver bowl, mounted on a wooden pedestal that was appropriately inscribed. This was really a high point in my life to be so honored on a nationwide basis.

An important milestone in Housing Police operations was the installation of a citywide radio band to dispatch messages to our men with their walkie-talkies. We began operating on July 20, 1976, which enabled us to be in constant contact with our men, thereby expediting response to complaints and incidents. We were then considered the fourth largest police force in the state.

Another step toward professionalism was that we were able to enroll sixty-three of our men in classes in Criminal Justice at Temple University. The Housing Authority passed a resolution commending our men for their academic and professional interest.

As the year neared its end in 1980, I made the decision to retire. I had moved to New Jersey, and I had a problem fighting traffic to and from work. On December 29, 1980, I handed in my resignation. I had long looked forward to retirement, as I had so many things that I wanted to do, one of which was to do some writing.

My last day of work ended with my cleaning out my desk after five o'clock, and a long day's work on January 16, 1981. To celebrate, I took Vivienne, my sons, and their wives out to dinner. The celebration continued on January 19, 1981, when a small group of my friends had a luncheon for me at Pagano's Restaurant. On February 5, 1980, my extended family accompanied me to City Council Chambers where the Honorable Joseph E. Coleman presented me with a Councilmanic Commendation, sponsored by the Honorable John C. Anderson and co-sponsored by all of the other councilpersons.

The grandest celebration of all was held at the Penn Mutual Building on February 27, 1981. The Philadelphia Chapter of the National Association of Black Law Enforcement Executives sponsored it, with Retired Chief of County Detectives Gilbert Branche and Captain Harry Anderson of the Housing Police taking the most active part in presenting it. The list of speakers seemed to be the "who's who" in Philadelphia politics, police, fire, civic organizations, as well as many out-of-town police officials.

For the next few months I had mixed emotions as many of my friends and co-workers either stopped by or called to say that they were sorry about my leaving. Reflecting on my career, I remembered that the life of the black policemen has not always been a happy one. I had found this to be all too true when I first reported for duty at the old 33rd District only to have the sergeant take one look at me and say "My God, it gets worse." It was at this point that I began to question the wisdom of choosing law enforcement over the beautiful life I had as a student at Lincoln University.

Although I found police work very interesting, working conditions did not improve for me until I joined the Dick Anderson squad. It was there that I found more action and less stress. Working for a black supervisor made me far more determined to do good work, for I had the feeling that we were improving the lot of all black people. For years, there had been only one black supervisor in the police department, Robert Forgy, and he had not been permitted to wear a uniform. Within a dozen years of my joining the force, I was able to wear the uniform of a captain.

My eleven years with the housing police were a real joy. It was here that I finally had the feeling that I was on top. I had withstood a lot of pressure along the way, and I could look back on my many gains, and the gains of other blacks in the police department. I had the feeling that I had made a lot of the progressive changes happen, and that my career in law enforcement had been time well spent.

Compendium

Black police officers' struggle for equality within police departments has a legacy with attempts to not only increase their numbers, but also to strive for the highest ranks. Within five years of the appointment of the first black policeman in 1881, their number had increased to thirty-four, and a serious, but, unsuccessful effort had been mounted to obtain a promotion to the rank of district commander.

The loyalty of Black Americans has always been taken for granted. As a minority, blacks have aggressively fought for equal opportunity, within the laws of the land. They have served on the front lines in every war that America has been engaged in and have given a good account of themselves. This was particularly true during the Civil War when sixteen blacks were awarded The Congressional Medal of Honor. During any war, black citizens have been in the forefront of supporting America.

As for civil laws, most blacks, just like most whites, respect, obey and uphold the laws. Before and since the time that Richard Allen and James Forten organized a group of black men to defend Philadelphia in 1814, many blacks have wanted to be a part of public safety. After the Philadelphia Police Department was formally organized, every announcement of an impending entrance examination brought on an avalanche of black applicants. Yet, in practically every instance only a token few of them have been appointed, while many qualified and over-qualified black applicants were passed over.

When it came to promotions, the percentages were even worse. Even as I write this sentence, Philadelphia has one hundred and one white police captains but only seven black captains. Over the years, it has not been any secret that appointments and promotions in the police department have come about due to political expediency more than because of qualification or need. I would speculate that a survey of known dates of black appointments will reveal that the vast majority of them were made within the proximity of election days, beginning with the first appointment on August 6, 1881.

I have written about the "scratched" examination of 1940 that focused on the political aspect of feuding civil service commissioners. In spite of the public controversy surrounding that examination, it was not an isolated case. Suspicions continue to surface when examination results are known and many with good reasons. Further, gains not only were slow in the numbers of black policemen and ranking black officers, but integrating various squad and patrol cars proved to be even more difficult. Because the City of Philadelphia's administration was Republican from 1886 to 1952, with elections won by wide margins with white voters, politicians were less likely to court the black vote. To cull even the smallest crumbs from the Republican's table, blacks were compelled to register as Republicans.

With the national election of Franklin D. Roosevelt in 1932, as President of the United States, the Democratic Party began to rise in power as blacks gradually joined up. Having been totally disenchanted with the Republicans, blacks rallied to help elect Joseph S. Clark, a Democratic Party's mayor in 1952. Grateful for their support, the Democrats showed their appreciation and desire to retain the black vote by doing more for blacks. Blacks in the police department expected the Democrats to promote four blacks into the rank of sergeant. To their surprise, within a year, there were blacks promoted into every rank up to and including that of inspector.

Over the years, blacks have consistently proven that they are as intelligent, honest, loyal, brave and all-around qualified for police work as whites. In fact, many have been in the top percentiles of test scores. Very few ever have lost their jobs for being dishonest or failing to do their duty. Many have won awards and commendations for outstanding duty. Many baffling-crime cases have been solved by black policemen. Unfortunately, thirteen died in the line of duty.

While the plight of black public safety applicants and employees were moderately espoused by the news media and civic organizations, it wasn't until the birth of the Guardians within the police department and the Valiants within the fire department that the city administration began to take it seriously. Both organizations began with an emphasis on social events for their members. Within a short time, they realized their potential power and they began to utilize it to further the welfare of their members in the two departments. Networking, political contacts, news media, newsletters, and tutorial sessions, became their modus operandi. Each of those had some degree of success, but it wasn't until they threatened city officials with the use of demonstrations and finally, the courts, that they gained support for across the board fair treatment.

Another important aspect of the Guardians' activities, is an ongoing community relations program. Changing the perception and feelings of citizens toward police persons have worked through the Guardian's social programs such as, food programs for the needy and youth recreation programs. Their activities and participation in the historic Freedom March on Washington in 1963 was well publicized. Yet, not all the Guardians' do-the-right-thing positions have been accepted. The Fraternal Order of Police (FOP) bitterly denounced the Guardian's position against police overreaction in making arrests, and a deadly force strict policy—use of firing a weapon during an arrest.

The second half of the 20th Century has seen the use of police clerks and other civilian employees. Blacks have encountered few problems in getting those positions, possibly because of the low pay scale or because some white non-uniform person has fears about working in black neighborhoods. Definitely, integration is flourishing among police office workers, traffic enforcement officers, school crossing guards, police garage workers and truck operators. The upper ranks of the police department continue to have a few token blacks and they question their effectiveness. To equalize the ratio between the number of whites and minorities, the police department still has a long way to go.

Public housing organizations under the federal government have provided law enforcement careers for blacks and other minorities as part of police departments. Those organizations have many acres of buildings to protect and hundreds of tenants at the bottom of the socio-economic scale of society. But, the high number of blacks among the estimated 20,000 private patrol persons and security guards for private organizations, suggest many of them have been denied access to the police department for whatever reasons.

There has been an upsurge in the number of black state police persons during the past thirteen years. Affirmative Action programs and court-backed plans made it happen. Moreover, local, state and national long-established police organizations have shown a readiness to recognize and respect the concerns of black law enforcement persons through their representative organizations, such as, The National Black Police Association and The National Organization of Black Law Enforcement Executives. The Guardians are well known and respected by the public for its position on affirmative action that leads to a more representative police department of the community.

During former Mayor Frank L. Rizzo's administration (who is now deceased), the number of black police hires deceased while the number of blacks promoted into rank, increased. His administration was a bittersweet regime for blacks as compared with the empty promises of former Mayor William Green. Black police persons believed Bill Green would cause changes in their favor. When he was elected, they were overjoyed. He immediately appointed Harvey Crudup, a black deputy commissioner, highly respected by other blacks. Subsequently, his administration did nothing to help get blacks promoted throughout the ranks of the police department. There were always periodic meetings and public announcements of former Mayor Green's intentions.

When ranking black officers became eligible for retirement or the availability of well paying positions elsewhere, they gave up on breaking the "class ceiling" of the police department. From a high of eleven blacks as captain and above in 1979, the decline continued until it reached a low in 1981 of only three ranking positions with blacks, deputy commissioner, an inspector and captain. Weary of broken promises, on January 15, 1982, The Guardians boycotted Mayor Green's breakfast honoring Dr. Martin Luther King's birthday. The publicity shocked the administration and to save face, Mayor Green appointed a Task Force on Affirmative Action.

Their recommendations were disregarded by Mayor Green's Administration and it was business as usual in preventing blacks access to policy-making positions. The Philadelphia Inquirer, editorialized against his inaction; Congressman William Gray III held a congressional hearing; and the American Jewish Committee urged affirmative action for remedying discrimination.

Michael Churchill said, of the Public Interest Law center, "a need for some new procedure is obvious. Mayor Green issued an executive order that initiated the recruitment and training of minority applicants. Executive order 2-82, City of Philadelphia, for the first time in Philadelphia's history gave an opportunity to more blacks and Latinos to be recruited. More minority applicants than white applicants passed the police test.

When Mayor W. Wilson Goode, the first black mayor, took over the city government, he found himself with not only budget problems, but also with legal and civil service restraints that permitted very little in the way of affirmative action in the police department. The above has been recognized and reported in a detailed study of the Philadelphia Police by the 1987 Task Force.

Police Commissioner Gregore J. Sambor resigned after his leadership ability was seriously doubted after the police department's confrontation against the Move organization. Kevin Tucker, former FBI agent, and highly respected was appointed by Mayor Goode. He was a good law enforcement commissioner who made many appointments of bright officers. One of those appointments was Willie L. Williams, a career police officer who knew the system. Commissioner Tucker appointed the highly intelligent, ambitious black ranking police captain to inspector. He later rewarded him for his hard work as inspector with a promotion to deputy commissioner. After two and half years as police commissioner, Mr. Tucker took another position outside government.

On June 10, 1988, Mayor Goode appointed Deputy Commissioner Williams police commissioner. The right thing had finally happened. It was a real tribute to many men and women in the police department who had struggled for many decades to cause equality in the Philadelphia Police Department. Commissioner Willie Williams has proven himself to be a real public servant of law and order, and he is highly respected by many citizens.

BLACK POLICE TRAIL BLAZERS

Part I

It is a matter of record that blacks were appointed as turnkeys as early as the 1870s. On August 6, 1881, The Philadelphia Press reported that newly appointed black policeman, Louis W. Carroll, had been a turnkey at the 7th District Station House for four years. On the same day, *The Philadelphia Press* commended Mayor Samuel G. King for recognizing "the fitness of a Colored man for any position in the Department of Police (other) than that of turnkey in a station house."

First Appointed Black Policemen

The appointments of the first four black policemen occurred on August 5, 1881. It was surprising that Mayor King, a Democrat, made the appointments since most black voters at that time were Republicans. The appointments were widely reported in the press.

On August 6, 1881, *The Philadelphia Times* reported in a front page article: "Mayor King yesterday appointed four Colored men to his police force and early next week they will assume the club and shield and go forth to battle against crime and disorder. Whether they will figure wholly as peace preservers is a matter on which some affect to be doubtful. . .the members of the force are for the present dissatisfied at the innovation. The names of the men are Charles K. Draper, Alexander G. Davis, Louis W. Carroll and Richard Norton Caldwell. All appeared at the Mayor's office and, having filed the required papers and taken the required oaths, received orders for their uniforms."

The assignments were: Carroll and Davis, 5th District; and Draper and Caldwell, 19th District. Yet, at that time, all officers, as recruits, were designated as "substitutes" until there were openings as permanent policemen. Substitutes had

Black policemen in Philadelphia - 1900 (photo - courtesy of James E. Lee)

Police being interviewed for patrol car duty
L to R: (front row) Dr. John K. Rice, Assist. Dir. Public Safety, Herbert E. Millen, Esq., and James H. Malone, Dir. of Public Safety
(back row) Francis Moten, James Reid, Walter Wilmore, Ira Graham, Robert Fouche and Norman Tyree
(below) Tyree and Reid - October 14, 1940

Police Commissioner Thomas J. Gibbons swears in police captains
L to R: Austin Norris, Esq., Charles Baker, Rev. E. L. Cunningham, Rev. Marshall Shepherd, Thomas J. Gibbons, Det. Milton Smith, Councilman Raymond P. Alexander, Sgt. Frank L. Rizzo and Sgt. Joseph Downs - January 1952

to report daily. But, if all the regular men were on duty, the substitutes did not work nor were they paid for that day.

The Philadelphia Press also published an article on the same date, giving brief biographies of the four men: "Police Chief Samuel I. Givin administered the oath of the office to the four stalwart citizens of dark complexion. Richard N. Caldwell is very dark, 24 years old and resides at 1506 Carver Street. He is a native of Chester County, has always labored for a living when not engaged in the more seductive occupation of politics.

Charles K. Draper is 40 years old and lives at 920 Souder Street. He served three years and six months in the Navy during the war. . .He has been very active and influential in politics, is Secretary of Equal Rights Lodge, A.Y.M. and Captain General of St. Albans Commandry, Knights Templar.

Louis W. Carroll is 36 years old and weighs 158 pounds. He gave his residence as 711 Russell Street. Carroll previously had served as turnkey and, since his discharge as such, has been a coachman. He has been an active politician and is credited with efficient work for Mayor King in the recent municipal elections.

Alexander G. Davis is the only ex-slave. He was born in Germantown, N.C., thirty years ago. In color, he is a brightmulatto. Davis came north at the close of the rebellion and was educated at Lincoln University. After graduation he went south as a school teacher. He has recently lived at 415 S. Juniper Street.

The men all appeared intelligent, and Chief Givin remarked that the autographic handwriting of their applications were much above the average. Still, there are many disorderly persons left yet, and they may make the duty of the new men unpleasant for a while."

A Lieutenant Weir of the 5th District was quoted as saying, "Now that the promise has become performance I think the men are inclined to make less noise about it. At all events, I don't hear anything said, and those who don't like it have their choice, either to keep quiet or quit the force."

The black officers appointed immediately after the first four were: James H. Fray, June 18, 1882; John Williams, January 3, 1883; Lawrence Jackson, September 7, 1883; and David Truitt, James Davis, and Moses Wright, in the early 1880s as well. (Wright had been appointed a turnkey on September 7, 1880.) These blacks formed the nucleus of black officers who set the standards for others to follow: equality and efficiency in law enforcement in the City of Brotherly Love.

The number of black policemen on the Philadelphia force grew steadily as the black population increased. The U.S. Census reveals that, from the time of emancipation at the close of the Civil War, blacks migrated steadily from southern states to the North. Blacks were lured away from harsh treatment asshare-croppers in the South to less physically laborious domestic jobs in the North. The black population in Philadelphia in 1890 was 39,371, compared to 22,185 in 1860—a jump of 45 percent. Only 32% of the black population in 1890 were native-born Philadelphians; clearly, there had been an unprecedented, mass migration to the city.

Because of this influx of black residents, it is not surprising that the force of 34 black policemen dating back to Mayor King's administration had grown almost twofold, to a total of 62 by 1890. In 1854, the state legislature had set a standard of one policeman for every 600 citizens. The number of black policemen in 1890, in comparison to the number of black residents, nearly met that standard.

By 1913, the number of black officers again more than doubled, reaching a total of 124, almost all by political appointment. Ten years later, by 1923, the number again more than doubled. The total reached 268, which remained the record high for the next 35 years. Unfortunately, the number actually decreased to little more than 100 by 1950.

First Detective

George L. Williams had the unfortunate distinction of being the first black detective killed in the line of duty. Prior to joining the force, he was a catcher for the Cuban Giants baseball team. Williams was a good athlete, particularly known for being a heavy hitter.

At age 28, the Philadelphia native was appointed to the police bureau on February 18, 1892. He was assigned to the 19th Police District, then at 8th and Lombard Streets, at the center of the largest black community in the city. Williams resigned from the force on November 4, 1905, to go into private life. But he was reinstated on December 15, 1906, by Mayor John E. Reyburn, who had taken a great fancy to him. Williams was assigned to the North District, then at 23rd and Brown Streets. Amid much fanfare, he was promoted to the rank of detective on September 30, 1909, thereby becoming the City's first black detective. He worked out of the Detective Division in Room 111 in police headquarters, then located on the first floor of City Hall.

Often, it became necessary for him to receive assistance from personal friends in civilian life since he lacked police partners. Williams was well liked and well known for his daring exploits. Perhaps it was just those qualities that prompted him to single-handedly engage in a shoot-out with four men outside a taproom at 16th and South Streets on January 9, 1918. The four men, all with weapons, had been in an altercation with the bartender and had been ejected. When Williams attempted to apprehend Malcolm Trice, Samuel Coles intervened and without warning, drew his revolver and fired four shots—all which struck Williams at close range. Williams returned the fire, striking a man who was nicknamed "Planky." Williams was taken to Pennsylvania Hospital where he was pronounced dead. He was survived by a widow and five children.

The First Police Sergeant

Robert B. Forgy became a policeman on March 10, 1913. Not much is known of his early life, except that he was born in 1896, in South Carolina, and he was an avid hunter. On January 6, 1925, he became the first black promoted to corporal. He served well in that rank, despite the overt prejudices of the day. While serving as director of public safety, General Smedley Butler had created the rank of corporal. But when Butler left the position, the rank of corporal was abolished. Consequently, on May 1, 1928, Corporal Forgy reverted to the rank of patrolman. As some measure of consolation to him, he was assigned to plainclothes duty in the Homicide Division.

Forgy also was the first black to be promoted to the rank of sergeant, achieving this distinction on August 4, 1929. He was promoted by the Director of Public Safety, Lemeul B. Schofield, but he was not permitted to wear his stripes. Despite the promotion, he remained in the Homicide Division where he wore plainclothes. There were a few exceptions when he was given permission to wear his sergeant's uniform, as in the Elks' parade. As a rule, Elks' officials made special requests of the public safety director for parade permits and permission for Forgy to wear his uniform in the parade.

In the parade, Forgy usually headed a group of about a dozen black policemen, all were extremely proud to be marching down Broad Street, led by their one and only black sergeant. On August 26, 1941, the Elks held their annual conference in Atlantic City. Sergeant Forgy, in uniform, was chosen to lead his usual contingent of black Philadelphia police officers down Arctic Avenue—all marching as proud as peacocks. During an interview on July 18, 1939, Sergeant Forgy said that there were only 175 black patrolmen, six black detectives and one senior clerk in the Pawnbrokers Division. In 1932, Dick Anderson served for a few days as a provisional sergeant. Forgy remained the only ranking black officer until the Director of Public Safety, James J. Malone, appointed Anderson as an acting sergeant in 1943. It should be remembered that Sergeant Forgy and some other black policemen were pleased to be loaned horses to lead the Elks parade in 1944. Their heads were high as they rode horses to the applause of the predominantly black parade watchers.

Mayor Joseph S. Clark made Police Inspector Thomas J. Gibbons the new police commissioner. Gibbons had long shown that he was not only an honest man, but one dedicated to fairness in the assignment of black officers. Almost immediately, Gibbons transferred Sergeant Forgy to the 23rd District as a street sergeant in uniform. Though Sergeant Forgy was very pleased with his new assignment, at age 63 he found it difficult to climb in and out of squad cars. He chose Charles E. Marriott and James "Big Jim" Reid as his drivers. Sergeant Forgy died while in active service on March 31, 1953, just one month short of

40 years of service. Many believed that his irregular work hours precipitated his death.

Second Corporal

Charles T. Belgrove was appointed to the police bureau on August 9, 1906. He was well respected by his colleagues and he gained much-deserved recognition as an accomplished athlete. His tall, well-proportioned body was a delight to behold as he ran and won most of the track events he participated in. Then the police bureau had a physical fitness program that was very popular, both with the contestants and the public who came out in droves to see them.

On March 17, 1927, Director of Public Safety Butler appointed Belgrove a corporal, making him the second black corporal. But, like Corporal Forgy, Belgrove was reduced in rank to patrolman when the rank of corporal was abolished on May 1, 1928. He and Forgy were the only blacks to hold the rank during that period. Belgrove was consoled when he was assigned to plainclothes duty.

James N. Reaves, the author, has his own memories of being chased by Belgrove when he was 13 years of age. He had gone to the local barbershop to take a relative's list of numbers for an illegal lottery. When he saw Belgrove, he became frightened and he tried to hide the slips. Belgrove chased Reaves and he got his hands on the number slips, but did not arrest him because he and the barber were friends. Reaves learned his lesson, not to carry number slips.

Belgrove took the examination for detective and was promoted on April 1, 1930. He held that rank until June 30, 1945, when, due to political entanglements, he was demoted. Because of his ability as an investigator, he was assigned to the Special Investigation Squad under Sgt. Dick Anderson. As an old friend and co-worker, Anderson made sure Belgrove was treated well. Belgrove died while in service on April 16, 1946, just four months short of 40 years in the department.

First Motor Bandit Patrolman

Officer Robert E. Lee (1900-1944) was unable to trace his family lineage back to his namesake of Civil War fame, but he was proud of his uniform and devoted to his duties. Lee was born in Warrington, Virginia, on March 7, 1873. His family moved to Philadelphia in 1890, during the time of the great immigration of blacks from the South to the North after the Civil War. After working various jobs, he was appointed to the police department in 1900. Then, blacks worked mostly in domestic services, so to become one of 100 black policemen was quite an achievement.

Lee joined the force when police department transportation included bicycles and enclosed police vans known as, "Black Marias," with rear doors for prisoners' entrance and exit. It was perfectly acceptable to be assigned to ride a bicycle while on official duty. But when some of the more ambitious men began equipping their bikes with an attached motor, other policemen wanted to get into the act.

The Motor Bandit Patrol was born. Lee was the first black assigned to that unit, and he rode with the Patrol from the early 1920s to the mid-1930s. Being assigned to the Motor Bandit Patrol quickly made Lee famous in some parts of the black community. He married and became the father of seven children. He lived with his family in the Nicetown section of the City.

As a child, Roy Campanella, who later became a famous Brooklyn Dodgers' catcher, lived near the Lee family. The youngest son of Lee, Quentin, played baseball on the same community team with Campanella. Campanella wrote about Quentin in his biography, "It's Great To Be Alive" (Little-Brown Company, 1959, co-authored by Joe Reichler and Dave Comerer). Campanella said, "His daddy [Lee] was the first Negro policeman in Philadelphia to ride a motorcycle. I remember it was black with cream spokes. I can't tell you how proud we were of Officer Lee."

Quentin later became a city fireman, giving twenty years' service. Another son, James, served 20 years on the police force. The elder Lee served 41 years in the police department, many of them while assigned to the Motor Bandit Patrol, working out of the police station at 10th and Thompson Streets. He spent his last years in the police department as second grade patrolman, a rank which was discontinued in 1952. Then, it was the custom for elderly, sick and injured officers to be assigned as second grade patrolmen. They primarily remained around the police station and performed light chores, until retirement. Lee leisurely worked a foot beat in the 35th District before he retired. He died on May 15, 1962, at the age of 89.

Black Women in the Police Department

The term policewoman was the accepted appellation for that position in the early years. The term was also piggy-backed with the higher ranks such as policewoman sergeant, policewoman lieutenant, etc.

First Policewoman

Looks can be deceiving. At first glance, Rosa J. Satterwaithe looked like she might be employed in some less strenuous type of job, any position considered "women's work" in the 1930s. She was small of frame and of average height, and wore eyeglasses. Yet, her general demeanor belied the fact that she was indeed a law enforcement officer. She was one of the first women to join the Philadelphia force, and she was the first black policewoman.

Satterwaithe previously had been active in Republican politics in the 24th Ward in West Philadelphia. On March 2, 1936, because of her political activity, she was appointed a clerk in the Juvenile Division of Crime Prevention, the forerunner of the Juvenile Aid Division. While still working for the police bureau, she filed petitions to run for the state legislature in the Republican primaries. With much community support and little effort on her part, she won in the primary election on April 28, 1936. Finally, on August 31, 1936, she was sworn in as a permanent police officer.

But in the general election that fall, Satterwaithe was up against the rising popularity of the Democratic party, due to the well liked President Franklin D. Roosevelt. In spite of her spirited campaign, she lost the race. During the campaign, she had functioned simultaneously as a sworn policewoman. Those dual roles, politician and policewoman, ran counter to the thinking of some powerful political enemies. They managed to have her dismissed on December 31, 1936, only four months after joining the force.

Second Policewoman

The second black policewoman was Aleen B. Copper. She was provisionally appointed on January 1, 1943. Like Satterwaithe, she worked in plainclothes, and mainly with juveniles. Copper's tenure also was short. She died of natural causes on January 11, 1946.

First Policewoman Sergeant and Lieutenant

Annetta M. Sledge was a tall and statuesque no-nonsense lady who handled unruly culprits with ease. In that she was the only active black policewoman for a few years, she was in great demand by district captains to handle sensitive investigations involving both black and white suspects.

Sledge joined the police bureau on January 31, 1945. She was the third black policewoman on the force. She was assigned to the Crime Prevention Bureau, as were all other policewomen at that time. Although she was well educated and qualified for advancement, there were not any vacancies in the supervisory ranks. It took 13 years and numerous commendations before she was promoted to sergeant on January 6, 1958. As the first black female sergeant, she received wide publicity from black newspapers.

An upsurge in the number of blacks in the department and their upward mobility, coupled with her experience and capabilities, resulted in her promotion to lieutenant on August 11, 1967. Again, she had blazed the trail, as the first black female lieutenant. Sledge served the citizens of Philadelphia well for 24 years, until she retired on February 4, 1969.

"The Lady with Many Firsts"

In retrospect, it is difficult to imagine what the police department would have been like without Dorothy F. Cousins. "Dotty," as her close friends referred to her, accomplished so much and achieved more fame than any other female police officer in the history of the department - including Norma "Ma" Carson, the first policewoman, who served from 1936 to 1954. Cousins succeeded while remaining a lady at all times. Her co-workers said they never saw her get angry. Her five-foot, seven-inch frame was statuesque.

Cousins was reared as one of six children, who lived in the area around 20th and Dauphin Streets. After graduation from Girls High School in 1948, she worked at Sears and Roebuck and, later at the Philadelphia Navy Yard, before becoming one of the first women to be admitted to the Police Academy. Mayor Joseph S. Clark swore her in at the academy on April 25, 1955, with a mixed class of men and women.

James N. Reaves was her captain, and he said, "As her captain, I sent her and a policeman into a small hotel on Powelton Avenue, where they registered for a room for the night. Once in the room, they were to order drinks and, with this accomplished, identify themselves and raid the place. They managed to arrest 12 couples, who admitted they were not married to each other, plus the female proprietress. Cousins later said that, in spite of her initial fears, she enjoyed the experience, though she was appalled at the hotel activities."

Later, as a female member of the Juvenile Aid Division, she found that promotions came slowly. Finally, on August 11, 1967, she was promoted to the rank of sergeant. While remaining in Juvenile Aid, she was promoted to lieutenant on March 11, 1974.

Cousins' appointment to the rank of Juvenile Aid Captain on June 11, 1979, caused an unusual amount of excitement because she was the first black woman to be so honored. And, as if that wasn't enough, the excitement rose when she was appointed a police district captain. She was assigned to the Thirty Ninth District at 22nd Street and Hunting Park Avenue on December 22, 1980, filling what previously had been considered a man's job in the male-dominated police department. "I don't expect it to be easy," she said, "but I'm looking forward to the challenge. It's time a woman took command."

Police Commissioner Morton B. Solomon said, "This move is being made consistent with our policy that any woman can work anywhere in the Philadelphia Police Department." Other cities, such as Detroit, Chicago, New York and Washington, DC, already had female captains. In her new position, she supervised four lieutenants, eight sergeants, four corporals and 180 patrolmen. Her only complaint was that she had to wear the same type of uniform worn by the men.

On August 19, 1982, Cousins was promoted to the rank of staff inspector. On advancing to this rank, she scored a first for all women. A *Philadelphia Tribune* article stated, "The tempo of life has quickened for Cousins. . . but the apostrophes denoting trail blazing will hang forever after her name like a blue ribon." All the daily newspapers, as well as the broadcast media, carried stories on Cousins' promotion.

Also, her promotion made room for another black to ascend to a higher level. Harvey Crudup was promoted to captain at the same ceremony in which Cousins became staff inspector. Crudup was assigned to take over Cousins' former command at the 39th District. There are some police observers who said Cousins' promotion was a "kick upstairs," in order to remove her from her functions as a commanding officer.

Others, however, believed she was promoted by the administration because she was an excellent model to use, to demonstrate their equal rights position regarding female employees. It is possible that both opinions were correct. Yet, her promotion served to indicate the administration's commitment to upward mobility for blacks and women.

Following a short vacation, Cousins was anticipating going into retirement when she was appointed Chief of County Detectives on December 15, 1983, another first. She received so much public acclaim for her previous promotions that it was becoming old hat to her. But the fact remained that she had the distinguished honor of being the first female Chief of County Detectives. County detectives work as investigators for the district attorney. The majority are former city policemen and they sometimes work closely with the police department.

In January 1986, Cousins left the County Detectives office when the new Republican administration came into office. In March 1987, the Board of Directors of Philadelphia Housing Authority hired Cousins as overall head of PHA's security.

Cousins is an active member of St. Luke's Church on Germantown Avenue in Germantown. Cousins was the first female member of the local chapter of the National Organization of Black Law Enforcement Executives (NOBLE) when she joined in 1977. She served with distinction as a regional vice president from 1980 to 1981, for an area covering Pennsylvania, Delaware, Maryland and Washington, DC.

First Policewoman Detective Sergeant

Viola Mitchell is an achiever. She is constantly on the move. She became a police officer on July 15, 1968, and credits her success in passing the police test from her many years of struggling to get her high school diploma from Dobbins

High School. Mitchell received public attention when she became the first black female detective on February 26, 1979. She continued to prepare herself for further advancement. Her efforts paid off when she became the first female detective sergeant on December 15, 1980.

Besides her police work, Sergeant Mitchell has found time to serve in the Army Reserves. And, not surprisingly, she is a sergeant first class. Yet, she still doesn't allow herself to rest on her laurels. She currently is enrolled on a part-time basis at Saint Joseph's College in Philadelphia, where she is striving to earn a bachelor's degree. She said, simply, "I believe everyone should strive toward excellence in whatever he or she does."

By knowing Mitchell's character, it is not surprising that she was further promoted to the rank of lieutenant on September 13, 1984. Her promotion brought a feeling of reduced anguish to the other two black female sergeants who had despaired of any chance of promotion. Her latest assignment is with the Internal Affairs Division.

First Policewoman Wounded

In spite of her unfortunate distinction—as the first black policewoman wounded in the line of duty—Loretta Thomas was immensely proud of her achievements within the department. As a graduate of Overbrook High School in Philadelphia, she easily passed the police examination in 1978. At age 33, she was appointed to the department in 1979.

Initially, she was assigned to patrol car duty at the 23rd Police District at 17th Street and Montgomery Avenue. She generally worked alone, receiving a backup if she ran into problems. On December 16, 1980, Thomas responded to a "robbery in progress" call, and was the first officer to arrive on the scene at a check cashing agency and grocery store at 1521 N. 33rd Street. Upon her arrival, a pedestrian pointed to a fleeing man and said, "He's the one." Thomas chased him a short distance and pulled her car to a curb near the fleeing man. He turned and pointed a revolver at her, firing three shots, one of which struck her in the shoulder.

Another female officer arrived in time to get the description of the man and the license number of the car in which he escaped. The other officer called in the license number to police and transported Thomas to St. Joseph's Hospital. She was admitted in serious condition, and doctors operated to remove the bullet which was lodged just a few inches from her spine.

Two suspects were arrested at different locations, after a shoot-out with police. The gun and more than $1,000 in cash were recovered. Robert Smallwood and Theodore Harris were indicted and sent to court. Both were found guilty and given long prison terms.

Officer Thomas returned to limited duty on April 29, 1981. However, her recovery was slow and long. Although she attempted to perform limited duty, the excruciating pain from her wounds prohibited it. Finally, it became apparent that these injuries would preclude her from continuing an active police career. On January 16, 1986, with the help of the Fraternal Order of Police, she was placed on a permanent disability pension. Thomas now devotes her life to her teenage daughter who is approaching high school graduation.

First Assistant Director of Public Safety

In October 1986, a magnificent portrait of Herbert E. Millen was unveiled at City Hall. The Barristers' Association, a black lawyers' organization, had raised the funds to commission Powelton Village artist Rebecca Rose to complete the Millen portrait, which pays tribute to his many accomplishments.

Herbert E. Millen was born and grew up near Stroudsburg, near Lancaster County, Pennsylvania. When his family moved to Philadelphia, he enrolled at Lincoln University, where he graduated in 1910. He worked at the post office while a student at the University of Pennsylvania Law School. After passing the bar examination, he opened his law practice in South Philadelphia. Millen became active in community affairs and received an appointment as a special deputy attorney general for the State of Pennsylvania.

He also advanced quickly as a member of the Masonic Order, eventually becoming the Most Worshipful Grand Master of the Pennsylvania Masons. As an active member of the Republican Party, Millen sought its endorsement for a judgeship in the late 1930s and early 1940s. He was refused with the hackneyed expression, so commonly heard by black men, "The time is not right yet." He decided to run independently, after being refused the Republican endorsement for the state primaries, in May 1939. Though he didn't win, he gave a good accounting of himself at the polls.

The Democrats, headed by John B. Kelly, Sr., had come very close to winning the mayoralty in 1939. Blacks were attracted to Kelly in large part because he had the temerity to have his black private chauffeur commissioned as a state policeman, wearing a state police badge and uniform. His assignment was to continue to work as a chauffeur for Kelly, and to be his bodyguard. Many years later, some white policemen still were angry towards Kelly because of his chauffeur's state police appointment. Some felt Kelly had lost more white votes than he gained black votes.

Republican Mayor Robert E. Lamberton, placated blacks with his appointment of Millen as the first black Assistant Director of Public Safety on March 4, 1940. James H. "Shooey" Malone was Director of Public Safety, which involved both the police and fire departments. The political strategy involved in Millen's appointment was hailed by blacks as a big step for racial justice. Nevertheless, it left a lot to be desired since there was no black above the rank of sergeant, and there were no black police assigned to eleven police units: Accident Investigation, Foot Traffic, Harbor Patrol, Motor Bandit Patrol, Mounted Patrol, Operations Room Duty, Uniformly Marked Patrol Cars (Red Cars), Police Sanitation Squad, Police Garage, Police Academy and Vice Squad.

The one and only unit that had blacks in it was the Crime Prevention Bureau, the previous designation for the Juvenile Aid Division, and that was because Captain Thomas J. Gibbons, Sr. insisted on it. All other blacks were assigned to uniformed, foot patrols in the districts. In light of events of later years, it is almost inconceivable that police commanders could even pretend to suppress vice and crime conditions without utilizing the services of black plainclothesmen. This was all the more absurd when one considers the truism circulated at the time. "In spite of his lofty position, Assistant Director Millen would not even be permitted to direct traffic at Broad and South Streets. After all, The time was not right yet."

For the most part, during his tenure, Assistant Director Millen was low-key and he did not make too many waves. There were only a few times that Director Malone left the City, leaving Assistant Director Millen in charge. In other words, he could neither change existing policies nor could he establish new ones. His low-key methods were accepted as a proper means of making racial progress at the time, however slowly.

But Millen finally grew weary of his restricted role and resigned in June 1946. On June 8, 1946, *The Pittsburgh Courier* reported that he resigned "because the Republican Party refused to slate either him or any other black for the municipal judgeship vacancy." It termed Millen's resignation "the most courageous political action by a Negro politician in twenty years."

Eventually, because of pressure by blacks, Millen was appointed the first black judge by Governor James H. Duff. The announcement of his appointment was made at the *Philadelphia Tribune* Charities' Cavalcade of Music at Convention Hall on November 1, 1947. *The Philadelphia Tribune* hailed the appointment as a victory that it gladly celebrated since the newspaper had long campaigned for "a colored judge." Millen had an excellent record during his 12 years on the bench. Without a doubt, his expertise and deportment blazed the trail for many other blacks to wear the robe.

He died of a heart attack on July 26, 1959. He oftentimes had been upset, as a judge in juvenile court, as he witnessed the varied problems of the city's black youth. Some observers believe his compassion for poor black youth broke his heart.

First Aide to the Assistant Director

Hillary Johnston was one of the first black detectives in the City. When Millen became the assistant director of public safety on March 4, 1940, he chose

Johnston as his aide, making him the most powerful policeman in the department. Johnston had long dreamed of being a ranking police officer and now, in his new assignment, he felt secure in the thought that he would make it. But as luck would have it, Johnston never quite succeeded.

He was born June 19, 1890, in Chambersburg, Pennsylvania, the son of an Indian scout with the United States Army who had been killed in the service. Johnston attended schools for orphans in upstate Pennsylvania. He joined the Army and was sent to Officers Candidate School during World War I and became a lieutenant. After his discharge from the service, he joined the police bureau in Philadelphia in 1919. He worked mostly as a plainclothesman, and was appointed a detective in 1926. His son, J. Willard Johnston, was appointed to the police department on October 31, 1942. After a long stint as a plainclothesman, he was promoted to the rank of detective on January 1, 1953. Most of his time as a detective, he spent in the Homicide Division. He retired on June 10, 1964.

When interviewed about his father in 1983, Willard Johnston said, "Dad took the captain's examination three times and was ranked 7, 11, and 14, respectively, on the Civil Service lists. But, the time was not right. He was eligible on the promotion list, but they passed him up twice without a reason. On the third time, the Republicans who were in power pulled a deal with Negro leaders to keep from appointing him. They offered a middle-level administrative position of assistant recorder of deeds to the Negroes in exchange for not making my dad a captain. The Negroes, thinking that Negroes in Philadelphia would be better off with a man in a position to give many jobs rather than the one captain's job. The Negro leadership accepted the offer and Ernest 'Daddy' Wright, the leader of the 14th Ward, got the position." Consequently, Hillary Johnston was not promoted.

He remained as Millen's aide until the administration changed. He went back to the Detective Division, retiring in 1952. He later moved to Honolulu in the Hawaiian Islands to be near his older son, Hillary Jr. He died there on April 29, 1972, and was buried in the National Cemetery.

Second Assistant Director

A long-standing peculiarity in politics is that once a black person is assigned to a job, it continues to be a "black job" from then on. Consequently, after the resignation of Millen from his post as Assistant Director of Public Safety, the position went to another black man, Robert J. Nelson, who was sworn in on June 13, 1946. He was a former resident of Reading, Pennsylvania, and was well known statewide as a former member of the State Athletic Commission, on which he served from 1932-1935. In private life, he was a real estate broker, with a successful business in West Philadelphia. Like his predecessor, Nelson made no waves, but the records show that more blacks were taken into the police and fire departments during his tenure than during the previous fifteen years. This fact alone is a real accomplishment of his administration.

During Nelson's term as assistant director of public safety, Fire Marshall George J. Gallagher was suspended due to a probe of the fire marshall's office. Nelson took over active command of the fire marshall's office during the probe. But Nelson suffered a heart attack at home on February 3, 1949. He was taken to Philadelphia General Hospital, where he died twelve hours after being admitted, at the age of sixty-three.

Third Assistant Director

Political expediency prompted the appointment of Fredrick W. Matheas as the next Assistant Director of Public Safety. When Nelson died in office on February 3, 1949, it was generally expected that a black would succeed him since the precedent had been set, making the assistant directorship a "black job". The only unanswered questions in the black community were, who and when?

The most politically expedient time to make the appointment would be at a time close enough to election day to appease the black electorate and thereby gain their votes. Almost 10 months after the position was vacated, Mayor Bernard Samuels appointed Matheas to the position on October 24, 1949. The 67-year-old appointee previously had been the assistant superintendent of the Water Department's distribution of water. Matheas was a native of Bangor, Maine, who came to Philadelphia in 1910. He held a civil engineering degree from the University of Maine.

By 1912, he had advanced to the position of foreman of repairs in the Water Department. On January 1, 1922, he was promoted to a position previously unheard of for a black, the general foremanship. It took him another 25 years to receive his next promotion, assistant superintendent of distribution of water, on July 16, 1947.

Blacks were not overly joyful about the appointment of Matheas as Assistant Director of Public Safety because his previous position at the Water Department was not filled by another black. Yet Matheas served two years before resigning on December 31, 1951, just prior to the installation of the members of the new Democratic administration.

BLACK POLICE TRAIL BLAZERS

Part II

First Police Surgeon

While police surgeons are not police officers, they are being included here because, as professionals, they are given much respect and have a certain amount of input in policy-making decisions in the police department. Dr. John P. Turner was born in Raleigh, NC, and earned his medical degree from Shaw University. After moving to Philadelphia, he became active in both medical and civic affairs. In 1912, at the age of 27, he became a medical inspector for the public schools at $600 a year. On September 1, 1931, he was appointed the first black police surgeon in the police bureau. He held this position for 20 years, resigning on November 1, 1951.

Dr. Turner was widely known for his accomplishments, the most notable of which was becoming the first black member of the Board of Education in 1935. He also served on at least a dozen other boards of medical and civic groups. He died September 14, 1958. The Board of Education named the Turner Middle School in his honor.

Dr. Charles W. Maxwell came into the police bureau by way of provisional appointment during the heart of the depression era, on September 19, 1936. At that time, the police bureau was not hiring anyone. However, as a surgeon, he was sorely needed and the black community was overjoyed about such an important appointment. Mayor S. Davis Wilson and Director of Public Safety Andrew Emmanuel swore him in as the second black police surgeon in the city's history.

Doctors Maxwell and Turner were two of the 12 surgeons in the department. Although considered adequate at the time, the $2,200 salary seems almost like automobile allowance, compared to the present economy. When examinations were finally given later in 1936 for the position of police surgeon, Dr. Maxwell scored too low to be reached on the list for the few available positions. He left the police bureau on December 18, 1936.

First Black Police Entry Into Other Police Units

Being assigned to foot traffic duty never has been highly desired by police, based on the merits of the duty alone. Therefore, there was no rush on the part of black police to transfer into it. The compelling decision to accept that assignment usually is reached after a consideration of the benefits accrued.

On the negative side, there are several things to consider. The exposure to all types of weather conditions, and the constant danger of being injured or even killed by passing motor vehicles. There also are long periods of time on one corner or at some other site, restricting the freedom of movement enjoyed by police on normal patrol duty. On the positive side, however, are several other things to consider. The certainty of a steady tour of duty that enables the officer to obtain a second job or enroll in school.

Further, the opportunity to make close friends with people near the police officer's post, such as community leaders. The opportunity for regular eating and sleeping hours, plus time with families during those prime evening hours, are paramount. Nearly all policemen do traffic duty at one time or another, but mostly during school hours when children are going to and from the school buildings.

John King was the first black assigned to regular traffic duty in the early 1940s at 5th and Spring Garden Streets. King was a district policeman, and wasn't in the traffic division. He had daytime duty operating the old manual semaphore, that had signs designating "stop" and "go." "Kingie," as he was known, was proud of his work, since he thought of it as a milestone for black advancement in the police bureau. He even requested, and was given, permission to purchase a white hat, the same as those worn by the regular foot traffic police. The fact that "Kingie" towered over six feet tall and was a deep brown color made him a real standout in that white hat.

Permanent Foot Traffic Police

Police Superintendent Howard P. Sutton initiated the movement of blacks into regular traffic duty in 1948. He instructed Dick Anderson of the Special Investigation Squad to recommend two of his men to the Traffic Division. Anderson chose Policemen Mack Goffney and James Mobley, Sr. The determining factor in their selection was that both men were over six feet tall.

Mobley lasted only a couple of weeks because of his recurring back problems. Goffney remained until 1951, at which time other blacks were being routinely assigned to traffic duty. Goffney transferred into the Juvenile Aid Division. He later explained, "I was getting too old to stand around on those corners all day." In the Juvenile Aid Division, Goffney teamed up with Samuel Wyche and Sergeant James N. Reaves to form the first Gang Control Unit.

Police Accident Investigator

John W. Thomas was a fine, enthusiastic police officer. He graduated from Overbrook High School in 1934. After leaving school, he taught himself touch typing as a means of self-improvement. This later proved to be extremely beneficial in his quest to be assigned to the Police Accident Investigation Division. On October 3, 1950, he succeeded in obtaining this appointment, making him the first black officer in the Accident Investigation Division.

Thomas had joined the police force in October 1943 and was assigned to the old 14th Police District at 28th and Oxford Streets. After only a few months, he was transferred to the Vice Squad. In early 1945, he was reassigned to the 23rd District, on foot patrol. Thomas had long wanted to work in the Accident Investigation Division and sought political help in attaining this goal. After receiving many promises but no results, he became very critical of the black politicians, who had failed to assist him.

Finally, he decided to request a transfer by going directly to Assistant Superintendent Herbert Kitchenman and, two weeks later, he received the transfer. The men he worked with took a liking to him and were very helpful in getting him orientated. He became so efficient that in 1958 he was given a specialized job of following up on, and clearing, difficult hit-and-run cases. He remained in that position until he became disabled in 1962, when he went on light duty—paperwork and errands for the station house. Thomas continued at light duty until 1965, when he retired with full disability benefits.

First Top of Police List

An unprecedented event took place in Philadelphia's municipal government in the spring of 1953. A black person ranked number one on a civil service examination, and it was for a police officer's position. The event sent shock waves throughout City Hall, where some persons made their opinions ring out loud and clear. "The sky must be falling," said some. And others: "Surely the administration must be off its rocker."

But in more hushed tones, it was rumored that the Reverend E. Luther Cunningham, the new and first black civil service commissioner, had given test answers to black applicants. This rumor was made more tenable when an arrest took place involving a man who was alleged to have sold answers to commercial civil service examinations tutors.

Commissioner Cunningham heard the rumblings and became very uneasy.

At first, he ordered the Personnel Director, Frank J. Escobedo, to retest the first ten men on the list. But later, when faced with the fact that the retesting of ten men might cause undue anxiety and lead to a court fight, Cunningham settled for the retesting of the black man who was number one. Jerome Banks was not ordered to retake the test, but rather he was requested to do so in order to clear up any suspicions regarding Commissioner Cunningham or himself.

Cunningham's efforts were designed to prevent having the test decertified. Banks readily agreed to cooperate because he was anxious for the police appointment and he wanted to preserve the original list of successful applicants. Upon reporting to the Philadelphia Civil Service Commission, Banks immediately was escorted to the seventh floor. There he was met by six or seven people who took him to a secluded room. Banks must have felt as if he was being exiled to the Tower of London.

The second examination was exactly like the first 180-question test, except that all the questions were rearranged numerically. Banks did not find the second test difficult, though he disliked being watched as he filled in his answers. A few days later, the list of successful candidates was published. Banks was indeed, number one. He scored 99.81. On July 20, 1953, a large group of candidates along with Banks were administered the oath of office as police.

Although Banks was promoted to detective in January 1956, the black community was disappointed because he did not advance further in the police department. On December 4, 1963, he was injured in the line of duty and eventually was forced out of the department against his wish to remain a policeman. He received a disability pension.

First Provisional Appointments

John R.T. Roane was a highly energetic man who was always very solicitous of other people's problems. Among his co-workers, he was well known for his ability to do effective report writing. This ability probably was an important factor in his becoming the first black provisional police lieutenant.

Roane was born in Philadelphia on December 10, 1913. He was appointed a policeman on October 31, 1942. Upon completion of his training at the Police Academy, he served a short stint on uniformed patrol, a job he disliked. When he heard that Dick Anderson's Special Investigation Squad was to be formed, he immediately applied and was accepted. He spent most of the time working in the office. But he was soon recommended by Anderson to become a sub-operator, to work in the office of the police station a position that was certified and highly respected by the administration. Within a short time, he received the new classification by the administration, thereby becoming the first black to receive such an assignment.

When Police Commissioner Thomas J. Gibbons disbanded the SIS, Roane was transferred to the 16th District as a provisional street sergeant on February 2, 1952. Yet, he received no increase in salary, though he was assigned to command a shift of uniformed officers. When his captain discovered his ability to do paperwork, he was assigned to the district operations room. He was so efficient that on January 1, 1953, he was made a provisional lieutenant with an increase in pay to $4,900.

Unfortunately, Roane did not score highly enough on the lieutenant's examination list to be able to receive a permanent promotion. On December 24, 1953, when new promotions were made from the list, Roane was reassigned to his permanent rank of patrolman. After only a short period of time, he rejoined the SIS which had been reestablished under Captain Clarence Ferguson. Roane remained in the squad until his retirement on September 18, 1965. He then took a position as a nonteaching assistant with the Philadelphia School District. He served well in that position, primarily at Furness Junior High School, where he was well liked and respected. After a long illness, Roane died on November 27, 1972.

Milton S. Smith was an excellent student, yet he had to leave Central High School to take a job and help out with family expenses. His first job was as an elevator operator in 1916. Because he wanted more physically demanding work, he next took a job as freight loader at Franklin Sugar Refinery. Smith became a policeman on August 15, 1922, with an admitted assist from a Republican politican, Charlie Hall, for whom his mother worked as a maid. He became a plainclothesman on January 1, 1924.

On April 1, 1930, he was promoted to the rank of detective. As such, he joined a small but elite group of black detectives. He was assigned to the pickpocket squad and had the reputation in the community as being one of the best detectives in the department. From time to time, he had been assigned to be a bodyguard for heavyweight champion, Joe Louis, and Dr. Martin Luther King, Jr.

Smith was well liked by Commissioner Gibbons, who had been appointed to his position by the newly elected Democratic administration. It was generally believed that Gibbons would appoint a black captain early in his administration. Many detectives' names were bandied about as possible candidates, including Hillary Johnston, Cecil Joyner, Firman Hopkins and Clayton Brown. Considered also was Robert Forgy, whom Gibbons had transferred to uniformed duty as a street sergeant.

But, on January 16, 1952, Gibbons appointed Smith as the first black captain in the city's history. Smith was sworn in by Managing Director Robert K. Sawyer. Present to witness the ceremony were Civil Service Commissioner E. Luther Cunningham, Councilman Raymond Pace Alexander, Commissioner of Records Marshall L. Shepard, Sr., and Deputy of Records Charles Baker, and Attorney Austin Norris. The black newspapers had a field day over the appointment of the first black captain. Further proof that Gibbons liked Smith is the fact that he gave Smith his own uniform with captain's bars to wear. Ultimately, Smith gave this same uniform and bars to James N. Reaves in 1954 when he replaced him as the first black captain under civil service.

Smith's appointment greatly satisfied the black community and caused extremely high jubilation among aspiring black police. It appeared that the new administration had given a signal, that it would keep its word and promote black police. Smith was assigned to the 23rd Police District at 19th and Oxford Streets. Since he had no previous experience as a police supervisor, he made his way cautiously. He made no waves. Some of his black officers were critical of him for not being more firm in making decisions that would benefit them. But this same type of criticism has been leveled at many succeeding black supervisors.

Smith's command did not last long as enormous changes were taking place in the city's administration. Under the Republican administration, which went out of office in 1952, very few official promotions were made. The Republicans preferred to make "acting" or "provisional" appointments so they could have tighter control over the ranking officers. Therefore, when the Democrats took over in 1952, they found hundreds of "acting" ranking officers. Officials of the Fraternal Order of Police persuaded the new administration to hold open examinations for the five lower ranks of sergeant, lieutenant, captain, staff inspector and inspector. Any policeman could take any or all of the examinations.

A new city charter took effect in 1952, mandating permanent promotions from civil service lists. Consequently, an examination for the captain's position was held in 1953. Since Smith had only been appointed provisionally, he was required to take the test for a permanent promotion. Smith, however, refused to take the examination and appealed in vain to Commissioner Gibbons to have him exempted from it. To make way for the new captains, Smith was returned to his previous rank of detective on February 5, 1954. He decided against going back to work as a detective and took a leave of absence until he retired on March 10, 1954. Perhaps a note to Dr. Robert Chapman, Ph.D., indicated Smith's real feelings. "Resigned to go on pension, my mistake."

After his retirement, Smith got involved in politics and became a Republican committeeman in the 59th Ward. His constituents were so pleased with his performance that six Democratic legislators joined the Republicans in honoring Smith with a State of Pennsylvania Citation. He died on March 26, 1967, and he left a substantial amount of scholarship money in his will for needy students from the First African Baptist Church.

First Deputy Inspector

After two weeks of training as lieutenants—only halfway through the course— Ballard and Payne were again promoted, this time to the rank of deputy inspector. Although both men were on the captain's list, they waived their rights to that rank, precluding their becoming the first black captains under Civil Service. Their promotions were the talk of the black community, for this was far more than blacks had expected from the administration. But blacks should not have been so surprised since the Rev. E. Luther Cunningham, the first black Civil Service Commissioner, had promised that all appointments would be made on the basis of merit. In time, it was apparent that these men were eminently qualified for their new positions.

First Four Sergeants Appointed

The next appointments were made on January 6, 1954, when Leonard Jones, William Lindsay, Frank Winfrey and James N. Reaves were promoted to the rank of sergeant. This was further proof that the administration of Mayor Clark and District Attorney Richardson Dilworth was living up to its commitment to deal fairly with everyone in the police administration, black promotions were made intermittently and taken for granted. Oftentimes, news of promotions created such little interest that it did not even reach the press.

First Lieutenant In Detective Bureau

Leonard T. Jones was dubbed affectionately by his men, "the Little Colonel." He was a strict disciplinarian yet this did not minimize his character for it was generally recognized that he ran an efficient and effective squad. Jones was born in Camden, New Jersey, but he was raised in Philadelphia where he graduated from West Philadelphia High School in 1931. He holds a degree in liberal arts, with a concentration in criminal justice courses, from Thomas Edison State College in Princeton. He also has a certificate in Security from Villa Nova University as well as one in State and Local Government from the University of Pennsylvania.

Jones joined the police force on October 1, 1942. Upon completion of training at the Police Academy, he was assigned to plainclothes duty. He worked with the U.S. Army and Navy Disease Control Units from 1942 to 1946. After those assignments, he was reassigned to the 16th Police District until 1950, when he was borrowed by the U.S. Treasury Department to work in the Narcotics Bureau. On February 1, 1951, he returned to the police bureau and was assigned to the Special Investigation Squad.

With all his drive, education and experience, he could not be held down for long in any one rank. Therefore, on January 6, 1954, he was promoted to sergeant. He was assigned to the Homicide Division, becoming the second black of that rank in the Detective Bureau. Two months later, on March 9, 1954, he was promoted to lieutenant and remained in the detective division.

Shortly after James N. Reaves became a captain in the 16th District in October

1954, Lieutenant Jones was transferred there at the request of a group of black politicians who wanted to see more blacks in command positions in uniform. Although Jones resented this move at first, he made the most of it.

Jones retired honorably from the department in 1968. He immediately went to work for the School District of Philadelphia, in its Internal Security Unit. He specialized as a training officer until he retired in 1978.

As a member of the Masonic Order, Jones served in a number of offices. While he was a lieutenant, he became aware of a number of policemen who were Masons and had problems attending meetings because of chainging work shifts. He called together a group of them and discussed the possibility of forming a Masonic Lodge primarily consisting of policemen. After a series of meetings with these officers, they organized the Herbert E. Millen Lodge 151. The lodge name honored the first black assistant director of public safety who had served as head of the Pennsylvania State Grand Lodge of Masons. Lodge 151 was granted a charter by the State Lodge in November 1961, with Jones serving as Most Worshipful Grand Master for two years.

First Staff Inspector

Edward M. Payne came closer to being the first black police commissioner in 1966 than any other black aspirant up to that time. He managed to become the second runner-up for the position of Philadelphia's police commissioner. Payne was born in Mississippi on May 27, 1911. While still a child, his parents migrated to Philadelphia and he graduated from West Philadelphia High School in 1930. Because of the Depression, jobs were hard to come by so he applied for entry to all branches of the military service. The Army replied that they had only one unit for blacks, a cavalry unit stationed in Texas with an extremely long list of applicants, so it was doubtful his application could be acted upon in the foreseeable future.

The Navy said they used blacks only as food handlers in the galley and they already had more applicants than openings. While the Marines never bothered to respond, the most disconcerting response came from the Coast Guard. They said they did not use blacks at all and it was doubtful they ever would.

Payne worked as an elevator operator at a time when it was considered a high-class job for blacks. He next worked at the Philadelphia Post Office as a substitute. His interest in volunteer work with juveniles led him to part-time and, later, full-time work through the W.P.A. with the Wissahickon, Wilmot and Benezet boys clubs. During this time, Payne also received assignments as a boxing referee, becoming the first black in the state to hold a referee's license. He had been appointed a referee by State Athletic Commissioner Robert Nelson, one of the first blacks in that position.

Payne was appointed to the police force on November 15, 1940. After Police

Academy training, he was assigned to the old 38th District, currently the 18th District. But Payne made such a striking figure in uniform—six feet, two inches in height with broad shoulders—that Captain Henry Brown had him transferred to the district in which he commanded, the old 1st District at 20th and Fitzwater Streets.

After about two years in uniform, Payne was transferred to plainclothes duty in the Crime Prevention Bureau, the forerunner of the Juvenile Aid Division, located at Quince and Pine streets. While in that unit, he teamed up from time to time with Thomas Chisholm, John Cury, Charleroi Gray, Clarence F. Jones, William "Puny" Norman, John S. Smith, Horace White, John Reid and James N. Reaves.

As a result of a disagreement between Payne and police authorities about departmental policies, he was transferred to Dick Anderson's Special Investigation Squad in 1950. Because of his educational background and investigative police experiences, he was assigned to desk duties. He remained in the unit for one year.

During his years in the Crime Prevention Division, Payne took numerous criminal justice and traffic courses at various colleges and universities. His interest and credentials were so impressive that he was transferred from the SIS to the Philadelphia Police Academy in 1951 as an instructor with the rank of acting sergeant. He was the first black officer assigned to the academy as an instructor on a permanent basis.

On January 1, 1953, he was promoted to the rank of Police Academy Training Instructor, becoming the first black promoted to that rank. He proved to be so proficient in his assignment that he was instructing men of all ranks up to, and including, inspector.

When the open examinations were held in 1953, Payne took them for all five ranks. When the promotions were made, he was among the first four black lieutenants, along with Ballard, Edwards and Jones, to be appointed. After some in-service training as lieutenants at the Police Academy, he and Ballard were called to City Hall and sworn in as deputy inspectors (later renamed "staff inspectors") on January 7, 1954. These promotions—along with the promotions on the previous day of the four black sergeants, Jones, Lindsay, Winfrey and myself—were the real signal that the administration meant to keep its word concerning the upgrading of black police.

As a deputy inspector, Payne immediately went to work specializing in community relations. He organized a program that involved community meetings that were held in schools and recreation centers at which the top commanding officers and community leaders discussed community problems. He also participated in organizing a program known as "Clergy Briefing." He invited members of the clergy to the Police Administration Building for discussions on community problems and provided tours of the building on Friday nights. After some of these meetings, the clergy also would be invited to tour various police districts. When they accepted, they rode with the senior ranking officer in a patrol car in the district.

In September 1956, Payne and Reaves attended the conference of the International Association of Police Chiefs, held in Chicago. They were the only black members in attendance and the first black ranking officers in attendance in the thirty-one year history of that organization.

On November 10, 1956, Payne took a leave of absence to go to Liberia with his wife, Mildred, to assist in reorganizing and training that country's National Police Force. This was under the auspices of the U.S. State Department. In December 1957, he received an additional leave to complete his work in Liberia, returning home November 10, 1958. On resuming his duties in Philadelphia, he was assigned as a relief inspector of uniformed forces in various police divisions.

On July 31, 1962, Payne, one of the most highly respected and well-liked officials in the department, retired. He returned to the State Department for a two-year stint as a Police Training Specialist. His next assignment was in Washington, D.C., training new foreign service employees for overseas duty. His last two-year stint was spent in Recife, Brazil. He retired from the state Department in 1966 and returned home.

In the spring of 1966, Mayor James H.J. Tate convened a panel to select a new police commissioner to replace Howard R. Leary, who resigned to become police commissioner of New York City. Payne put in his application for the position. Although the search was nationwide, the black community was very hopeful. There were two blacks on the selection panel, Judge Thomas Reed and Robert Williams, who later became a judge. The selection process narrowed the choices down to four men: Bernard Germeier, police chief of Tucson, Arizona; Acting Commissioner Edward J. Bell; Staff Inspector Millard T. Meers, and Payne. On April 30, 1966, the panel announced that Germeier was its first choice, but he declined the appointment. The committee next recommended Commissioner Bell and he, of course, accepted. That is how close Philadelphia came to having a its first black police commissioner in 1966.

Because he was not ready for full retirement, Payne accepted a position with the American Red Cross. He became a paid executive in charge of Disaster Services. His duties were to organize programs and volunteers to assist victims of disasters. He served faithfully and well until he died of natural causes on January 17, 1970.

First Inspector and Chief Inspector

Allan B. Ballard, a native of Greenville, South Carolina, was appointed to the police force on May 16, 1941. He had graduated from Virginia Union

University and was a teacher in the public school system of Bluefield, West Virginia, for a short time. He supplemented his meager salary by playing the trombone and trumpet with a small combo. On his return to Philadelphia, he tried his hand at being a salesman. Finding he did not like that type of work, he accepted a position as the assistant to the executive director of the Wissahickon Boys Club. He served well in that capacity until he joined the police force.

The first ten years for Ballard's police career were spent as an undercover man for the vice squad. He worked in partnership with Policeman Herbert Higgenbothem. They gathered intelligence for the vice squad to make arrests. Because of their covert assignment, few people knew that they were policemen. They reported directly to their commanding officer.

Many times they were "arrested" and brought in along with a group being raided, only to have their superior officer slip them out the back door of the station house. This worked well until, one day, things became a bit sticky when one of the men arrested complained that Ballard and Higgenbothem were the only ones being released. Consequently, the undercover men had to go before the magistrate. Needless to say, they were discharged. Ballard often told the story of the time that a raiding policeman, thinking he really was a bum, began beating him with a blackjack. He ran to Captain Craig Ellis to be rescued.

When Commissioner Thomas J. Gibbons took command of the police department in 1952, one of his first administrative actions was to disband the vice squad. All of the members of the squad were returned to uniformed duty except Ballard. He had such an unblemished record that Commissioner Gibbons transferred him to the Juvenile Aid Division. It was here that he was provisionally made a plainclothes sergeant with a pay increase on January 1, 1953.

As mentioned previously, Ballard was promoted to lieutenant on December 24, 1953, and after an incredibly short two weeks of training, he and Payne were made deputy inspectors on January 7, 1954. On August 9, 1954, the black community was surprised to learn that Ballard had been made a full inspector and assigned to the North Central Police Division. Most of his time as an inspector was spent in the North Central Division although he was assigned to the West Division for a little more than a year.

Ballard became one of the most respected police officials of his day. His men loved him because he did active police work along with them, and he showed he cared about them and their families. Ballard's effectiveness became increasingly more noticeable by community leaders. The community's respect for his accomplishments was evident when a dinner was given in his honor on February 17, 1959, at McAllisters Catering Building on Spring Garden Street. More than 300 people attended, heaping praises, gifts, and an outpouring of affection on him.

Ballard felt later that he had gone as far as he could in the police department. He submitted his retirement papers and applied for a position as a teacher. His appointment to the faculty at John Wanamaker Junior High School was announced on July 28, 1961. But he decided not to accept based upon advice from his political friends. He remained with the police department.

During his off duty hours, Ballard pursued his hobby of woodworking by building his own home in New Jersey. Many of his subordinate police officers tried to volunteer their assistance, only to have him politely refuse their help. He wanted to avoid any conflict of interest.

As community pressures mounted for his further promotion, the Civil Service Commission relented and the Personnel Department gave an examination for chief inspector. Ballard was one of the top four on the list, and he was promoted on December 4, 1961. A new division, the Police Community Relations Division, was set up especially for him, with its headquarters in the Police Administration Building. In spite of the obviously important work ahead of him in community relations, Ballard was given only 12 men and a lieutenant, Chester Gathers, to work on a city-wide basis.

Yet, he demonstrated outstanding ability in organizing his programs and within a short period of time other units were added. The Police Band, School Crossing Guards, Traffic Safety Officers, and the Visual Aids Unit, (police artists making composite sketches of suspects, and departmental films and posters) were managed by him.

One of the lesser-known functions of his office was to investigate citizen complaints of police harrassment and brutality. When the investigation reports were completed, they were sent directly to Police Commissioner Howard Leary. The commissioner reviewed them and sent them on to the Police Advisory Board. If the board thought they were valid, they would hold public hearings and submit findings and recommendations back to the commissioner. The commissioner would then accept, alter or reject the board's recommendations.

Unfortunately, Ballard did not live long after becoming a chief inspector. He served only ten months before being hospitalized with a long and painful illness. He died on December 26, 1962, at the age of fifty-six.

Reaves succeeded Ballard at the helm of the Community Relations Division. At that point, he was the highest-ranking black police official in any major city on the East Coast, including Boston, New York, Baltimore and Washington, DC. By his appointment to succeed Ballard, the city administration specifically sought to keep a black police official in a highly visible position. This was necessitated by the accelerated number of civil disturbances, in particular those at Girard College, Girard and Corinthian Avenues; the central Philadelphia Post Office at 30th and Market streets; the Strawberry Mansion School construction site at 32nd Street and Susquehanna Avenue; and the North Philadelphia tinderbox area.

It should be noted that except for the eleven months that Richard Edwards served as provisional deputy commissioner of community programs in 1964, no black attained a rank as high as that held by Ballard until Arthur Matthews was promoted to chief inspector almost seventeen years later on June 11, 1979.

BLACK POLICE TRAIL BLAZERS
Part III

First Fraternal Order Of Police (FOP) Vice President

James E. Lee is a "chip off the old block," as the saying goes. Like his father, Robert E. Lee, he joined the police force and was a staunch member of the Fraternal Order of Police. He joined the police force on June 28, 1946. He was so popular in the F.O.P. that, in spite of being called crazy, he ran for vice president in 1958 and won. Not only was he the first black vice president of the F.O.P, it also marked the first time a black became a lodge official other than as a conference delegate.

After graduation from Gratz High School, Lee had worked at the Midvale Steel Co. As soon as he was eligible, he took the police department examination and was appointed. His first assignment was in his home district, the 36th at Germantown Avenue and Lycoming Street. After a short stay in his home district, Lee joined Dick Anderson's Special Investigation Squad. He essentially preferred being a uniformed man and served only two years in the squad before returning to his district.

Later, Lee, Richard Drayton and George Williams were reassigned by Superintendent Howard P. Sutton to Highway Patrol. He loved this assignment, if for no other reason than he was following in the footsteps of his father who was the first black member of the old motor bandit patrol. Officers in the Highway Patrol are distinctively attired in jodhpurs, puttees and storm trooper's hats. Except for two short stints of plainclothes duty, including a period of time with the venerable Detective Firman Hopkins, Lee spent his last sixteen years in the department in the Highway Patrol. It became his first love.

F.O.P.'s National Conference - Miami Beach - 1953
Bottom-center-first-row-right: James N. Reaves and Vivienne Reaves

James N. Reaves, retirement ceremony in squad room at 22nd District - July 30, 1965
L to R: Chief Inspector Robert Selfridge, Joseph L. Reaves, Vivienne L. Reaves, Alan Reaves and Deputy Commissioner Frank Rizzo

James N. Reaves retires with good wishes from colleagues
L to R: Captain Anthony Wong, Captain Richard Bridgeford, Chief Inspector Robert Selfridge, Deputy Commissioner Frank Rizzo, Staff Inspector Edward M. Payne, Staff Inspector Frank Nolan, Captain Matthew Miller and Lt. William Mitchell

Lee was elected to four terms as vice president of the F.O.P. He also was elected as a delegate and attended national conferences in Florida, Louisiana, Nevada, Arizona and Kentucky. As a lodge member, he said, he was always treated well by the other members at the conferences. He recalls that he had one overt experience with racism. During the 1958 police convention in New Orleans, Dennis Knight and he were not permitted to stay at the conference hotel. They were disappointed and angry, but they felt much better staying in the home of a friend. It proved to be much more interesting because they had someone who took a special interest in them and made sure they received a full tour of the city. "They really treated us royally," Lee recalled.

As a member of the F.O.P. Legal Aid Committee, Lee happily recalls casting the deciding vote that enabled three black officers to obtain legal aid for departmental charges against them. When the first vote was taken by the committee, Lee was absent and the request was denied. Later, when Lee arrived at the meeting, at his insistence a second vote was taken. The legal aid was approved. This action ultimately saved their jobs, as they were successfully defended by lawyers.

Lee retired from the police department on October 12, 1966, and was hired into the Philadelphia School System's security operations.

First Thrill Show Queen

The Thrill Show has been an annual event held at the John F. Kennedy Stadium. Policemen and firemen display their unique skills and daring acts of bravery. The goal is to raise funds for scholarships for the children of policemen and firemen who have been killed or permanently injured in the line of duty.

A queen is selected to reign at the show. Beauty and talent contests are held locally in various sections of the city. A finalist is chosen as the citywide queen from those sections. The first Thrill Show was held in 1955, and a queen has been selected each year. Although young black females have been contestants in each of these contests, it wasn't until the 12th Thrill Show on September 9, 1966, that a black queen was chosen.

Fern Anita Matthewson, a 19-year-old junior at North Carolina State College, was the 1966 winner. She earned the distinction of being the first black Thrill Show queen. She lived with her uncle, Norman Tyree, a retired Philadelphia detective, and worked at the John Wanamaker department store in the summer. Her chances of winning were greatly enhanced by the fact that she had attended the Philadelphia Modeling and Career School. For the black community, the real thrill of the 1966 Thrill Show was to see the black queen riding down Broad Street into the stadium, atop a flower-bedecked float with her court of four maiden attendants.

First Puerto Rican (Hispanic)

Gilbert Velez was born in Yauco, Puerto Rico, in 1926. He first became a policeman in San Juan, where he soon became fascinated with the techniques of fingerprinting. To perfect his skills and knowledge in this field, he came to the U.S. in 1952 and enrolled in the Pennsylvania Institute of Criminology. Upon completing the course in fingerprinting, he took a Civil Service test for a position as a fingerprint technician with the Philadelphia Police Department.

Velez was elated when he learned he had come out at the head of the list. In the meantime, he had to work at odd jobs until his appointment was finalized. When he was appointed on January 10, 1956, he became the first Puerto Rican-American employee in the department. In Philadelphia government, it seems, blacks and Hispanics are the only minorities that engender controversy. In many cases, blacks and Hispanics have allied themselves for their common good.

Velez has done well at his job and has increased his proficiency by enrolling at Rutgers University where he earned his bachelor's degree in political science. He enjoys his work to the extent that he continues to work long after becoming eligible for retirement. Also, he is an active member of the Spanish-American Police Association.

Physical fitness is Velez's hobby and his physique is living proof. He and several policemen work out with exercise equipment in his home, and he hopes to someday organize a fitness program in the police department.

First Philadelphia County Detectives

The Philadelphia District Attorney appoints all county detectives. They serve at his pleasure and are subject to be replaced with each change of political administration. Earl Barnes was the first black policeman in that office. He transferred from the Philadelphia Police Department shortly after Mayor Joseph S. Clark took office.

Earl M. Barnes was the classic example of a "workaholic," a high achiever who took his work seriously. Long hours and difficult problems were routine with him. His morale was constantly boosted by his understanding wife, Trudy, who was just as busy in public life as he was.

Barnes, a native Philadelphian, was born on March 3, 1912, and he graduated from Central High School in 1928. At age 19, he went into newspaper work at the old *Philadelphia Independent*. He worked his way up through the ranks to become the managing editor.

While police work always appealed to him, he entered the department not as a policeman but as a clerk. As such, he had the distinction of being the first black police clerk. He was appointed on January 16, 1941, and assigned to the

23rd Police District at 19th and Oxford Streets where he worked for Captain John Dooner. His appointment was hailed by black policemen of the district because it meant that for the first time they had someone in the front office with whom they could relate.

Nationally, economic conditions were on the upswing as preparations for World War II accelerated. For the first time in a decade, appointments of blacks to the department rose to about three percent of all recruits. Barnes also was on the police list, and was appointed to the position of patrolman on November 1, 1941.

His previous work as a newspaper reporter and police clerk proved to be excellent experiences, enabling him to go into the Detective Bureau after only a short stay in uniform at 28th and Oxford streets. He quickly showed his expertise at solving crimes while working in partnership with Detectives William "Kid" Asher, Milton Smith and William Peterson. His aggressiveness won him numerous awards and plaques. Probably his most outstanding arrest was that of William Norman, the killer of a State Store clerk in the Pennsylvania State Store at 8th and South streets in 1943. For that arrest, he won *The Philadelphia Inquirer's* Hero Award.

After the change in the political administration in 1952, Barnes became the first black to be transferred from the police department into the District Attorney's office. In 1959, he took the Civil Service examination for county detective and was appointed on September 28, 1959. He continued his brilliant career until his retirement on August 25, 1969. After retirement, Barnes soon grew weary of relaxing and took a position with the Public Defenders Office. He enjoyed his work but eventually ill health caught up with him and he died on December 29, 1976.

The first black nonpoliceman appointed as county detective was James "Big Jim" Robinson. He had been a longtime city employee in the Recorder of Deeds Office and transferred to the County Detectives office in 1955. Old-timers remember him mainly by the fresh carnation he always wore in his lapel, summer and winter. He served well and remained there until his death on September 5, 1967. Other early black appointees were: George Wilmer, James Shorter, William Peterson, Ralph Jones, Talmadge Jackson, Robert Smallwood, and Joseph A. Hall.

First Chief of County Detectives

The first black chief of county detectives was Gilbert M. Branche, who served from January 3, 1978, until his retirement on December 15, 1983. He was succeeded by another black appointee, Dorothy F. Cousins, the first female and first black female in that position. Without a doubt, Chief of County Detectives

Gilbert M. Branche was one of the most powerful black professional law enforcement officers that Philadelphia had during the 1970s. He also was one of the most militant and articulate of top-ranking black officers.

Branche was born in Philadelphia but attended high school in Darby, Pennsylvania. He graduated in 1950 and went on to Virginia State College. In 1951, he joined the U. S. Air Force and was honorably discharged as a staff sergeant in 1955. He joined the police department in 1957 and was assigned to the Highway Patrol. In 1961, he was promoted to detective and was assigned to the South Detective Division. After only a few months, he was transferred to the Homicide Unit. While in the Homicide Unit, he wsa promoted to sergeant in 1964 and lieutenant in 1967.

In 1968, he transferred to the District Attorney's office and was put in charge of the Homicide Unit. On April 14, 1969, he was promoted to captain and, in January 1970, was made the acting deputy chief of county detectives. He climbed the next step to deputy chief on May 11, 1970.

In 1976, there was a change in the administration and, on July 26, Branche was transferred back into the police department. But, this time, some eyebrows really were raised as he came back as an inspector. He was stationed at police headquarters and placed in charge of a number of staff-supporting units, including the Criminal Records Unit. In January 1978, he took a leave of absence and went back to the District Attorney's office, where he was made the chief of county detectives. He reported directly to the new District Attorney, Edward Rendell, and was put in charge of office administration.

Chief Branch has received more than 30 commendations and he was awarded a City Council Resolution for Meritorious Service in 1968. He also has been awarded many other civic and professional awards, including the 1980 County Detectives Association of Pennsylvania Distinguished Award. He earned his bachelor's degree in Political Science from the University of Pennsylvania, holds certificates from Penn State University, and took Business Administration courses at Marywood College. He was the first black from Philadelphia to attend the F.B.I. Academy.

Branche was a founder of the National Organization of Black Law Enforcement Executives (NOBLE) in 1976. He served as Greater Philadelphia Chapter President from 1977 to 1983, as regional vice president from 1978 to 1979 and from 1982 to 1983, and as national president from 1979 to 1980. In 1980, he was selected by the Law Enforcement Assistance Administration as one of twenty-one persons chosen in the United States to be a commissioner for the Accreditation Project for Law Enforcement Agencies nationwide. Recognizing his valuable contributions to law enforcement, NOBLE presented him with the James N. Reaves Distinguished Service Award in October 1986.

Branche retired on December 15, 1983, after twenty-six years of service to the city. While still vigorous and active, he accepted a state appointment in the

Department of Welfare as chief of the Frauds Investigation Division. One newspaper commented on the fact that his combined annual income of salary and pension was more than the salary of the governor. Within a short period of time, because of his expertise and effectiveness, Branche moved into the higher echelon of the State's administration. He became the deputy secretary of the Department of Welfare.

First Deputy Police Commissioners

Richard "Dick" Edwards, the first black deputy police commissioner, was a classic example of the Horatio Alger story. He was catapulted from the rank of lieutenant to deputy police commissioner in one giant step. In the process, he bypassed the ranks of captain, staff inspector, inspector and chief inspector.

As unusual as this action was, Edwards proved to be equal to the task, as his personnel record clearly proves. Not only did he have a good education, he also had a personality that made quick friends—a characteristic which served him well as chief of the Police Community Relations Division.

Edwards was born in New Bern, South Carolina, but he grew up in Philadelphia. He first came to public attention when he was elected as the first black captain of the Central High School football team, leading it to the City championship in 1938. His football prowess and fame as a guard and linebacker brought him offers of full scholarships from numerous colleges and universities. He chose to attend Westchester State College for a year, before transferring to Howard University in Washington, DC. After two years at Howard University, he left school in 1944 to become an electrician at the Philadelphia Navy Yard.

On June 28, 1946, Edwards joined the Philadelphia police force and did uniformed work in the 16th Police District at 39th Street and Lancaster Avenue. In 1948, he transferred to Dick Anderson's Special Investigation Squad. He soon teamed up with John Grant and together they concentrated on narcotics arrests, for which they earned several commendations. In fact, they were so successful that they were transferred to the Narcotics Squad in 1951.

Edwards took the detective examination and was promoted to that rank in 1953. He was the first black assigned to the North West Detectives Division. In 1953, open examinations were given for all policemen for all ranks up to that of inspector. Edwards did well and was one of the first four black lieutenants appointed to that rank on December 24, 1953, and sent to the Police Academy for supervisory training. Upon completion of this course, Edwards was assigned to uniformed duty in the 31st Police District. A few months later, he was transferred to the North Central Detective Division.

Within a few weeks, Edwards was reassigned to the Police Academy along with Lieutenant Chester G. Gethers, as instructors. It is generally known that the new City Charter of 1952 made provisions for more than two deputies. However, all deputies other than the allotted two appointees would have to take a civil service examination if they wanted to serve in the rank of deputy for more than one year. Consequently, on January 6, 1964, Frank Rizzo, Edward J. Bell, John F. Driscoll, and Edwards were appointed deputy commissioners.

Political insiders, knowledgeable about matters inside City Hall, gave credit for Edward's appointment by Mayor James H.J. Tate to City Councilman Thomas McIntosh. Driscoll was assigned to a newly created position while Edwards was placed in charge of the Community Relations Division. In this new position, Edwards served well and was highly thought of by the community. However, in compliance with the City Charter, a new examination was held by the Civil Service Commission with hundreds of contestants competing. When the list of successful candidates was published, neither Driscoll nor Edwards scored highly enough to be considered. As a result, both men reverted back to their original ranks on December 5, 1964. Edwards remained in Community Relations.

As a result of previous examination for captain, in which he scored highly, Edwards was appointed permanently to that rank on January 11, 1965. He remained in Community Relations and did a splendid job, receiving numerous local, state and national commendations. Edwards died on October 17, 1966, bringing to a close a most colorful career.

Donald M. Gravatt was the second black deputy police commissioner. He was the fifth black to serve in the non-Civil Service appointive positions of the top echelon of the Philadelphia Police Department, and was, by far, the most powerful of the five. This hierarchy includes deputy police commissioners and assistant directors of public safety—all policy-making positions.

Gravatt came closer to serving in all ranks leading up to his position as deputy commissioner than any of his black predecessors. He skipped only the ranks of staff inspector and chief inspector. The first three blacks in the top level position of Assistant Director of Public Safety were: Herbert E. Millen, Robert J. Nelson, and Fredrick Matthias. However, none of the latter had previously been policemen. The fourth, Edwards, became a deputy commissioner without previously serving as a sergeant, captain, staff inspector or chief inspector.

By virtue of his education and experience, Gravatt was eminently qualified to fill the appointive position of deputy police commissioner. He was born in Philadelphia and came up through the public school system, graduating from West Philadelphia High School in June 1949. He did undergraduate work at Lincoln University and at St. Joseph's College in Philadelphia. Upon graduating from St. Joseph's University, he received a bachelor's degree in sociology and psychology, finishing in the upper third of his class while working full time on the police force.

He was appointed to the police department in July 1953. Upon completing his training in the Police Academy, he was assigned to plainclothes duty in the District Attorney's Office. Following that, he spent two and a half years in the 16th Police District. After closely observing and recognizing his potential, James N. Reaves assigned him to the Operations Room from which the majority of promotions were made. He was the first black regularly assigned there.

Gravatt was transferred to the Juvenile Aid Division in June 1957. After a year and a half, he was promoted to the rank of detective in November 1958. For the next five years, he worked in various divisions as a detective. In November 1963, he was promoted to the rank of sergeant and reassigned to the Juvenile Aid Bureau. From there, he was transferred to the 12th Police District for a short stay in uniform. On April 10, 1967, he was promoted to the rank of lieutenant and assigned to the 16th District, remaining there for a year before his promotion to the rank of captain on June 6, 1968. While serving as a captain for nine years, he was at various times in charge of three different districts, the 23rd, the 18th and 22nd.

It was rumored in 1976 that Mayor Rizzo would not permit Captain Gravatt to advance any further due to the bad chemistry between the two of them. Yet, in spite of this, the mayor did not interfere when Gravatt's name was placed near the top of the list for inspector. He was promoted to that rank in June 1976. However, the black community was a bit disgruntled when he was assigned to "Night Command"—tantamount to being punished or hidden in a less desirable position—rather than to a uniformed division.

In July 1979, Gravatt took the examination for promotion to chief inspector. When the results were published, he was more than a little perturbed. As the only college graduate out of the twenty-seven candidates, he was rated no higher than tenth on the list. He was not advanced in rank.

In 1980, William Green was elected mayor on the Democratic slate. Green had campaigned hard in the black community to retain the black vote that had become disenchanted with the Democratic party during the Rizzo Administration. One of his campaign promises was that, as mayor, he was going to appoint a black deputy commissioner of police. Green was particularly solicitous of the Guardian Civic League membership.

Upon assuming office, Mayor Green sought their input as to whom the black deputy commissioner should be. A delegation from the Guardian Civic League met with the local chapter of the National Organization of Black Law Enforcement Executives (NOBLE) and requested their opinion. After a brief discussion of all possible candidates, two members were nominated, Chief Inspector Arthur Matthews and Don Gravatt. Gravatt was selected over Matthews. The selection was made known to the body of the Guardian Civic League and the membership concurred with the choice of Gravatt.

His name subsequently was submitted to Mayor Green. On January 7, 1980, Gravatt was made a deputy police commissioner, the second black ever to hold that position. The black community accepted the promotion with mixed emotions. Gravatt had become a deputy commissioner but he was less than enthusiastic upon learning that he wouldn't be in charge of either the uniformed patrol or the detectives. Instead, he was placed in charge of the Administrative and Services Division. This was a monumental change from a long-established system of organization. Since the new City Charter of 1952, the practice had been that one deputy commissioner directed the detectives' division and the other directed the uniformed forces.

Ordinarily, Gravatt is an outspoken person, yet he remained low-key throughout Mayor Green's administration. Mayor W. Wilson Goode was elected in 1983. Shortly after the election, upon being questioned, the mayor said he would not consider Gravatt as a candidate for police commissioner. The general thinking was that Mayor Goode wanted another black, Leo Brooks, for managing director, and he was afraid of too much static from the white community if he also appointed a black police commissioner.

Mayor Goode's statement brought an outcry from the members of NOBLE. Gil Branche, president of the local chapter—being mindful of the November 9, 1983, appointment of a black commissioner in New York City—protested to Mayor Goode on behalf of NOBLE. Branche managed to extract a promise from the mayor to interview Gravatt and other black candidates. The interviews were held and Gravatt, though not chosen as a commissioner, finally was selected as the deputy commissioner in charge of uniformed forces.

This was just another example of changing the rules of the game whenever the blacks appear to be winning. To those of us who constantly observe the way that political appointments are made, the outcome was not unexpected. The white community would have been distraught with both the managing director and commissioner of police being black. Since Gravatt accepted the change, albeit reluctantly, NOBLE no longer pressed the issue. Gravatt was sworn into the new position in January 1984.

In his own way, Gravatt, proved to be effective in advancing the cause of upward mobility for black police. In his new position, he was able to assign blacks to positions of high visibility other than in the uniformed ranks. In many cases, they were able to gain valuable experiences that would enhance their capabilities for being promoted to positions of greater responsibilities. Yet, Gravatt was very anxious to become the police commissioner. He believed that his experience in the previous ranks and various investigative and administrative positions more than qualified him for the appointment.

Although his new position as head of the uniformed forces appeared to be a step upward, it just wasn't what he ultimately had wanted. After a few weeks in that position, he retired on May 11, 1984, going directly to a new position as head of security forces for Temple University in North Philadelphia.

First Homicide Inspector

Without a doubt, Arthur J. Matthews was one of the best prepared police officers in the Philadelphia Police Department to command a major operations department, in the history of the city's police force. His education, military and civilian work experiences made him eminently qualified. Matthews graduated from Benjamin Franklin High School in 1948. He enlisted in the U.S. Army in 1951 and served in Korea as a radio repairman, attaining the rank of sergeant. He was honorably discharged in 1953 and returned to his former position at the Philadelphia Navy Yard.

He remained there until he entered the police department on February 20, 1961. Soon after becoming a policeman, he enrolled in courses at Temple University. He also took courses from the University of Pennsylvania, Pennsylvania State University and Michigan State University. He also attended seminars in criminal justice wherever they could be found. As far away as Montreal, Canada, he attended seminars. His expertise was such that he became a guest lecturer during FBI seminars, and classes at West Chester College, Penn State University, Temple University and the Community College of Philadelphia.

Matthews' steady rise in the police department: policeman, February 29, 1961; detective, March 1, 1965; sergeant, November 1, 1965; lieutenant, June 6, 1968; captain, October 28, 1969; inspector, July 22, 1974; and chief inspector, July 1, 1979. However, his promotions did not attract much attention until he became a captain and was placed in the Homicide Division. This was a first for a black captain. It is considered one of the most prestigious positions in the police department. Upon making the promotion, Frank Rizzo, then a police commissioner, said, "He is an outstanding police official." Matthews considered it an honor that Inspector Fredrick Ruffin give him his own captain's bars and pinned them on him.

When Matthews became chief inspector in 1979, there had not been a black police officer to hold that position since Ballard in 1962. There was much speculation that Matthews surely would be the next deputy commissioner. Indeed, Matthews was very much in the running for that position until Donald Gravatt was selected over him on January 7, 1980. At first, Gravatt's advancement to the deputy commissioner position caused much jubilation in the black community. However, as fate would have it, the community found that its joy was tempered with the news that Matthews was retiring.

Matthews, fearing a demotion from his new post due to an expected reduction in the police force, retired seven months later on August 20, 1980, to protect his chief inspector's pension. Like so many of the other high-ranking blacks who retired, he joined the security system at Harrah's Casino in Atlantic City. He became its director of security.

BLACK POLICE TRAIL BLAZERS
Part IV

First Park Police Captain

Francis C. Walker was the first black captain in the Philadelphia Park Police. His ten-year tenure was the second longest tenure as a black captain. James N. Reaves served as a captain only ten months longer than Walker. He was born in Baltimore, Maryland, and attended public schools. Morgan State College awarded him a B.S. degree in 1951 after four years of struggle. After college, he joined the United States Army and he was commissioned a lieutenant in the infantry.

After leaving the Army, Walker was appointed a patrolman in the Fairmount Park Police of Philadelphia on July 27, 1953. At various times, he took criminal and social courses from the University of Pennsylvania and Temple University. The FBI instructed him about the control of civil disorders. Promotions came slowly, but steadily. He was made a sergeant in July 1956 and a lieutenant in July 1961. He took the examination for captain in 1967 and placed highly enough on the list to be considered for an appointment.

They were about to pass him up for a new list that recently had been published. The top men on the new list were called to be sworn in, but Walker's name was missing. When word of the incident passed among certain black civic leaders, pressure was brought to bear upon Mayor James H.J. Tate. On August 28, 1967, Walker had his own small, private swearing-in ceremony in the Mayor's Reception Room, with family and civic leaders. Mayor Tate praised Walker's record. Walker remained with the Park Police until his retirement on August 21, 1967, even though the Park Police had been merged with the Philadelphia Police Department.

After retiring, he served for a time as an instructor of security officers. In December 1977, he received an appointment that ranks among the most prestigious positions ever attained by a retired black policeman. He was made executive secretary of the Pennsylvania State Athletic Commission, a position he held until August 6, 1988. Walker also continued to be active in a number of civic organizations, the YMCA, Boy Scouts, the Kappa Alpha Psi Fraternity and the St. Francis De Sales Church.

First Dectective Captain

Moorey D. Green was the first black captain to command a detective division. There are seven detective divisions in the city with boundaries that correlate with the uniformed police divisions. It is the desire and hope of almost every policeman to advance to the rank of detective, with its accompanying prestigious status. And to say that one has become a detective captain is tantamount to saying one is well on his way up the chain of command.

Green attended Philadelphia Public Schools, and he graduated from Gratz High School in 1952. He joined the United States Army in 1953 and he was honorably discharged in 1955. On February 20, 1961, he was sworn in as a Fairmount Park Policeman. He was promoted to sergeant on October 11, 1965, followed by his promotion to lieutenant on December 4, 1967. He continued his higher education with part-time studies at Temple University between 1967 and 1972. During this time, he earned credits in the liberal arts, criminal justice and leadership supervision.

With an outstanding record as a lieutenant, he was promoted to captain on March 12, 1973, and assigned to uniformed and special patrol. In his new rank, he showed so much promise that he was selected to attend the FBI Academy in Quantico, Virginia. Black police considered it a very rare honor for one of them. While he was there, he attended an executive-level training program for law enforcement officers at the University of Virginia.

On July 1, 1978, he was assigned to the West Detective Division at 55th and Pine streets. This has been the largest division, encompassing twenty-five square miles with a population of about 350,000 people. Moreover, Green supervised five lieutenants, four sergeants and seventy-two investigators. During his tenure in the West Division, there was a decrease in the crime rate while the rest of the city experienced an increase. His records also showed an eight percent increase in the number of crimes solved.

During the late 1970s black promotions slowed down and almost stopped in the early 1980s. The latter motivated Green, after eight years as a captain, to seek challenges elsewhere. He retired on September 11, 1981. Green selected a new challenge, the Harrisburg, Pennsylvania Police Department. As technical assistant to the director of public safety, he was responsible for crime investigations and training. Actually, he took flight from an urban area to enhance his chances for upward mobility. Green did well at his new post, remaining until

July 1985, when he accepted another position in Harrisburg. He became the chief of special investigations for the Pennsylvania Department of Welfare.

First Sheriff

John D. Green was born and raised by his family in North Philadelphia. He graduated from Gratz High School and he was accepted into Lincoln University, the oldest African-American university in September 1965. While still a student there, he took the Philadelphia police examination and he received high marks. In May 1969, he left Lincoln and he became a member of the Philadelphia Police Department. He did not like working rotating, shifts and he requested steady day work. This was soon granted, enabling him to see more of his family, and he enrolled at Temple University. He completed work on his undergraduate studies, and he received his B.A. degree in 1971.

Besides a short period as a plainclothesman, Green worked several patrol districts in uniform. In 1976, he was promoted to sergeant, working both in uniform and in plainclothes in the detective division. Because of his dislike for certain police practices at the lower levels that affected black police, he joined the Guardians. As a new member, he became very vocal and rose quickly through various offices. On September 9, 1981, John Green became the fifth president of the Guardian Civic League. After his election, he said that his main objective was "to elevate the organization to the status of being a major force in the city. Because we are black police officers, we can act as a continuing mechanism to bridge the gap between the police department and the community and, along with that, try to explain to the grassroots people what is really a complicated process." That statement summarized the influence that his administration would have on the course of progress for black police in Philadelphia.

During his term as GCL's president, the tempo of affirmative action in recruiting, hiring and promoting minorities reached its peak. The incident that sparked the most positive action was the Martin Luther King breakfast boycott on January 15, 1982. This action brought about a quick response from the city administration. Many GCL proposals were accepted and some new policies were implemented. As president of GCL, Green was placed in charge of a newly established recruitment unit. This unit assisted in preparing five hundred minority applicants for the police department. Green can point with pride to the fact that he was able to obtain the funding to complete the renovation of the GCL home. This resulted in Philadelphia being chosen by the National Black Police Association as the site for its home office.

Green's interest in his community has extended beyond the Guardians. During the Philadelphia primary election in August 1987, he upset the Democrats' party-endorsed candidate for sheriff. That put him up against Republican William J. Cole in the November general election. John Green won. His election as a Democrat was of particular interest in that the Democratic party failed to back him in the spring primary election.

In spite of that, in the general election, he received just as many votes as the Democrats' front runner, the mayor. He became Philadelphia's Sheriff, the first black. Black Philadelphians were proud of what they had done, they voted for him. With Green as sheriff, the State now had top-level law enforcement positions held by blacks. A Sheriff, Deputy Police Commissioner, Superintendent of State Police, Superintendent of Prisons, Deputy of Drug Enforcement Administration; and Agent-in-charge, Federal Bureau of Investigations.

First Police Commissioner

From the perspective of Philadelphia's black citizens, the appointment of Willie L. Williams as Philadelphia Police Commissioner on June 10, 1988, was of as significant importance as that of electing the first black mayor. They strongly felt that, in spite of the fact that the president of City Council, the sheriff, the superintendent of schools, managing director, and personnel director were all black individuals.

W. Wilson Goode was appointed managing director of the City of Philadelphia by Mayor William Green in January 1980. Goode was constantly badgered by the black community to influence the appointment of the first black police commissioner. At the same time, there were many, black and white citizens, who feared a backlash from having blacks fill too many top-level positions.

Goode settled for the appointment of Donald Gravatt, a black police inspector with an excellent reputation, to be one of two deputy commissioners. When W. Wilson Goode became mayor in 1984, he flexed his political muscles a bit more aggressively by assigning Gravatt to a major police operating command. Yet, it seemed, the mayor, still felt uneasy about placing a black man in the police department's top post. Gravatt resigned with bitter disappointment.

Mayor Goode chose Captain Harvey Crudup, the senior black captain at the time, to fill Gravatt's shoes in June 1984. In doing so, he bypassed William Lindsay, the only active black inspector. It was speculated that this occurred because of Lindsay's coziness with former Mayor Frank Rizzo. Harvey Crudup was a low-key deputy commissioner for four years. However, it is to his credit that he managed to avoid involvement in the MOVE controversy in spite of whispered criticism that he should have been involved.

A truer measure of his good judgment and character was that he was not implicated in the corruption scandal that rocked the department during his tenure. It resulted in the arrest and the imprisonment of his fellow deputy commissioner, James J. Martin, and over thirty policemen.

Finally, the long anticipated event happened. In November 1985, Commissioner Gregore Sambor retired—some said with substantial nudging from Mayor

Goode. Sambor had been deeply involved in giving directions to the police in "The Move" confrontation. There was destruction of a neighborhood's block and the death of Move members. The story of the event filled international and national newspapers for months. Philadelphia's image had been damaged.

While many thought Crudup would be a shoo-in, Mayor Goode thought otherwise. Crudup wasn't even used as a temporary caretaker during the so-called nationwide search for a permanent replacement. On January 1, 1986, Kevin M. Tucker, a former Secret Service official, assumed command of the department. Tucker served well during the investigation of departmental corruption. As a move to strengthen his position, Tucker formed a Police Commissioner's Council to review progress in the police department. This group of business and civic leaders worked hard. The council's chairman, William B. Eagleston, released a report on December 29, 1987. It stated that they were satisfied that Tucker had been rebuilding police morale.

It seemed that Tucker was so well liked by Mayor Goode that he held onto him into his second administration that began in January 1988. In March 1988, Mayor Goode made another change in the police department's administrative lineup, causing a lot of eyebrows to be raised. Deputy Commissioner Crudup took a leave of absence when Mayor Goode appointed him to replace Rex Uberman as executive director of the Youth Study Center. Willie Williams, who had been appointed an inspector in February 1986, replaced Crudup as deputy commissioner in March 1988. This appointment was expected since it followed the usual pattern of replacing blacks with blacks.

Four months into the new administration, an unexpected event came about. Tucker announced he was leaving the department to take a position with Provident National Bank. Mayor Goode decided to replace Tucker with Williams, the latest appointment of the three deputy commissioners. The mayor said that he had given consideration to others in the department, but he believed Williams was the best man for the job.

Commissioner Williams has charisma and he is physically over six feet tall with a well built physique. He has brought value and respect to the police department. Unquestionably, he has been loyal and courageous in fighting for the rights of the police. Yet, he has not hesitated to discharge police guilty of breaking police departmental regulations or societal laws. Moreover, he is bright, and articulate in providing the strong leadership necessary for police to fight against crime in one of the largest cities in America.

The F.O.P has been in a constant struggle with him. As the legal bargaining body for all police, it has challenged bitterly many of his professional decisions. In spite of the latter, he has maintained a good relationship based upon fairness. His top-level staff have followed his leadership in dealing fairly with all police.

James Clark, the first deputy, and for the first time in the police department's history, two civil service chief inspectors, George Craig and Richard Neal are black. There are more blacks in top-level positions, then ever before. Further, Williams has been an active member of NOBLE, since he was a lieutenant. He served as president of the Philadelphia Chapter of NOBLE, and as NOBLE Region II's vice president. His brilliance and know-how have been recognized by the national body of NOBLE. Williams was elected national president of NOBLE on August 1, 1991.

BLACK POLICE KILLED IN THE LINE OF DUTY

Conrad E. Gibson

Black policemen in Philadelphia received a severe jolt when two of their members were killed in the line of duty within a matter of hours on October 4, 1919. *The Philadelphia Tribune's* article of October 11, 1919, stated that both men,—"Conrad E. Gibson and Charles B. Jones—were in the process of making an arrest. Gibson was killed accidentally by his own revolver when it fell from his holster and discharged. The incident happened in the late evening in front of the police station at 20th and Federal Streets, in the 17th Police District. He was immediately taken to Polyclinic Hospital where he was pronounced dead upon arrival."

Gibson had been appointed to the police force on October 12, 1905 at the age of 22. He had completed 14 years of service at the time of his death. He had lived with his wife and sister on Wilder Street. His funeral was held there, with hundreds of officials and other citizens attending.

Charles B. Jones

The Philadelphia Tribune also reported on the death of Charles B. Jones. Jones was 32 years old and lived on Lombard Street. He had only two years with the force, having been appointed on May 12, 1917. "Early last Sunday morning Charles B. Jones, a colored policeman on plainclothes duty from the 19th District, was shot and killed at 13th and Rodman Streets when he attempted to break up a craps game which was going at full force on the pavement. The shooting occurred in the morning. Although Jones was shot in the temple and his neck broken by the downward course of the bullet, he continued fighting until he died. He succeeded in winging one of his attackers."

186

Jones was pronounced dead upon arrival at Polyclinic Hospital. Shortly after the incident, police arrested two brothers, Charles and Elijah Miller, but not before Charles Miller put up a big fight. He was found to have a .38 caliber gun on his person and was badly bleeding from the wrist. Both of the brothers were charged with the homicide of Officer Jones.

William T. Page

On April 21, 1929, Officer William T. Page was shot to death by unknown persons while patrolling his beat at 24th and Delancey Streets near the Delancey Garage. Page was assigned to the 19th Police District at 12th and Pine Streets and had been instructed to be on the lookout for holdup men who had pulled several robberies in the western end of the district.

A witness on the scene had been attracted by the sound of gunfire. He saw a small-sized green automobile pull out of the garage at a fast rate of speed. There was one man driving and two were standing on the running board. They escaped west on Spruce Street. The case is still being carried as unsolved by the Homicide Squad. Page died in the Polyclinic Hospital from a single gunshot wound to the head. The investigation that followed revealed that Page had fired two shots at the holdup men.

Page was a native Philadelphian who attended the public schools. He was 36 years of age, the father of four children, and was a member of a well-respected family with many friends. His funeral was attended by more than two thousand people, including five hundred policemen along with the Police Band. Director of Public Safety Lemeul B. Schofield and Magistrate Edward W. Henry also were in attendance.

In a press release, Director Schofield said, "Page died performing his duty as a brave and efficient policeman." *The Philadelphia Tribune*'s May 2, 1929, editorial stated, "It is hoped that the death of Officer Page has not been in vain; that, because of his death, a ray of light may break through the dark clouds that encircle Negro policemen and perhaps light the way for those of his group who pound 'beats' with little hope of day. Perhaps, after the martial strains have died away, those in authority will reflect upon the bravery of the deceased and, by proper promotion of some of his brothers, pay just and fitting tribute to the Hero Cop who died with no thought of reward other than to do his job well."

In retrospect, it is easy to deduce that Officer Page's death and The Philadelphia Tribune's editorial had a salutary effect on the course of events in black history. Almost three months to the day of the publication of the editorial, Policeman Robert Forgy was promoted to the rank of sergeant, the first black officer to advance to that level. Therefore, it is my resolute opinion that Officer Page did not die in vain.

Eugene Chavis

On May 20, 1944, Eugene Chavis, was only days away from retirement, as he walked from the completion of his tour of duty on Woodland Avenue. In the intersection at 43rd Street, he was struck by a car. It was driven by a hit-and-run driver. The car pushed him under the wheels of a trolley car. He was taken to Philadelphia General Hospital whereupon he was dead on arrival.

Chavis was appointed to the force in 1921. He was 65 years old at the time of his death. In those days it was common for policemen to work until their compulsory retirement age. Chavis was survived by a wife and daughter. He was given a full hero's funeral with hundreds of policemen and officials present.

Six days after the accident, police investigators arrested William Mathis, who admitted hitting Chavis. It turned out that the car Mathis was driving had been stolen.

William B. Chapman

His wife said he was "as good as gold." And we, the men who worked with William B. Chapman, knew him to be a good police officer, dedicated to his job. Chapman was appointed to the police force on February 1, 1945. His first assignment was at the 12th Police District at 8th and Jefferson Streets. Chapman was killed by David Allen on June 13, 1948, while working the beat near Darian and Poplar Streets. Chapman had attempted to arrest Allen, a 19-year-old fugitive from justice, on the corner of 8th and Poplar Streets. Two women had complained about his insulting them. Instead of leaving, Allen took a swing at Chapman, who then placed Allen under arrest.

Chapman marched him to a police call box at Darian and Poplar Streets. He tried to call for a police wagon, but as he opened the call box, Allen pushed his head into the heavy iron box, causing Chapman to fall. Allen then pounced upon Chapman, seizing his service revolver, and fired four shots into him at close range. He then fled to Reno and Orkney Streets, where he was arrested ten minutes later by two uniformed patrolmen. Chapman was taken to St. Luke's Hospital where he was pronounced dead.

Later, it was determined that Allen had arrived in Philadelphia only five months earlier from Georgia. A warrant had been sworn out against him for criminally attacking his aunt. On November 10, 1948, Allen was found guilty of first-degree murder and sentenced to life imprisonment.

James J. Auter

James J. Auter, a native of Dillon, South Carolina, was only 27 years old when he died. Auter loved police work. He was introduced to it while serving as a military policeman in Japan during World War II. Upon being discharged, he immediately applied to the Philadelphia Police Department. His appointment came through on July 19, 1953. After completing training at the Police Academy, he was assigned to the 9th Police District, and the captain chose him to work as a plainclothesman.

But, unfortunately, Auter's civilian police career was short-lived, due to a most untimely accident. It happened on October 15, 1953, while he was working with his partner, Albert Savich, investigating illegal gambling activities. While patrolling near the intersection of 18th Street and Ridge Avenue, keeping a suspect location under surveillance, Auter dropped his revolver to the pavement. When he attempted to pick it up, it discharged and a bullet struck him in the head. He was rushed to St. Joseph's Hospital where he was pronounced dead upon arrival. An investigation revealed that Auter's service revolver had a defective trigger spring.

Harry L. Davis

Harry L. Davis was an "eager beaver." He had been appointed to the police department on September 14, 1965. On March 9, 1970 at 1:40 A.M., a police radio transmission instructed policemen in patrol cars to respond to a burglar alarm in a taproom at 23rd and Catharine Streets, in the 17th Police District. Davis, at age 35 years of age, was the first to arrive on the scene. Without waiting for a police backup, he entered the bar alone, only to be confronted by a man with a gun. The man, without hesitation, turned and fired a single shot which struck Davis in the chest. Out the side door with the gun, the man fled. Davis was taken to Graduate Hospital. Police Commissioner Frank L. Rizzo arrived at the hospital to show his concern for the officer's welfare and to reassure the officer's family.

Police arriving on the scene gave chase as the suspect turned and fired at them. The suspect ran, with police in pursuit, to 2232 Catharine Street. The policemen followed him into the house, where they found him in bed fully clothed and with the gun under the bed. The suspect was later identified as James Hudson, a 40-year-old resident of Tasker Homes. Hudson was arrested and charged with first-degree murder. At a hearing before Judge Edward S. Cox on March 24, 1970, he was held without bail for trial.

In spite of the best medical attention, Davis, after lingering on for about a month, finally died on April 6, 1970. He was given a hero's funeral with hundreds of police, the mayor, the police commissioner, and other dignitaries attending. On January 26, 1972, Hudson was found guilty of first-degree murder and sentenced to life in prison.

Douglass Alexander

Alexander was born in Rochester, New York, on August 23, 1918. He attended a private school and worked at the Eastman Kodak Company until he enlisted in the Air Force during World War II. He earned his flying wings under Colonel Benjamin O. Davis, Jr. at Tuskegee Air Base in Alabama. He flew combat missions in Japan, and he was awarded the Purple Heart Medal for being wounded. While in the service, he married and became the father of two daughters. In 1945, he received an honorable discharge and returned to civilian life in Philadelphia with his family.

In 1951, a friend of his encouraged him to apply for a position with the police department. He was appointed in August of that year and he was assigned to the Motor Bandit Patrol. In 1955, he was promoted to detective and assigned to the Homicide Division where he earned thirteen commendations. Douglass Alexander had the unfortunate distinction of being the second black detective killed.

On February 9, 1972, Detective Alexander waited for friends in the Choo Choo Bar at Chew and Meehan Streets. At about 3:45 P.M., a man entered the bar and sat down near its front door. A few minutes later, a second man entered the side door with a shotgun. He announced a holdup. As the stickup man herded the patrons toward the rear of the building, Alexander pulled his service revolver and fired two shots. The man with the shotgun blasted Alexander's chest. Without any money from the holdup, the two men drove away in a maroon Chrysler.

Within minutes, the district police arrived. Alexander was driven to Germantown Hospital. Mayor Rizzo and Commissioner Joseph F. O'Neill immediately arrived at the hospital to visit Alexander before he died. Mayor Rizzo said, "Crimes like these deserve the death penalty." Commissioner O'Neill added, "He was one of the finest guys that I have run across, an excellent detective and an excellent man." In the meantime, the stickup men were captured.

The funeral was held at Holy Temple at 60th and Callowhill Streets, with the police department presenting full hero's honors with numerous city officials and hundreds of police taking part. As for the stickup men, Joseph Watson and Arthur Perry were sentenced to life in prison.

Michael S. Lingham

As an 18-year-old, Lingham was appointed to the police department on October 5, 1963. He was born in Philadelphia and graduated from West Catholic High School. He attended West Chester State College until his appointment as a police academy cadet. Four years later, on November 15, 1967, he was promoted to detective. His promotion to sergeant came on January 20, 1971. Lingham was an excellent investigator and leader.

On March 18, 1974, as a member of the Narcotics Squad, Lingham was shot three times by James McClain, who was arrested on the scene by other police. Lingham had attempted to serve a search warrant. A search of the premises revealed 22 pounds of marijuana, two pistols and other drug-related paraphernalia.

Lingham was taken to Graduate Hospital. Less than a month later, he died in the hospital as a result of his wounds on April 14, 1974. A full police hero's funeral was held at Our Lady of Victory Church at 54th and Vine Streets, with a full contingent of city police and police from the surrounding areas appearing in the line of march. The procession was led by Mayor Rizzo and the police band. Captain Harry Anderson and Inspector James N. Reaves followed with a contingent of the Housing Police.

Artimus Johnson

Johnson was born on January 9, 1943, in Winnsboro, South Carolina. He came to Philadelphia in October 1965 and he became a policeman in February 1968. Prior to being assigned to the Narcotics Squad in March 1973, he had worked in the 15th District and the Highway Patrol. On October 20, 1975, Johnson and Robert Smith, as undercover officers purchased "speed" in a house on North 13th Street. After the buy, they identified themselves as policemen.

Artimus Johnson was critically wounded after twelve shots had been fired. Harley, a drug dealer, was arrested by other police as Johnson, bleeding from a chest wound, was rushed to Temple Hospital. A search of the house by police found a .38 caliber revolver and nineteen bags of heroin while Johnson died in the hospital.

A hero's funeral was held for Johnson. A full police contingent was led by Police Commissioner O'Neill. Civic and religious leaders praised Johnson during the ceremony. Thereafter, Guardian Civic League members and Housing Police, led by Captain Anderson, travelled in a bus to South Carolina to attend the graveside ceremonies.

William Daniels

Daniels was 21 years of age when he joined the police department in 1962. In 1966, he was promoted to corporal and assigned to the Labor Squad. His mother, Grace Daniels, was the Democratic ward leader in the 44th Ward. He coached baseball in the Little League. On December 16, 1975, at about 8:15 P.M., Corporal William Daniels sat talking with friends in a bar at 58th and

Christian Streets. More than likely, he was talking about boxing or chess, his favorite endeavors. Suddenly, they were surprised by four stickup men. Patrons held their hands up into the air while the stickup men took valuable things off of them. As Daniels stood up, one of the stickup men fired two shots into the unarmed Daniels.

The four men ran out of the bar into the neighborhood street. Acting on a tip, two blocks away from the bar, the police found the four men hiding in a crawl space under a porch, while Daniels was rushed to the hospital. Later, he died. Daniels was given a full hero's ceremony at his funeral.

William Washington

Prior to joining the police department, he served in the United States Army from 1968 to 1970 in Germany and Vietnam. After his discharge and while still a policeman, he continued to be a part of the Army as an Army Reserve sergeant. By January 1980, Washington, 30 years of age, was engaged to be married.

On January 16, 1980, Edward McNeill, who lived in the 2200 block of Bonaffon Street, engaged with his wife in a heated argument. With her two children, she fled for her life. From inside the house, McNeill fired his rifle at them as they entered a nearby neighbor's house. His wife called the police.

Washington and his partner, Officer Edward Brinkman, were working on a burglary detail in plainclothes when they responded to the call of the disturbance. As they approached the house, McNeill fired and Washington fell. Brinkman took cover and called for assistance. With a gunshot wound in the head, Washington was rushed to Mercy Catholic Medical Center. In the meantime, the police on the scene barricaded the street and surrounded the house. A telephone line was established with McNeill for him to surrender. After his minister and sister arrived, he surrendered. He was arrested and charged with homicide.

Mayor William Green, Managing Director W. Wilson Goode, and Police Commissioner Morton B. Solomon arrived at the hospital to visit him. He could not be saved from death. He was given a hero's funeral in the Trinity AME Church at 27th and Cumberland Streets.

James N. Mason

Appointed in 1976 to the police department, he was well respected. At 36 years of age, with five years of police service, Mason enjoyed being a policeman and operating his delicatessen. On May 7, 1981, Mason and his partner, Officer James Singletary, responded to police radio instructions to go to the Mantua Hall Housing Project at 36th Street and Fairmount Avenue. They did not find any crime in progress. In his patrol car, Mason sat while writing the incident report.

Suddenly, there was the sound of two gunshots and Mason slumped over the steering wheel. Officer Singletary called for assistance and about twenty police responded. Mason was rushed to Presbyterian Hospital with a gunshot wound in the head. He never regained consciousness.

Police searched the housing project but were unsuccessful. About twelve hours later, Anthony McMillen, 18 years old, who lived on the 11th floor of Mantua Hall, told police in the Police Administration building that he had witnessed the shooting. However, later he admitted he actually had done the shooting.

Mayor Green, Managing Director Goode, and Commissioners Solomon and Donald M. Gravatt met with Mason's family. Mason died on May 10, 1981. The funeral was held at Pilgrim Baptist Church at 854 N. 15th Street, with over 1,000 persons attending, including three hundred police. Mayor Green later stated, "If people could see the grief suffered by the families of slain policemen and could get a sense of anger that we ought to have about mindless thugs, perhaps more could be done."

THE RISE OF BLACK POLICE ORGANIZATIONS

National Black Police Association

As the racial demonstrations and riots of the late 1960s subsided, the 1970s were a time of growth nationwide in the number of black police. It became increasingly apparent that if they combined their efforts into organizations of black police, they would be a potent force for change in the overall way of life for blacks and other minorities. Approximately a dozen existing black police groups already had flexed their muscles with some degree of effectiveness.

A seminar was held in 1971 at the University of Michigan for the purpose of finding a way for police and communities to have more harmonious relationships. Willie Johnson, president of a Detroit black police organization, was the driving force in bringing this seminar to fruition. The Philadelphia Guardians were represented at the seminar by Harold Arnold, James Holley and Harold James. Also in attendance were Howard Carrington and Robert Lamb of Community Relations of the United States Department of Justice, Peggy Triplett of the Law Enforcement Assistance Administration and a number of others from across the nation.

After the scheduled sessions, a small group, including those mentioned above, met privately several times and brainstormed about forming a national organization. As a result, an agreement was reached, calling for a coalition of black police groups to meet in St. Louis to form such an organization.

In August 1972, black police representing 29 organizations in 25 cities in 14 states came together at a conference in St. Louis. Their purpose was to lay the groundwork for a national umbrella-type organization. After numerous seminars and countless hours of brainstorming, the National Black Police Association was born. Moses Baldwin of New York City was elected its first president.

Three of NBPA's purposes:

* To improve the relationship between police departments and the black community

* To establish free and rapid flow of communication through a national network
* To work toward reforms in existing departments in order to eliminate police corruption, brutality and racial discrimination

Out of the coalition grew the idea to bring legal action to increase the number of blacks and other minorities in the various police departments. In quick order, Detroit, New York City, Chicago, and Philadelphia initiated litigation to bring about proportionate representation of minorities in their respective police departments.

The first nationwide NBPA conference was held in Atlanta in October 1973, with more than 400 representatives attending. The Philadelphia contingent, led by Holley, voted James N. Reaves, retired police inspector, Philadelphia, recipient of one of the national awards: "For Outstanding Dedication Towards the Goals of the National Black Police Association."

From the inception of the NBPA, GCL members have played important roles in its history. They have served on all the important committees, chairing many of them, and serving as regional representatives to the national board. James was elected president and Holley was elected secretary for one term in 1976. In February 1984, Philadelphia was selected as the permanent national headquarters of NBPA, with offices in the GCL building on Girard Avenue. GCL President John Green and other GCL members were highly elated at the selection since it makes their duties for NBPA easier to perform. Green was chosen to serve as NBPA's national information officer, to facilitate communication among its member chapters.

As envisioned by that dedicated few in Detroit in 1972, the NBPA is indeed a concentrated and effective force in the field of criminal justice, with about 21,000 members now enrolled.

National Organization of Black Law Enforcement Executives

Another new arrival on the scene of law enforcement for black police officers in recent years is the National Organization of Black Law Enforcement Executives (NOBLE). NOBLE consists of executive police officers with the rank of lieutenant and above. It is a nationwide organization roughly paralleling the International Association of Chiefs of Police, though NOBLE's membership is much smaller, with about 1,040 members.

NOBLE is the outgrowth of a conference of black law enforcement executives called by three nationwide criminal justice agencies. The conference was held in Arlington, Virginia, from September 6th to the 8th, 1976, specifically to discuss a means of "reducing crime in low income areas." Sixty blacks from 55 cities in 24 states attended—that included Inspector Fredrick Ruffin, representing Philadelphia.

Peggy Triplett, representing the Law Enforcement Assistance Administration, conceived the idea of a black police chiefs' group. She met privately with Newark Director of Police Hubert Williams, Atlanta Director of Public Safety A. Reginald Eaves, and New York City Deputy Chief William Bracey. They agreed on a plan to propose at the Arlington conference, which would change the direction of the seminar while continuing to address the crisis in the nation's urban centers. These officials realized it was vital that high-level black expertise be given greater consideration and latitude in the development and implementation of policies and programs that would effectively deal with crime in America.

It was hoped that the principle thrusts of NOBLE would be:
* To develop. mechanisms that will facilitate the exchange of information among black police executives
* To become spokesmen for black police executives in law enforcement
* To establish effective means and strategies for dealing with racism in the field of criminal justice
* To work for immediate implementation of programs to increase the number of black police officers at all levels delivering police service

Conference members eagerly seized upon the opportunity to interrupt the planned conference procedure for the purpose of greater importance: NOBLE was born. The conference members agreed that law enforcement needed a vehicle by which minority citizens could voice their concerns about urban crimes and problems.

Hubert Williams was unanimously elected temporary chairman of the organization, with Eaves and Bracey the co-chairmen. Also, participants selected Atlanta as the site of the first annual convention, to be held in June 1977.

Subsequent conferences were held as follows: St. Louis, 1978; Detroit, 1979; Inglewood, California, 1980; Baltimore, 1981; Kansas City, Kansas, 1982; Atlantic City, 1983; Chicago, 1984; Miami, 1985; Washington, DC, 1986; Oakland, California, 1987; New York, NY, 1988, and Atlanta, GA, 1989, Houston, Texas 1990, and Philadelphia, PA, 1991.

NOBLE is divided into six regions, and a number of local chapters have been organized. The Eastern Region has been designated 2, and the Philadelphia chapter is named the Greater Philadelphia Chapter. Former Chief of County Detectives Gilbert M. Branche served as Greater Philadelphia Chapter president from 1977 to 1983, as regional vice president from 1978 to 1979 and from 1982 to 1983, and as national president from 1979 to 1980. Also, former Chief of County Detectives Dorothy Cousins and Willie Williams served as regional vice presidents from 1980 to 1981.

While NOBLE has been instrumental in bringing about a lot of changes in the criminal justice system, it is not nearly as effective as it could be. The problem is that only about one-fifth of the membership constitutes bona fide police chiefs—that is, the top law enforcement officers for each jurisdiction.

However, this fact has not deterred NOBLE's efforts; each year it gets stronger while gaining more recognition among other national law enforcement agencies and top-level governmental officials on the local, state and national levels.

Within ten years, the number of black chiefs of police skyrocketed from three to thirteen in the fifty largest cities in the nation, culminating with the appointment of Willie Williams in Philadelphia in 1989. The other cities with black chiefs of police are: Atlanta, Baltimore, Chicago, Cleveland, Detroit, Houston, Long Beach, Miami, Newark, New Orleans, New York, and Washington, DC.

There are 212 other jurisdictions with black police executives. Georgia leads all others with a total of sixteen, while Louisiana and Missouri each have ten.

Richard Edwards, Deputy Police Commissioner - 1964

James N. Reaves, Inspector (photo - courtesy of Frank Winfrey)

Donald M. Gravatt, Deputy Police Commissioner - 1983

Police Commissioner Willie Williams

Police of the 31st District
L to R: (seated) Sgt. William Trommer, Lt. Joseph O'Brien, Captain James N. Reaves, William
O'Brien and Sgt. Thomas Grady - March 8, 1959

Dorothy Cousins - Chief of County Detectives

Annual Dinner with Special Investigative Squad (SIS)
L to R: seated - Leonard T. Jones, John Butler, Preston Washington, Tinsley Halliburton and
James E. Lee
back row - James N. Reaves, Theodore Jordan, John Grant, Reginald Owens, J. W. Johnston and
Frank Winfrey - November 14, 1986 (photo - courtesy of Lorin Hill)